Hope you ol... M...
Best W
Joh

2⁰

Climbing a Florida Mountain

John Freshwater

With Thanks...

To an incredible wife who made it all happen. What a ride! And our three wonderful kids who came on board. I hope the experiences we all shared will serve you well. And thanks for bringing such nice people into our family.

To Rob McGibbon for suggesting we put pen to paper and then staying around to guide me through.

And to Ron Marr for not only being a key part of the plot, but also for providing some valuable writing guidance along the way.

Front Cover Illustration and lots of other help: Susan Freshwater (we like to keep it in the family).

 And certainly not least. To Barbara Fowle for her tearful show of enthusiasm after reading the next to final draft. You gave me the encouragement to go ahead and finish the job.

Order this book online at www.trafford.com/07-0921
or email orders@trafford.com

Most Trafford titles are also available at major online book retailers.

Note for Librarians: A cataloguing record for this book is available from Library
and Archives Canada at www.collectionscanada.ca/amicus/index-e.html

Printed in Victoria, BC, Canada.

ISBN: 978-1-4251-2690-2

*We at Trafford believe that it is the responsibility of us all, as both individuals
and corporations, to make choices that are environmentally and socially sound.
You, in turn, are supporting this responsible conduct each time you purchase a
Trafford book, or make use of our publishing services. To find out how you are
helping, please visit www.trafford.com/responsiblepublishing.html*

*Our mission is to efficiently provide the world's finest, most comprehensive
book publishing service, enabling every author to experience success.
To find out how to publish your book, your way, and have it available
worldwide, visit us online at www.trafford.com/10510*

www.trafford.com

North America & international
toll-free: 1 888 232 4444 (USA & Canada)
phone: 250 383 6864 ♦ fax: 250 383 6804
email: info@trafford.com

The United Kingdom & Europe
phone: +44 (0)1865 722 113 ♦ local rate: 0845 230 9601
facsimile: +44 (0)1865 722 868 ♦ email: info.uk@trafford.com

10 9 8 7 6 5 4 3 2

Author's Note

When I first took up what was going to prove for me, an unpublished writer, to be a difficult challenge of writing this book, I had absolutely no concept of the underlining theme. Most definitely I didn't set out with an agenda to tell a sad story, but one that would try to capture, with a degree of honesty, the highs and lows in our lives since leaving the English shores almost a quarter of a century ago.

The book idea originated after a drive across south Florida's Alligator Alley, when taking an old family friend, visiting us for my son's wedding, over to Miami to catch a flight back to England.

The young friend, Rob McGibbon, the son of a former business partner, who had written several books himself, had listened diligently to my response to his question *"So what's been happening in your life since we last met?"*

I realized only as he was grabbing his bags and opening the door at the terminal curbside that I had spoken non-stop for the entire two-hour journey. Before I could apologize for boring him, he cocked his head to one side and said. *"That's a great story...you really must put it down on paper"*

But like so many people with a story to tell I did absolutely nothing about *"putting it down on paper."*

At that time I was chauffeuring at The Ritz Carlton hotel in Naples. It seemed inevitable that whenever I greeted a guest at the airport and soon after we started the 45 minute journey back to the lavish hotel, the conversation would follow a similar pattern. *"I can tell from your accent you weren't born in Florida...what brought you to Naples?"*

And just as inevitable, at journey's end, and after listening to one or two of our experiences, the departing farewell would include..."*Fascinating stuff. You really must write a book"*

And so the project was started. Memories of experiences past were revisited. The sad occasions, the happy ones and the remainder that fell somewhere in-between were relived. And then, as the first draft was nearing completion, an interesting fact was noted...sadly it was that four characters that had played important roles in our story have died along the way.

Firstly there was Janet, the psychic we met at a friend's party a few weeks before departing on our new adventure. My wife was anxious to hear what she saw in our future and pinned Janet into a corner for most of the evening. In the car on the way home I was curious to hear what the psychic had predicted. My wife explained that it turned out to be disappointingly very little. She said Janet seemed very hesitant as though she was holding something back. Apparently she kept repeating the same phrase. *"In the end everything will turn out ok and you will find contentment..."*

Many times over the years, as we have struggled on that journey, we have reminded ourselves of Janet's statement and drew strength from knowing that in the end... *"everything will be ok."*

Ironically, the attractive young psychic could not have seen much in her own future, succumbing to cancer shortly after our meeting.

To qualify for our investment visa we had to purchase a business. The one we wanted, a small marina, was already under contract to another English immigrant, named Phil O'Connor, who went on to make considerable wealth from the venture. For us, we turned our attention towards a health spa instead. But far from giving us financial success, the spa caused us great emotional and financial hardship that eventually broke the bank.

Sadly Phil never got to enjoy his wealth, dying at a young age of fifty.

During one of our worst financial moments we receive the heart-breaking news that Mo's mother is suffering with terminal cancel. We were left with no other choice than to do whatever was necessary to get the family over to England to say our final 'goodbyes'. The trip that was budgeted for little more than the thousand dollars for cut-price airline tickets, turned out to be almost a twenty-thousand dollar mess when I was prevented from re-entering the U.S. and sent back to England for a four-month unwelcome hiatus.

Finally, just as I was completing the final update on the epilogue, we read in the local newspaper that Nelson Faerber, the lawyer who had played such and important role in our legal battles and whom we had been paying back his fees over the years, had been charged following a pedophile investigation.

Last week he committed suicide by shooting himself in the head with a handgun. He leaves a wife and three children. On the day of his death we received a note from him in the mail. It reads as follows:

"Dear Mo and John,

Thank you for the payments you have made to me on the old invoice. I very much appreciate your commitment. However, I think we should call it even now. Your friendship over the years has been invaluable to me. Though we do not often meet, you and your family are wonderful and good people and it has been my honor to be your friend."

Introduction

The fiery red disc begins its final descent in the clear, fluorescent, bright blue sky, almost bringing to an end yet another glorious sun-soaked day for the hundreds of families who have come out here to enjoy one of the world's most beautiful beaches.

Few scenes around the world can compare with the kaleidoscope of magical colors that will flame the sky when the disc takes on the form of a jello-like blob and finally melts into the horizon. Over the years, since the day it was first discovered, tens of thousands of artists have brushed canvasses while photographers have clicked shutters and poets have penned verse, all in a noble attempt to capture this majestic, if not magical, scene. For the rest of us we have simply stood back, opened our eyes and tried to absorb its breath-taking beauty.

Tucked away on the south west corner of the Florida peninsula, this area of postcard beauty is more than a just a beautiful beach...more than a pristine town called Naples...*it's our home and the place we call paradise.*

As the warm gentle breeze skates off the Gulf waters, I'm taking my wife's hand and leading her to a spot a few feet in front of the gentle swaying sea oats where the sand is soft and smooth. The hardy plants have been tiered to form a natural protection barrier between the beach and the grand, multi-million dollar beachfront homes that stretch both southwards and northwards, almost as far as the eye can see.

Mo is squeezing my fingers as we both sink to the ground. Only her mother has ever called her by her given name of Maureen. "Can't think of a better place to be right now," she says with a smile.... "It's just so peaceful."

"Can you remember that very first time we came here?" I ask as I reach across and pull two beers from the weathered and scratched blue plastic cooler. She offers a gentle, affirmative nod as she smoothes out the old, crumpled, bright-yellow bed sheet and takes up a cross-legged sitting position. As she leans back on her arms to stretch her back, I make sure she sees my approving smile as I slowly track the path from her khaki shorts down to her painted toes. The long shapely tanned legs haven't lost their appeal in the thirty-four years we have known each other. But she thinks they have and has mentioned many times that she loves it when I give those approving glances, and finds it reassuring when I tell her how much I still enjoying looking at them. I pull back the tab from the top of one of the ice-cold cans and hand it to her. She grabs it quickly, lifting the can to her lips to suck up the frothy liquid which is beginning to bubble out of the hole. She smiles her thanks and gives a little throaty giggle.

"Of course I can remember the first time here." she smiles, and then pauses before adding in joking fashion..."I just try to forget everything in-between." I wonder for a moment if she is really only joking.

We both know that our twenty-four years in America have not been easy, but even during the worst moments there was never a time when we felt like packing up and returning to our country of birth No, Naples, Florida, is our home, the place we both fell in love with the first time we saw it.

The memories are numerous. Some we will want to treasure forever, others we would prefer to forget. The passing of time helps. The bad times went on for just too long. The constant battles of trying to stay financially afloat, the emotional stress brought on each time we thought we had lost everything that matters… and then all the effort and determination that goes into trying to climb back.

And yet why did we ever think we had it so bad? We were still more fortunate than most. We always had each other and that alone proved time after time to be power enough to make us strong again.

The streaks of light are now beginning to change as the last of the sunglow begins to fade like those unhappy memories. We change position to make ourselves more comfortable. With arms draped around each another, we both feel an unspoken bond. One that comes from sharing many exciting pleasures, as well too many disheartening setbacks.

I suddenly realize we are sitting on almost the exact spot where we witnessed this view for the first time in the summer of 1981. Back then, the beach was quiet, almost deserted, but today we are still among a large crowd, which bears testament to the phenomenal growth of Naples. There are vacationers - clearly identifiable by the lobster-pink glow - beginning to slowly pack up their beach gear. There are the deeply weathered faces of the locals strolling along the frothy water's edge. There is a strong sense of camaraderie as both groups are drawn together by the unmistakable force that is the charm of Naples beach at sunset. And there is also an anticipatory sparkle in everyone's eyes as they wait to witness the "Green Flash" – supposedly the split-second moment when the horizon ignites into an emerald hue, just as the sun sinks beneath the water. Legend says that those who see it will enjoy a lifetime of good fortune.

"Yeah right!" We have said many times. "We'll believe it when we see it," Despite countless visits to this beach, the Green Flash has always eluded us. But as we learned to laugh at the ephemeral notion of good luck, we also took out insurance by allowing ourselves somewhere deep inside to keep an open mind about its existence. Perhaps tonight it will happen and we can spread a personal word that the Green Flash really does exist. And tomorrow our mountain of debts will disappear.

The small groups of people between the water and us are in no hurry to move. Close to the gentle breaking surf we hear the joyous giggles of children proudly finishing a sandcastle which, Mo suggests with some sadness, will soon be lost to the incoming tide. The scene reminds us of the days when our three children were much younger.

Our gaze turns to watch lovers of all ages strolling hand in hand and we silently wonder if, like us, they are recalling moments from the past, or planning dreams of the future. Darting streaks of pink and yellow are now illuminating the sky and to the south we can just make out silhouettes of fisherman casting their lines from the easily identifiable landmark of the pier.

The sun has just a few seconds left before it disappears completely. We squint towards the horizon, searching for anything that resembles a flash. The last remaining sliver of what now has become orange slips away and we hear a few cheers from somewhere along the beach. We see nothing to resemble a flash and are highly suspicious of anyone who claims they have. We keep searching the horizon but see nothing but the clear line of the horizon where sky, filling with strobes of constantly changing bright lights, meets the Gulf waters.

With Mo's head nestled into my chest, I turn my head to take in the sprawling multi-million dollar houses with their manicured lawns and stunning gardens surrounded by swaying palm trees. To me, these homes have become symbols of their owner's success and undeniable proof that America truly is still a land of wealth and opportunity. Even now, I still passionately believe it. Mo and I have experienced our fair share of troubles in the pursuit of that elusive dream. Long ago we began comparing our lives here to that of climbing a mountain. There were times we felt we were close to the summit, only to slip and fall. Whatever had happened, we would simply start climbing again, just like everyone has to. Even on the most perilous days, we seemed to have been held by a safety rope that prevented us from falling too far. As each new struggle began we never lost sight of the fact that we consider ourselves blessed. Our Florida mountain is located in the land of our choice, rising from a town which we think is paradise.

Naples now boasts - if that is the right word - of being the second fastest growing community in America, after Las Vegas. Throughout our time here, the town and wider areas have transformed around us. Property prices have soared, development has spread and business has boomed on a massive scale. Unfortunately, much of this wealth and opportunity has passed us by and, if anything, our American Dream has been, in some ways, an ongoing nightmare. Perhaps we should have heeded that vague warning from the psychic lady we met at a party just a few weeks before leaving England. *"Eventually, you will find contentment."*

Did she really see our future? As the years have flown by, we have often asked that question. Did she see the problems we would face with immigration, business corruption, court battles, as well as threats of bankruptcy and deportation? What did she see that night that she refused to share?

Tonight we are at peace. I don't want to be reminded of the worst day of my life...

Chapter One

This has to be the worst bloody day of my relatively young life. Here I am, a year before my fortieth birthday, supposedly living in paradise with my wife and our three young children, and our world is crumbling around us.

What this jury forewoman is saying has hammered the final nail into our coffin. We have not only been slipping and tumbling down our mountain, but now we are about to come crashing to the bottom.

This softly spoken woman, reading from a sheet of white paper she unfolded when she first stood up in front of her silent and attentive audience, just doesn't get it. She just doesn't get it at all!

How can this woman and the other five cronies seated around her understand what has been going on in the courtroom for the past two days? How could they? They have just found this son-of-a-bitch sitting just a few feet away from our table guilty of fraud and now, who would possibly believe it, they are ordering me to give this bastard more of my bloody money!

My brain is spinning out of control. The room is cool but I'm feeling hot. All of a sudden I feel nauseous. For a few seconds I'm thinking I may bring up what little breakfast I ate this morning, spew it all over the large wooden table and desecrate the little piles of court papers neatly stacked by our attorney's assistant along the front. I have to control myself as I look up and scan the room for the umpteenth time. Apart from the lady mouthing the words there is absolutely no other sounds or movement in the courtroom. The judge is sitting low in his chair with his head bowed to one side and resting in his cupped hand. There is no way of knowing what he is thinking, although later we will find out that he is just as shocked as we are at this jury's findings. All eyes are still firmly fixed on the gray-haired lady standing on the left side of the first row of the two-row jury box. Further over to her left is the blown-up tax return that dramatically offered compelling evidence when it was hauled into court. It stood there like some kind of token, positioned carefully by my attorney Nelson Faerber in a way the jury could feast their eyes on it for the entire two days. To everyone who could read it, it offered an irrefutable argument that we were right and he, the defendant, was so shamefully wrong.

He had sold us the business with a false set of books including a healthy looking tax return that he later amended but chose not to show us, our accountants or the immigration people. The company profits from an unidentified separate land deal had mysteriously vanished from the amended papers, leaving a business that, instead of being profitable, had been hemorrhaging money badly from day one.

But have we won?

The words of the jury lady, now gently wafting though the courtroom, are confusing. Nothing is making any sense. Desperately my mind tries to grasp what I'm hearing. My gaze shifts from the easel and works to refocus on this ongoing drama.

Just moments ago we heard the first part of judgment that the defendant has been found guilty of stealing our money - or in legal terms, guilty of civil fraud. We weren't at all surprised. Now, all we want to hear is how the shattered financial pieces of our lives are going to be put back together again. It's an easy thing for this jury to do. We had never looked for easy riches or unearned wealth; just an opportunity of getting back to status quo. Or to put it more simply, the position we were in before this con man entered our lives.

But the second part of the judgment isn't saying that at all. It is confusing. I cup a hand to my ear and listen. On one hand the jury is awarding us damages. On the other, in response to the defendant's counterclaim for the money we still owed him on the purchase of the spa business (and which we refused to pay when we realized he had duped us) the judgment is ordering *US* to pay up. In some twisted reconcile, this jury believes the two should be a similar amount, so the damages they are awarding us are the same as the money owed on the promissory note. They simply cancel each other out. But worse still, the defendant in his counter claim had sued us for his attorney's fees, and the misguided jury feels it is fair for us to pay those too.

Are they brain dead? Do they really understand what they are saying and the effect it is going to have on my family? It will be nothing short of disastrous long-reaching consequences in our already bruised and battered lives. Apart from ruining us financially, they are also threatening our chances of staying in our paradise, the place we have learned to call home.

Whichever way I look at it, we are about to lose everything.

The jury forewoman stops reading. She lowers her sheet of paper and looks up, offering a gracious smile towards the judge. The air conditioner kicks in and gives off a gently humming background noise to break what I sense to be a roomful of embarrassed silence. For a moment no one moves. The scene is frozen.

I'm brought back into focus by the sharp pain in my hand. Mo's fingernails are digging deep into the skin. The glazed look in her eyes tells me she has drifted for a moment to some far away place…away from the reality of what is happening in this south Florida courtroom.

She slumps forward and I can see the gentle shaking of her rigid body. She looks up and glares at the sixty-something year old lady, dressed smartly in the dark blue business suit, who is now taking her seat. Tears well up in both eyes as the soft lips part and she repeatedly mouths the word *'why, why, why'*

A few feet from us the defendant is hugging his attorney, whose back is positioned towards us. When the attorney turns around and our eyes meet, it is with an obvious show of embarrassment. I'm not sure if he is embarrassed by the hugging, or by the verdict, or both.

Our attorney's arm comes over my shoulder. "I'm sorry," he whispers. "I just don't understand it."

We all look on as the Judge thanks the jury for giving both their time and their diligence and releases them. We all stand as he rises from his chair, picks up his papers and he too leaves the room. We are left once again wondering what is going on. Nelson and his assistant pick up their briefcases in silence as we all move slowly towards the large double-doors. Outside the building, we stand in the bright, late afternoon sunshine, looking at one another. I'm aware of people coming over to offer condolences; as if we had just lost a loved one, but I'm in such a daze I don't recall their expressions of sorrow. Mo and I hang around, hoping that Nelson can come up with some type of explanation that can ease the pain we are feeling. I just feel sick, believing that a major injustice had been perpetrated. My impulse is to find the jury and ask each one of them how could they possibly arrive with such a verdict. Why was I, my wife and my family being punished?

Did they not understand anything they had heard over the past couple of days? I found myself asking again. It was such an easy decision for them to make…but in the end they screwed up.

Nelson is very subdued. He doesn't even attempt to offer any further explanation. He merely throws up his arms in a gesture of defeat and suggests we go home and meet up in the next day or so. He looks as weary as I feel. With the hot afternoon sun beating down, Mo and I walk across the sun-baked parking lot towards our vehicle. It had been left in the shade under a tree but now it sits there fully exposed to the burning rays. I open the doors and we wait a moment for the gentle breeze to cool down the inside. We can only stand there in silence, leaning against the hot metal frame, looking at each other and shaking our heads. There is nothing we can say that will comfort the pain we are feeling. We sink into the seats and I push the key slowly into the ignition switch. The engine fires up and I look down to see that the gas gauge is showing empty. I remember I had spent the last of the cash in my wallet on our last visit to the courthouse coffee shop. I look across at my wife and ask if she has any money for gas. I should have guessed the answer. She reminds me she gave me her few remaining dollars when we left the house this morning. With nothing left on our credit cards, we drive home in silence, wondering if we will make it before the tank runs dry.

Looking back on that memorable day I can easily recall that my mind was still reeling as we walked into our house. It all seemed like a dream. Nothing seemed quite real, until the children came rushing out to greet us. I can't recall exactly what we told them, but I know we watered down the story enough for them to know we had won but didn't get back all of our money. They would learn the truth of the full judgment in time.

The following days were beyond depressing. Although we had the children around, and our various part-time jobs to keep us busy, there were still many moments when Mo and I obsessed over the court case. We had not only used up the remaining available cash on our credit cards, but had also taken out an equity loan on the house to meet the attorney's fees. We were heavily in debt and there was no way our current income was going to cover our outgoings.

I could see that Mo was getting more and more despondent about our situation. Her whole persona was changing. Instead of being full of life, being someone everyone enjoyed being around, she looked exhausted and unhappy. Sensing the pain she was going through made me feel both guilty and useless. I daren't mention the fact that, with no business to run, we had lost our investment status in the eyes of the immigration department. How soon would it be before the authorities came knocking at the door to tell us we had to leave the country? I didn't dwell on that thought for too long.

But for the time being, this was still our home. We had given up so much to stay here that we weren't going to give up without a fight, and whatever it took to start the climb back up our mountain.

Apart from working various daytime jobs, Mo also took a job waiting tables six evenings a week. She was ready to collapse each night when she walked through the door. I will never forget the day we got a phone call from our elder son Kieran's fourth grade teacher. She said she was very worried about Kieran.

"Is he in trouble?" we asked.

"Oh no, nothing like that," said the teacher. "In class today he just buried his head in his arms on the desk and started bawling."

This was so unlike Kieran. After I thanked the teacher and hung up the phone I asked him what was wrong. He looked up at me with such sad eyes and said that he was so worried about his mom because "she works too hard!" My heart broke.

Mo told me years later that, during this entire period, she just wanted to stay in bed each morning and hide under the covers. She also admitted to having violent thoughts about getting back at the owner of the spa. I think it was fortunate she never saw him on the road when she was driving around town!

Our second son, Dominic, has since told us that his most poignant memory of those troubled times was sitting in the back of the old Cadillac with no air conditioning. As we drove past McDonald's he called out for us to stop. He remembers his mother and I looking embarrassingly at each other and saying we were sorry, but we just couldn't afford to buy him a McDonald's today. Kids remember the strangest things.

Chapter Two

With the sun finally set, the first twinkling stars begin to appear high in the darkening sky above the houses and trees away from the beach. The variety of colors is beginning to blend into one solid mauve mass. The offshore warm breeze is kicking up a little, and although the temperature is still in the eighties, Mo's body is giving off a little shiver. Most of the groups around us are gathering their beach stuff together and heading out to their cars.

I take a moment to brush back strands of blonde hair that have fallen across her forehead. "Remember how it all started?" she asks softly?

"Of course I do," I answer smiling back. "How could I possible forget?" My mind drifts into the past.

The first thoughts of moving from England to America started somewhere between *It's A Small World* and *Space Mountain*. I imagine this is pretty much the standard feeling for numerous families on holiday at Disney World, as everyone is seduced by the timeless wonder of the theme park and the colorful beauty and heat of Orlando.

Looking back now, I know that the magic of Disney, and ultimately that of America, was being indelibly caste over our lives as Mo and I and our two sons raced excitedly between the rides. Our daughter Kirsty was too young for the trip – she was just eighteen months old - and was back in England being looked after by family. I distinctly remember one scene as Kieran, then aged five, and Dominic who was four, kept circling us in breathless excitement after riding on Space Mountain. They were on an uncontrollable high as they regaled us with the story of their bravery. Nervous giggles punctuated the tale as dark haired, little tough guy Dominic attempted to explain how "cool" it was zooming in their jet rocket capsule through the scary darkness.

Isn't a kid's laughter gloriously intoxicating? I noticed it was also affecting others around us as several older couples stopped to listen to the boys' thrilling adventure. These curious onlookers appeared to hang on every word and I guessed that they were recalling similar stories told by their own children, maybe even their grandchildren. One white-haired gentleman gently nodded his head in a personal show of approval, while his wife leaned heavily on a walking cane, slowly rolling her twinkling eyes and beaming a warm smile.

For most people though, the fantasy of an exciting, carefree life in America's Sunshine State is quickly dismissed as unworkable, and the dream vanishes by the time they are back in their home state or country flipping through the holiday photos. But for us, the desire grew stronger with each exciting new day in Florida.

This was as happy a time as I can ever remember, and perhaps selfishly, I was aware that I never wanted it to end. It wasn't just about being with my family on this exciting holiday, for there were other, far greater forces at work. I was suddenly hit with a realization of what life was and what it could be, and I was consumed by an unmistakable blast of pioneer spirit. Maybe I was also a little giddy with the generous exchange rate – we were getting $2.25 for every pound, so not only did I feel that life was richer here, I actually *was*! Simply put, I didn't want us to leave Florida and live one day longer under the gloomy gray skies of England.

It is easy to recall pinpointing the particularly decision-making moment. It was when we were watching American history uniquely unfold at The House of Presidents and I started debating the situation in my mind. I told myself that such a thought to drop everything and move was absurd. I remember looking up at the life-like statues on the stage before us and wondering if my feelings were real, or like those models, unreal and false. Maybe I was just deluded by so much holiday fun, which, as everyone knows, cannot last forever. In the darkened theatre I found myself looking around at other fathers sitting with their families, eyes glued to the performance, and I wondered if any of them were experiencing such an unsettling dread of returning home. I decided at the time that these odd feelings would soon pass.

But of course, they didn't. They only grew stronger and became so intense that I couldn't hold back from sharing them later that same day with my wife. If I was expecting a sarcastic, negative response I was immediately proven wrong. "I'm feeling that way too," was Mo's simple reply, which caused my confused mind to spin even faster. We kept thinking and fantasizing as the ten day trip continued at a frenzied pace. If we needed any more encouragement, it came as we waited in the blazing sunshine outside our hotel to board the airport shuttle bus.

This was near the end of October and the Florida temperature was hovering in the mid-80s. I made a quick phone call to my office in London, and the ensuing conversation stoked a fire inside me that would never be doused. Back in England, I was told, it was cold, raining and utterly miserable. An all too familiar picture came into my mind as I imagined disembarking at Gatwick Airport and driving home in the chilly drizzle with the long, dark winter months ahead of us. It made me shudder and I could already feel the sadness that would set in, the longing for the sunny skies and the up-beat exhilaration of Florida.

It was not that we had a bad life in England – far from it. With my two partners, we ran a successful publishing company, as well as other lucrative businesses, which had given our family a lifestyle many would envy. We lived on a tree-lined private estate in a five-bedroom, detached house with a large garden; two new cars – my Jaguar and the family Volvo estate - sat on the long driveway. Our sons, Kieran and Dominic, went to private schools and there was always enough money to buy pretty much anything we wanted.

Mo and I enjoyed a social life that included dining at London's best restaurants and often, due to the business, we were mixing among the leading celebrities of the day. What more could we possibly want? Yet, here I was, plotting to move four thousand miles away from our lovely home and financial security. Surely, I'd had too much sun, I'd get over it.

But I couldn't.

It wasn't just Florida that inspired the move. Mo later admitted that while the attraction of the sun, sand and surf were a big motivation, she believed we were actually suffering an early mid-life crisis; I was thirty-five and she was thirty-four and we both needed a change and new challenges. It was as simple and as complicated as that.

I have often wondered, if we knew back then some of the problems we were going to face over the next quarter of a century, would we have still made the move? I would say, without any doubt, the answer would be yes. My only one regret has been the pain and pressure that our adventure has put on Mo. It was certainly the most frightening day of my life when my solid rock began to show cracks.

It came at a time when Mo was doing substitute teaching at the nearby middle school. After working various jobs she was desperately trying to get back to her first love of teaching. But because she didn't have a college degree – she attended a three-year teaching college in England to acquire a teaching diploma – she didn't qualify for the required Florida's Teaching Certification. The only work available to her within the Collier County school system was running the ISS (Inside School Suspension) class. This was hardly the type of teaching Mo desired or had been trained to do. This unit was where the kids came when they got into trouble. Most days she was seeing the same familiar faces. Kids who had no desire to study, and just wanted to disrupt those that did. It was a place to kill time, until the end of day bell sounded and they could get away from the environment they most certainly didn't enjoy.

Unlike many others who worked in ISS and seemed satisfied with merely throwing a book in front of the kids and demanding they just remain quiet, even if that meant resting their heads in the folded arms and sleeping for the entire day, Mo actually set about trying to provide some positive tutoring. Years later we would often run into kids in the local supermarket who had been in that ISS class and came up and greeted Mo with a warm and friendly hug. Some were able to turn their lives around and find a positive work ethic. I was always pleasantly surprised and proud by the numbers who thanked Mo for getting them back on the right track.

When each school day ended, Mo would grab her bag and change into her waitress uniform. For five, sometimes six evenings a week during a ten-year period, she would serve up ribs and chicken at the nearby barbeque restaurant. At the same time, I was trying to stay busy doing various day jobs, picking up work wherever I could. Yea, I often felt I had lost some dignity, especially on the occasions when I was out there almost begging for work. But you quickly learn you have to do what you have to do and we were just trying to survive. On the nights Mo was working evenings, I always made sure I was home to take care of the children.

Although she would rarely complain, it was no secret that Mo had grown to hate her evening job. She was burned out which was hardly surprising. She would arrive at the restaurant around 4.30 pm after leaving her day job, and wouldn't leave until after ten. I desperately wanted her to give it up, but she would always argue that to continue for "just one more season" would help get us out of debt.

I knew there was a serious problem as soon as she walked through the front door that October evening in 1999. Her usual friendly, if weary, smile had given way to a pale ashen face. He eyes were red and watery, and I could see from the streaks down her cheeks that she had been crying. Before I could ask what was wrong she asked me to drive her to the hospital. Her voice was shallow and weak. "I think I'm having a heart attack."

On the way to emergency, with head bowed and resting in the palms of her hand, she quietly explained she hadn't felt well all evening. At first she thought the slight chest pains were caused by nothing more than indigestion, from chunking down the sandwich she always ate during the few minutes between finishing whatever job she was doing during the day and arriving at the restaurant.

Instinctively my foot was pushing down harder and harder on the gas pedal. Mo was sitting up straight and massaging her arm. I didn't need to ask any questions. I needed to get my wife to a doctor…like now!

Without emotion in her voice, she said she only began to panic earlier when she felt this numbness in her arm, followed by the pain spreading across her chest. She realized at that point that something was seriously wrong.

Mo mentioned her fears to another waitress, Carol, whose husband is a paramedic. The urgent tone in the husband's voice on the phone made it clear he had no doubts. "Get Mo down to emergency as soon as possible. Call an ambulance if you have to."

Despite Carol's pleas, Mo refused the idea of taking an ambulance. She said the pain and the numbness was subsiding and she felt well enough to drive herself. Once in her car she decided it would even be ok to take a quick diversion to stop by home and let me know what was going on. It was only when she was driving into our street that the panic and fear overcame her and she burst into tears.

We were driving faster and faster, swerving in and out of the late evening traffic. My own heart was beating faster and I was aware of tears welling up my own eyes. For the first time a thought flashed through my mind - *was there a real danger I could be losing my partner?*

As we screeched into the hospital car park, someone standing in the brightly-lit lobby of the emergency room saw me lifting Mo out of the car and helping her towards the glass automatic doors. The young onlooker, dressed in scrubs, sensed the emergency and came running out with a wheelchair. He sat Mo down and hurriedly pushed her inside. In just another few minutes she was lying on the bed with nurses hooking her up to heart-monitoring equipment. It was later that night when we were told that tests showed that one of the arteries was ninety percent blocked.

"A heart attack wasn't too far away," said the cardiologist reading from papers on his plastic clipboard. "We need to schedule her for an angioplasty tomorrow morning".

Although there were some minor complications during surgery, and a stent had to be inserted to keep the artery open, Mo left the hospital the following day feeling very relieved. Although the problem had been diagnosed in time and hadn't caused any heart damage, we both took the incident as a warning that her lifestyle had to change.

Conscious of the words of the cardiologist - that Mo should reduce the stress in her life - we made our way to the hospital's billing department to explain that we had no insurance and very little money to pay the hospital bill.

Not taking out hospital insurance was not simply an irresponsible act on our part. We simply couldn't afford the $500 a month premium.

Actually, the hospital office staff couldn't have been more understanding and helpful. Hospital records showed that, even without insurance coverage, we were paid-up on all previous hospital bills. The young man at the desk said he saw no problem with the hospital accepting a payment plan. We could pay the new hospital charges on a monthly basis. We would, however, have to make our own arrangements to pay the doctors.

As we left the hospital and made our way to the car it seemed that we had dodged the bullet once again. Still, we also knew that changes had to be made in our lives. We had been vulnerable for too long. But a solution wouldn't be easy to find. Because of our investor-only immigration status, I was still technically unable to be employed by a company that provided health care benefits.

It was several weeks later that the financial impact of Mo's surgery came to the forefront. Each day we were pulling a steady stream of doctors' invoices from the mailbox. Once again we had reached that "oh so familiar" point where we hated going to collect the mail. We knew we would only find bad news, and today it was going to be really bad news.

The green hospital envelope said it all; the final figure for Mo's surgery was more than $24,000!

We had arrived in America with nearly half a million dollars from the sale of our home and business. The day we placed the hospital bill on the growing pile we estimated we were more than one hundred thousand dollars in debt.

Chapter Three

If we thought our day in court was the worst day of our lives then it didn't take long for us to have cause to reconsider that thinking. How does anything compare with a day when my wife receives news that her mother has been diagnosed with terminal cancer? And if that wasn't sad enough, more bad news was quick to follow. While Mo was dealing with the pain of her mother's death, I innocently became involved in my first major confrontation with U.S. immigration, which, as we soon came to realize, could so easily have resulted in our family being kicked out of Florida.

Not for the first time, and it certainly wouldn't be the last it seemed, just when we appeared to be making progress on our mountain, our climb had come to an abrupt standstill.

Mo's mother Sheila was one of those sweet, shy ladies adored by everyone she met. She had spent her entire working life caring for geriatric patients at Epsom Hospital, just outside London. With husband Tom, who she doted over, the couple had raised three daughters, with Mo being the eldest.

Sheila loved the couple of visits she had made during our early days in Naples, which she readily admitted had opened her eyes to a whole new, excitingly different world. Despite her admitted shyness, which she fought with rugged determination, she had succeeded in adopting an adventuresome spirit. And dear old, easy-going Tom, was just happy to tag along.

Until the news of her illness, we had expected and hoped that she and Tom would be paying us regular visits; long vacations where they could spend quality time with our children. But sadly it wasn't to be. Instead of looking forward to their lengthy stays and the opportunity to explore together our adopted country, we found ourselves planning a trip back to England to say our final farewells to this lovely lady.

The trip came at a time when I had returned to my journalistic roots and, with Mo's help, I was publishing a free distribution advertising publication. It was a business project that had kind of fallen into our laps.

Mo's last daytime job had been selling advertising for a small publishing operator in town. She had taken the job not knowing anything about selling but that did little to impede her progress. She quickly became successful and when we decided to publish our own publication, she brought those newly acquired skills into our venture. But although our publication was enjoying some considerable success, which had exceeded our guarded expectations, each slow summer period proved to be a financial drain on the business. Now, even after eighteen months, Mo and I could still only pay ourselves a very modest and irregular salary. This was made harder to accept knowing that if we were able to pay Mo her true sales commissions, our lives would have been so much easier. But our hands were tied. We knew it would be financial suicide to try and extract any more money than we were already taking. So this sad and unexpected trip to England would have to be conducted as an extremely low budget exercise.

We searched everywhere for days, seeking out the best deals until eventually we found what we believed to be the very lowest fares. There was no doubt in our minds that this would be a tiring trip, especially traveling with three young children. We were also to discover why it was a discounted flight. It added hours to the journey, flying us out of Fort Myers, backwards to St. Louis, before crossing over the Atlantic to London. At the time of making our reservations we had no idea, and how could we, that St. Louis airport would soon be playing such a critical role in our lives, a role we could have gratefully done without.

For some time I had been serving as coach of our son Dominic's soccer team. I had agreed to travel with the club's four teams to a tournament in Colorado, with the club paying my travel expenses. The arrangement was that Dominic and I would spend a week and a half in London, come home and meet up with the teams, and fly out to Colorado Springs three days later. Mo and our other two children would return to Florida a few days later.

As one might expect considering the circumstances, the family trip to England was hardly a happy one. We could only watch as Sheila's health deteriorated before our eyes. Her doctors gave her but a few weeks to live – no more than a month at most - as the cancer had spread through much of her frail body. We felt helpless as we hung around the house. Poor Tom was a broken man who, until his own death nearly twenty years later, would never recover from the devastating loss of his partner.

After discussing the situation with Mo's family shortly after arriving, we all decided we shouldn't stay any longer than originally planned to await Sheila's passing, whenever that was to be. With her two sisters and other family members around, and her doctor visiting her daily, we knew she was in good hands. We also knew we had done the right thing in coming over to say our goodbyes. But as the days slid by we also knew there was a need to get on with our own busy and complicated lives.

Despite the somber mood around the house we all tried to remain positive and cheerful. We divided our time as best we could, conscious of trying to spend as much time as possible with our children as well as exposing them to many of the exciting sights of London. After all, in their young minds, this was still supposed to be a vacation. We showed them the places where they were born, and revisited the big expensive house we had left behind. It was funny to see the boys' eyes light up at the sight of the mock Tudor-style house set among an acre of manicured lawns, and giggle with excitement at being reminded of their exploits of playing their fantasy games together among the hedges and shrubs. They adored The Tower of London, and got a big kick out of listening to the speakers standing on their soapboxes and arguing with the rowdy audiences at Hyde Park Corner.

But all too soon, it was time for Dominic and I to return alone to the States. We left with mixed emotions. Sad at knowing this would be the last time we would see Mo's mother, but also feeling hyped that we were off to start on another exciting adventure. After saying our emotional farewells and driving in silence to the airport, we were soon boarding our plane and taking our seats for the long trip back across the Atlantic.

It was late in the evening when Dominic and I disembarked the aircraft and began following the straggling line of other weary-looking passengers making their way to immigration at Lambert Airport. After nearly nine hours in the air, we were both feeling drained and exhausted, neither of us looking forward to the second leg and another three hours of airline travels. The adventure spirit had long been lost somewhere over the pond. We tagged on the back of one of the four lines of passengers and shuffled our way towards the row of immigration booths deep inside the terminal building. Knowing we had a two-hour lay-over before boarding our connecting flight back to Ft Myers, we were in no hurry. By the time we reached passport control we noticed we were not only the last in our line but also realized that all the other lines of passengers had already moved through immigration and were snaking their way into the baggage area.

Nonchalantly I handed over our passports to the man sitting behind a computer screen inside an open booth. Instinctively I smiled a cheery "good evening".

"Where are you heading?" he asked without raising his head in a surprising, not too friendly manner.

"Naples, Florida," I replied, continuing to smile towards the top of his head.

"Business or pleasure?" he asked in a more inquiring tone.

"Neither. We have our home there," I answered.

"Really! Is this your permanent residence?" he countered, still not bothering to look up from the two passports laid out on the desk in front of him. I nodded and added something about having my own business there.

The officer's attitude hardened as he walked out from behind the desk and asked us both to "step this way".

I now knew that something was definitely not right, but I couldn't imagine what it might be. I suddenly became aware of the tiny hairs on the back of my neck standing up as my confused brain tried to rationalize all the possibilities. I knew our passports were current, and I also knew we weren't carrying anything in our luggage that could cause a problem.

In silence, like two little children following in line behind their teacher, we were led to a small room. As the door closed behind us I took in the stark features of the surroundings. There was a desk, four chairs and bare walls. Suddenly it felt very cold and I became conscious of trying to conceal the shiver running down my spine. The somber setting made the situation somehow appear even more serious and threatening.

Without speaking, the officer gestured for us both to sit down. I had now come to accept there was something seriously wrong, but what? I was at a complete loss in determining what it could be. It didn't help that Dominic was looking at me with a puzzled expression, and I couldn't give him any answers. I could only look back, pat his arm, and attempt to give him a confident looking, if false, smile.

"Is there something wrong?" I asked, cutting into the silence. The officer was now seated behind the metal desk, flipping through the pages of our two passports for a third, or maybe it was the fourth time. "Could be," he replied. "This visa in your passport doesn't allow you to re-enter the U.S. on a permanent basis. In fact, from what you have told me, it could be considered that you are trying to enter the country illegally!"

What! This was ridiculous, I thought. Our passports and visas are all current, having been stamped and renewed just a couple of months prior. What was happening here? This just wasn't making any sense at all.

In my friendliest manner, conscious of not wishing to offend, I asked the officer if he could explain exactly what was wrong.

"These are temporary visas that allow you stay in the country, but they do not provide for re-entry. For you to do that you would need to get them stamped again by the American Embassy in London."

At that moment I felt crushed. I could not believe I was hearing the man correctly. What was he suggesting? Was he really saying we were going to have to return to London to get our passports stamped with a new visa?

"Can't we get them done here?" I asked pleadingly.

"No," he replied coldly. "It has to be done in the country you are exiting from."

Something was definitely not right. Here we were, in this unfriendly cold place, at the mercy of a seemingly hardened bureaucrat who was displaying nothing less than a cynical attitude towards us. In almost a sadistical manner he seemed to be taking pleasure over our plight. He needed to hear we were definitely not one of your typical illegal aliens. We had been living legally in Florida for four years, had invested and lost nearly half a million dollars. We had followed all the rules and yet, here we were, possibly facing a scary situation of being kicked out of the country on some technicality by an immigration officer who had no idea of what we had endured. Where was the justice in that?

In three or four sentences I hurriedly blurted out our brief family history covering the past four years, but clearly he was not the least bit interested. He merely lifted his eyes towards the tiled ceiling and shrugged his shoulders. He didn't even try to hide a bored sigh.

I had to think of something, and quickly, to try and save the situation. Flying all the way back to London was certainly not an option. My mind was in full gear as I desperately sought a way out of this mess.

With all the composure I could muster, I politely asked the officer if I could meet with his superior. I needed to speak with some other person. Someone who would show a little more compassion.

I realized I was running the risk of offending this official by suggesting I go over his head, but I couldn't think of anything else. The officer pulled himself slowly out of the chair and looked down on me with a cold stare. I could see my charm was not working. He was clearly pissed!

There was a long, cold silence…"I will make a phone call, but the charge is fifteen dollars!" he retorted with almost a snarl.

I gulped down my anger, thinking it was wise not to question why I was being charged a fifteen dollar fee and wondering at the same time where this money would be going. I made a mental note that one day

I would check to see if this really was a legitimate charge and not just some cash benefit going directly into the immigration officer's back pocket.

I peeled off three five-dollar bills from a very thin money clip and placed the notes on the desk. The officer walked back to the desk, picked up the money and placed it in a brown envelope, as if to give the appearance that this payment was on the level. He told us to wait while he went off to make the phone call, leaving both Dominic and I shuffling nervously in our chairs.

Although he left the door open, and I could see him supposedly making a call from another office, I couldn't hear anything of what he was saying into the phone.

As I desperately tried to lip read, my attention was suddenly interrupted by the tightening grip of Dominic's hand. His nails were digging painfully into my fingers. I knew he was scared to death at what was happening to us but there was nothing I could do to make him feel any better. He didn't speak but continued shuffling nervously on the plastic cover seat, causing the plastic to make a plucking sound as it peeled away from his sweaty skin. We sat in silence, not knowing what to say to each other, just looking towards the open door and feeling the situation growing more intense by the second. I was now beginning to feel very frightened as I put my arm around my son's shoulders, not sure who was comforting whom. "This will all be sorted out in a moment Dominic," I said in a wavering voice that croaked emotionally from a dry mouth.

A few minutes later the arrogant officer sauntered back into the room. He didn't need to speak. His face told me the answer. "My superior says there is nothing he can do. You have to return to London."

"That's it!" I stammered, my anger rising. "Then I would like to go before a judge or magistrate," I blurted out.

The immigration officer had seemingly been waiting for a reaction. Now he was able to fully exercise his authority. Can you believe he was actually smiling now as he stretched to his full height and pushed out his bloated chest. Clearly he was reveling in the intimidation. "You can do that, by all means, but a court hearing will likely take a couple of days to arrange and we will be left with no choice but to keep you in custody until then."

I know now that I should have tried to call a lawyer at this juncture, but I had become so confused that it simply didn't enter my mind. Quite honestly I was feeling a little shell-shocked.

Held in custody! This situation was becoming more bizarre and idiotic by the minute. Held in custody, for what? I had openly told the officer I had a home and business in Naples. I didn't want to run off anywhere. Goddamn it. I wanted to stay.

I tried taking deep breaths as I attempted to collect both my thoughts and composure. If I had called an attorney at that moment, as I learned much later, the outcome could have been vastly different. Instead, confused and shaken and with young Dominic frightened to his core, I reasoned to myself that if I returned to London I could possibly get this matter sorted out in one day, allowing my son and I to fly back before the weekend when I was supposed to be in charge of taking the soccer kids to Colorado.

"How do we get back to London?" I asked the officer.

"You have to board the very next available flight," he said in a cold, matter-of-fact tone.

"And who pays for that?" I asked. "You do!" he said sternly, clearly becoming irritated by my questioning.

"And what happens if I can't afford the air fares?"

His expression suddenly softened, like a cat toying with a mouse. I could sense he was beginning to really enjoy this game.

"No problem! Uncle Sam will pay..." a long pause and a sickening smile..." but we we'll stamp the word '**DEPORTED**' in your passport. Most likely you'll never be able to return to this country again!"

The only credit card I had available for use was my American Express which had been acquired in more affluent days back in England. Mo and I had agreed this would only be used in dire emergencies. I had no problem convincing myself that this bizarre situation easily qualified.

If these events had reached a crazy level, it was soon to advance to an even higher plateau. Code red! What I had experienced so far was already worse than any nightmare and we were now about to discover it was still far from over.

"I need you to promise me that you will return to this office immediately after purchasing your tickets," the officer lectured me. "Otherwise I will have to place you in restraints."

I could only shake my head in disbelief at what I was hearing. Clearly the officer was enjoying this game but I couldn't understand why. Trouble at home? Dislike of Brits? Or maybe just a fun way to break up a boring night shift.

There was nothing left to consider and certainly no alternatives. Reluctantly I offered a verbal promise as Dominic and I were waved away and permitted to make our way to the line of airline ticket counters on the departure floor above. It was now after 9:00 p.m. and the rest of the airport appeared almost as deserted as the immigration hall. Upstairs, there were few travelers lounging in chairs and beyond them I could see the ticket counters which seemed, from this distance, to be totally abandoned. Now late into the evening, all airport activity appeared to be closing down around us.

We headed quickly towards the TWA booth where, as we moved closer, I was relieved to see a woman in uniform appear from a door and take up a position on the other side of the chrome counter. The sign above her head simply read "Tickets."

She looked up as we approached and gave us a cheery smile. My mind was beginning to come out of its cloud and my thinking was becoming a little clearer. Given an option, I really didn't want to explain to this friendly woman, with the motherly-type of demeanor, that we were, well, kind of being deported. But if explaining our situation could get us a cheaper airfare, I was prepared to forget my personal embarrassment and confess to anything!

Remembering we had paid less than $1,000 for five, round-trip air tickets out of Florida, I had in mind a realistic and, hopefully, an affordable figure as we waited for the woman to access the price and availability from her computer screen.

"Here we are," she smiled. "We can squeeze you both on the next flight but you will have to hurry. They are beginning to board now". And, almost as an after thought, added. "That will be $950 for you sir, and $750 dollars for your son."

"Seventeen hundred dollars! Come again," I blurted out.

I was asking myself once again if the situation could get any worse. This couldn't be right. There had to be a mistake. But apparently not as she repeated the prices again, this time lowering her voice as if trying to make the figure sound a little more reasonable and we were getting a deal. I was about to turn and walk away from the counter when I recalled what the officer had said about us getting on the first available flight. I knew he would be checking on our status and would be exercising zero tolerance. I feared there would be no hesitation on his part over placing me in handcuffs. In fact, I truly believed now that he would actually relish that opportunity and I still didn't understand why. And what about poor Dominic?

"This really is a serious problem for me," I said, turning to face the confused lady once more. "We are kinda being deported and I'm desperately short of money. There's a death in the family..." I let the full explanation drift away. "Is there any possible way we can get cheaper fares?" I was not faking the emotion in my voice.

"I'm sorry to hear of your problems but there is nothing I can do. The plane is now full and there are already three people waiting on stand by."

I hesitated for a second before accepting I had no other choice. I reluctantly handed over my credit card. It was then that my ten year-old confused son looked up at me with appealing eyes, as if possibly understanding for the first time what was happening, and quietly whispered, "Oh no dad... not more airline food!"

With our tickets in hand, we literally ran back to the escalator and down to immigration where our sadistic officer was waiting to scrutinize our tickets. Appearing satisfied as he handed them back, he sarcastically wished us "bon voyage." What a bastard. I jerked the tickets from his outstretched hand as Dominic and I turned to make our way back towards the departure lounge.

We had to hurry but first I needed to make one quick phone call before boarding the plane. Although it would be after 2:00 a.m. in London, I felt I should let my wife know what was happening. She would be expecting a call from us as soon as we arrived in Naples, which was supposed to be in four hours time. Instead, we would be halfway across the Atlantic on our way back to England.

I couldn't imagine what it must have been like for Mo. Her mother was passing away before her eyes, and I was waking her in the middle of the night with this unbelievable story. I pumped every coin from my pockets into the phone and dialed the number. The phone rang just twice before Mo's soft 'hello' came on in an inquisitive, sleepy whisper. I tried to keep the story as simple as possible so as not to alarm her, but who was I trying to kid? A feeling of alarm or panic is a given when you are being told that your husband and son have been refused entry into what had become your homeland. I tried relating the basic facts without pausing...and to make it sound a lot less than it really was. But obviously I wasn't doing a good job. I could sense the growing panic in her voice as she began asking questions. Rather coldly I was forced to cut the conversation short. We had a plane to catch, and I knew I would be facing the gleeful inquisition tactics of the immigration officer and all the repercussions if it left without us.

On board, we settled into what had become the all too familiar squashed and uncomfortable environment of the economy section. Even before we had settled, one of the flight attendants came to us, looked at the seat number above our heads, and asked for our passports. I was amazed that word had filtered through so quickly. The attendant, in matter-of-fact tone, explained the passports would be held by the captain and handed back to us on our arrival into London. I had to smile to myself, wondering where the flight crew expected Dominic and I to disappear to, cruising 30,000 feet above the Atlantic Ocean. I sensed the inquisitive lady in the window seat next to me was feeling a little uneasy about being so close to a couple of 'fugitives'.

I felt deflated over what was happening and in no mood to argue. I accepted the flight attendant was only following orders and I voiced no objection and decided not to make any smart comment as I handed over the two documents.

I may have dozed during the night but doubt it. Too many thoughts were racing through my mind as I kept recalling the events of the past few hours and how I was going to find a solution. I noticed a sleeping Dominic hadn't touched his tray of food.

As arranged, Mo was there to pick us up at Heathrow Airport. It was sad to see the look of distress and sadness on her face. Her mother was still hanging on, but only just, she explained. I quickly changed the subject and began filling her in with all our details as we drove back to her sister's home where she was staying. The time was a little after 8:30 a.m. and I was exhausted. But this wasn't the time to be thinking about sleep. I needed to take a shower and change the clothes I had been wearing for the past thirty-six hours before heading out to the American Embassy in London's Grovesnor Square. I hadn't had a wink of sleep for two days but the adrenaline rush in my body was all I needed to keep me moving. I was conscious of only one thing. We were facing a big problem and it needed fixing.

My train ride to central London came at a time when recent bombings in the city had caused a tightening of security at all government buildings. As I was soon to discover, the American Embassy had the tightest of them all. The big notice at the top of the embassy steps announced entry was by appointment only, except in a case of emergency. I had no problem believing my situation certainly qualified for that.

At the side door marked "visas" I could see, as I approached, two uniformed guards checking everyone entering the building. As I moved within earshot I could hear the man in front of me being asked if he had an appointment. When he replied 'no' he was rather curtly directed to read the sign on the wall which said the same as the big one in the front of the building. Letting out a gentle sigh he moved on without further discussion. Clearly his situation was not an emergency. I had to believe his eyesight wasn't that good either.

Taking note, I approached the soldier standing on the left of the door with a blatant, if false, air of confidence. A six foot something frame took a step forward and blocked my entry. The soldier, looking no older than a high school graduate, was now posing the same question to me. Before replying, I made sure he could see me reading the notice on the wall behind him. I looked squarely into the young man's face and answered: "No, I don't have an appointment," and quickly adding without pausing "It is definitely an emergency though."

To my surprise and relief the young guard appeared satisfied and didn't pursue the questioning. He merely stood back and waved me inside the door. I puffed my cheeks and sighed with relief, but the slowing of my pulse was to be short-lived. In the hallway were yet more barriers, as well as a brigade of more security people, some checking bags and purses while others checked off names listed on a clip board. Once again I tried to show confidence as I made my way towards the first table.

"You have an appointment?" I was asked by the pretty young lady dressed in a starched, white military uniform.

"No I don't, but I do have an emergency," I said. It wasn't difficult to assess from her inquisitive look and the pause in her voice that she was waiting for the particulars of that emergency.

"I got refused entry into the U.S. last night and it's imperative I'm back in Florida by the weekend." There was no need for me to try to sound desperate. Desperation had been my constant companion since this debacle first started back in St. Louis. Again I was both surprised and pleased that she also accepted my response without further inquiry.

After showing the contents of my pockets and submitting to a brief pat down, I was directed to join the line leading into a large reception area. Inside another door I was handed a plastic number and told to wait to be called. For a second, my mind went back to the deli counter at our local supermarket in Naples, where we also waited for service with a numbered ticket in hand. How different were the two situations I mused.

Fortunately I had to wait only a few minutes before I was summoned to one of the small cubicles at the front of the room. The seriousness of the situation now hit me like a hammer blow – not that I have ever been hit by a hammer before, I have to admit. I suddenly realized that the direction of my family's future depended on what was about to take place.

The young lady sitting behind the counter in a cubicle with the number eight above it looked friendly and attractive. Positive start I thought. She spoke with a soft calming voice. "How can I help you?" she asked.

I tried to be succinct as possible, without deleting or editing any of what I considered to be important points in my dealings with the immigration officer at the St. Louis airport. She listened intently, thumbing through the two passports I had pushed under the glass screen. I felt my luck might be changing with this sympathetic listener. As I continued to speak, my anxiety began to ease.

"… and I really do have to get this matter sorted out as quickly as possible, so I can get back to take these young players on their soccer trip. Do you have children?" I threw out, believing a little input on my volunteer work, and a mention of children, wouldn't do me any harm. She didn't respond.

"Can you see I have a real emergency here?" I pleaded.

The woman looked up, and for a second I thought I detected a hint of compassion in her smile. But before she could respond I was suddenly aware of another figure standing behind her. A man's head dropped down over the woman's shoulder.

In a brusque voice the middle-aged man took over. "This is no emergency! We can't deal with this matter today. We will have to wait 'til the paperwork gets to us from St. Louis." His voice took on a more threatening tone. With passports in hand he retorted, "Trying to enter the United States illegally is a serious matter!"

His words hit like that hammer feeling again. It seemed I had just encountered the long lost brother of the St. Louis immigration officer. In retrospect, I truly think at that moment I went into a state of shock. My legs started to tremble before almost buckling under me, as the full impact of what he was saying hit me like a cannon ball…not that I know what that feels like either. I held on tightly to the edge of the wooden counter below the glass screen. I felt weak all over as a light-headiness swept through my head. I took a deep breath as I desperately tried to regain some composure.

"There was absolutely no way I was trying to enter illegally, sir." I was conscious that my voice sounded as weak as the words which tumbled out. "I believe my visa to be valid. I had no way of knowing I couldn't use it to re-enter the country. No one told me I couldn't."

The man behind the grill was clearly running the show and, just as clearly, he wasn't going to allow the young woman to show me some of the compassion I still believed from the look on her face she was willing to offer.

"That may be proven to be so," said the still gruff sounding supervisor, "but there is absolutely nothing we can do until we receive a full report from the officer who stopped you at the airport." He raised his voice one octave as to make it clear this was the end of the discussion. He stood up straight – showing off a now familiar puffed-out chest that I reasoned must be something they teach in immigration bureaucrat school - and turned to walk away.

"How long will it take for the report to get here," I blurted out while he was still within earshot.

He turned back, stroking his chin. "Ohhhh, I can't really say. Why don't you come back here in FOUR MONTHS."

Suddenly I felt defeated.

Chapter Four

As I walked from the white stone embassy building I was reminded of earlier times when I came here to pick up our first visa that allowed me to move my family to the place where we now call home. It wasn't easy then, and I knew my new challenge wasn't going to be an easy one to overcome now. But I wasn't going to be beaten. I knew I was going to do everything that was required to return to my paradise.

It was a typical grey, cool, blustery day as I pulled up the collar on my light summer jacket. My body shivered as my mind went back to memories of warm sunshine and clear blue skies and the vacation that started our roller coaster journey.

After that Disney holiday in October, 1980, I kept the momentum going by meeting with an immigration lawyer in London and by Christmas we fully committed to the move by putting the house on the market. At the end of January, I was back in Florida, alone, in a hired car with a list of places to see. I felt like a European prospector from the 18th century looking for land with gold. In more modern terms, I guess I was looking for a place from which we could all find the American Dream. Sounds a bit foolish and dizzy now, especially considering how things turned out, but that's what it was all about really. Crazy as it may sound, I had no preconceived plan or detailed research to test out. In fact, all I had was a list of towns scribbled on a piece of paper and the only criteria in my head was that our new home needed to be close to the beach. If we were going to travel four thousand miles to find a new home, there's no way we were going to end up in the nether regions of some choking city. No, it would have to be a place my family would regard as paradise, or we'd forget the whole thing.

After a fitful night in a basic hotel near Miami Airport, I pulled out a map from the glove compartment of my rental car and headed north on Highway I-95, the congested Atlantic coast Interstate Highway. There is a corridor of communities scattered at regular intervals all the way along this coastline. I quickly passed through the high-rise condominiums of Ft Lauderdale and then into the smaller communities of Pompano Beach, Boca Raton, Delray Beach and Boynton Beach. I threaded my way through each town desperately looking for a reason to stop and investigate further, but whichever new place it was, nothing enticed me to slow down, let alone stop. I just kept driving and crossing names off the list. I suppose I was panning, like a true gold seeker, and I simply knew in my heart that I would instinctively know the place where I wanted us to live the moment I saw it. If it meant I had to drive the entire East Coast of Florida to find that elusive new hometown, then so be it.

I got as far as West Palm Beach and then I stopped. To this day, I don't know exactly what made me do a U-turn, but I had this gut feeling that the East Coast was not for us. I looked at the other names on the list and thought, no, I've seen enough on this side. My next thoughts turned to the one name on the West Coast, which was written down: *Naples.* Mo and I had heard about it purely by chance, after meeting a real estate lawyer at a party in London. This friend of a friend had recently become involved in various property deals in Naples and he held our attention as he explained that it was a beautiful area, not yet facing the pains and perils of rapid growth or urban sprawl. He spoke of the slow pace, of how Naples consisted of a couple of good restaurants and a plethora of pristine beaches. He said there were opportunities to be had in this growing town and that he could feel a certain vibrancy when he was there.

Best of all, he thought it would be an idyllic place to raise children. As my mind wandered to the illusion of Naples, I suddenly felt uneasiness. What was it really like? Would it be like the other places I had seen? Maybe the West Coast is just a replica of the East. Maybe Florida was not for us after-all. I pushed these negative thoughts away as I gassed the car and hit the road.

Most people only discover Naples when they need a rest stop somewhere between Tampa and Miami. Certainly, in the winter of 1980, Naples was something of a forgotten town compared to the commercial places I had already seen on the East Coast. And it was certainly a world away from the hustle and bustle and tourist attractions of Orlando. It was only because of that party conversation that Naples got on my list at all, but the moment I arrived there and opened the car windows, I knew this would be our new home.

I breathed in the Naples aroma and smiled. It is difficult to describe the scent now but I suspect it is one borne from a unique blend of the beautiful flowers that grow all year round and the saltiness from the Gulf of Mexico. I loved it then as I love it now. I came across Fifth Avenue South, the town's main shopping street, and walked along it for the first time. This is a quaint and attractive thoroughfare lined on both sides by elegant shops. It was busy with the activity of shoppers, both with locals as well as with vacationers seeking warmth from the harsh chills of northern states. Naples was clearly not a destination for European tourists seeking the thrills of Disney World. More than anything, I was struck by the mosaic of color that filled the streets. Flowering window boxes and immaculately kept pots were on every shop-front patio. This was a town that clearly took pride in its appearance. To me, Naples had a distinct warmth and positive energy running through its heart. Back in the car, I had no idea where to start my exploration and for a few minutes I drove around aimlessly. I came to a crossroads - which I later discovered is called 'Four Corners' - and drove straight across and immediately found myself back on the main shopping street heading towards the gulf. A few hundred yards further on, past the shops, I first noticed the houses bordering the beach. Although partly hidden behind high bushes, I could see enough to appreciate they were magnificent estates with sweeping driveways and gardens filled with explosive red bougainvillea and various flowering shrubs. This was a sight completely new to me. Some of the homes were built in a Spanish style, with heavy tiled roofs and ornate arches. Others were of a traditional, one-floor Florida style, impressively large but lacking flair and imagination. That architectural flaw would change as the world's sophisticates discovered Naples. In the future we were to witness countless more extremely wealthy families moving to the area, most seeking higher quality architectural designs to match their lavish lifestyle. I would be there to witness, during what would be a relatively short period, newly constructed homes becoming so big that the local planning authorities would have to step in to regulate maximum sizes for both new and renovated constructions. But all this was many years down the road. On the day I took those first steps toward the white sandy beach, life in Naples was a whole lot more simple.

I had already taken off my shoes. Although the afternoon sun had heated the pavement, it was nothing like the unbearable hot plate that burned my soles the moment I stepped onto the golden sand. I quickly found a shaded piece of cool grass and looked around. The sky was a deep rich blue, the air was clean and fresh. The Gulf waters shimmered as blinding sunlight danced across the calm surf. I was totally convinced I had found paradise and hungrily breathed in the scene. This was *it* - home! I clearly remember the excitement when I phoned Mo later and told her what I had discovered. "You will love it here. The kids will love it here. It's perfect, magical. I can't wait to show you." Mo couldn't curb her enthusiasm. "Is it really that gorgeous?" she asked.

Now that I had found Naples, I knew there was no turning back. Alone in my hotel room that night, I was reminded of the meetings back in London I'd had with the immigration lawyer. I didn't know it at the time but I was destined to do a lot of business with both immigration and litigation lawyers during our time in America.   How could I possibly foresee what was going to be required, or all the crazy immigration bureaucracy that would come to rule our lives?

I have to admit I initially felt suckered by the deception of advertising when I arrived at Gudeon's office, just off Trafalgar Square, and climbed up three floors of a narrow and dangerously rickety staircase. I finally entered a tiny office which showed no signs of a successful business, and found a man in a shabby gray suit, checkered shirt and a creased tie, slightly hidden behind a cheap looking desk creaking under the weight of unattended files. He looked like a headmaster going through school reports.   His hair was thinning and swept back with the visible tracks of overly firm combing; plastic framed bifocals were pinched into a pitted nose. Clearly, the £1,200 fee Gudeon was charging me was not being spent on his attire, an assistant as I could see or, for that matter, a luxury office. And he clearly did not spend his money on an office with a view either - the outlook from a small window behind his desk was of a plain brick wall that seemed to be within a short arm's reach. One side of his cramped domain was covered with impressive framed diplomas and various legal qualifications, which basically did a decent job of covering the peeling paint. So, this was the man in whom I would be entrusting so much. I could never have guessed what a major role this physically unimpressive man was going to play in our lives. Although he was not exactly inspiring at face value, he would get us into America and years later he would ultimately fight in our corner when deportation seemed our certain route back to England. Thankfully, my random pick was going to prove to be a good one, and Ed Gudeon would, over time, be a valuable, if expensive, aide.

During our opening meeting, Gudeon had asked a barrage of questions, jotting down my answers on several printed forms. He rarely smiled, and my attempts at humor and banter were always met with a blank. In all the time I knew him, I never got as much as a chuckle out of Gudeon. To him, life was a serious business. When he finally looked up that day, he peered at me over his bifocals and I felt my first sense of alarm. He looked quite stern as he eased back in his peeling leather chair and for a moment I thought he was going to extol some type of reprimand.

"I have to tell you that your choices for getting a permanent visa are limited to one at best," he said in a deep and ever-so slow voice.

"You certainly don't qualify for a green card, but you may possibly qualify as an investor under an E2 visa, assuming you make a substantial investment in purchasing an established profitable business. That will permit you to stay for as long as you own the business. But be warned. American immigration is getting tougher on issuing these visas. Get out of the business you purchase and you are giving up your rights to stay in America."

I didn't appreciate it at the time but this last phrase would come back to haunt me. On what I took as a brighter note, Gudeon went on to explain that our new business could be any type, providing we could convince the "man at the embassy who authorizes investment visas" that I had the ability and financial wherewithal to run the operation successfully.

As I paced the hotel room in Naples, Gudeon's words came back to me. I formulated a plan to find myself a business and qualify for a visa. Over dinner, I scoured the local directories for the names of people I felt I needed to meet during my stay. The first contact was with Gil Pooler, a local business broker. His display ad appealed because the firm blatantly boasted of having "The Largest List Of Businesses For Sale." With growing confidence that I had found the perfect location, I now needed to find the perfect business. I phoned Gil's office and was pleasantly surprised to find him still working so late. I quickly explained my needs. He sounded cheerful and friendly and agreed to meet with me at his office the following morning. For the next two days I was destined to be a prisoner in his office as we poured over the countless number of enterprises he had listed for sale.

Gil was a waddling and wheezing advert for early death. A walrus of a man, he was grossly overweight and chain-smoked Marlboro Reds which had left a distinct nicotine stain on his heavy moustache. He wore baggy shorts and a polo shirt. I learned that after breaking up with his second wife a few years prior, he had followed his parents down to Naples from "up north." Unbelievably, he was only in his early thirties and told me he had recently started dating the attractive daughter of a local surgeon who was ten years his junior. She would become his third wife. It makes you wonder. Gil told me he had tried many different careers over the years; some he claimed were very successful and many, he admitted, were not. Gil turned the pages of his business listings and read aloud from the information sheets. I listened and said 'Yes' or 'No' and slowly we eliminated one business after another. Fortunately, Gil had an extensive inside knowledge of many of the listings, so we were able to discount a large number quickly for not meeting the three requirements I had previously set.

The first requirement was to satisfy me that the business would be one that Mo and I would enjoy operating together; there was simply no way we would move to another country and be unhappy in our work. Secondly, the business had to be making a good profit; we refused to purchase an unprofitable business, even one showing great potential. Besides, in order to satisfy the immigration services, the enterprise had to be healthy and operating heavily in the black, or we would not qualify. As Gudeon had explained, it wasn't just enough for the business to be able to support us as a family, the authorities would demand it showed potential for making continuing healthy profits. My third condition was a requirement to find a company we felt confident we could manage without a lot of aggravation. We did not want to relocate to where we considered paradise only to be entrenched in a miserably troublesome business. So Gil continued reading and I continued listening. And the pages kept turning. Lawn care services, pool cleaning companies, chemical supply wholesalers, pet shops, clothes shops, sports shops, hardware stores, car rental agencies, golf ranges, and car-repair garages. You name it, and it was for sale. And if we fancied owning a restaurant, no problem. Take your pick. There were more than twenty to choose from!

At first, the list had seemed inexhaustible, and as we moved from one thick file to another, I began to feel deflated. My hopes of finding a good investment were raised several times. From the promotional wording many businesses looked quite appealing and challenging, until Gil and I looked deeper and realized they were barely making a profit. Some were immediately discounted when I looked across at Gil and met a screwed up face shaking fiercely. I couldn't help but smile at some of the comments listed by the vendors. The general selling line was "shows great potential" which I quickly interpreted as: "We couldn't make this bloody business work, so please give us a stack of cash and see if you can!"

As time wore on, the files became thinner and by the second afternoon I was beginning to think we might not find a qualifying business at all. The Yellow Pages listed another business broker in town, but I had grown to like Gil and felt I could trust him. I appreciated that all the information he was giving me came directly from the business owners. It would be down to me to check it out later. Buyer beware!

Finally, around four o'clock on the second day I was left with two businesses that appeared to meet the criteria – a small Naples marina and a health and exercise club. The limited information in their blurbs made them sound very attractive. The marina, with its docking berths and boat rental business, looked like a prosperous and fun operation. I knew next to nothing about boats, but felt confident I had the capabilities of managing this type of operation with the right help. Gil phoned the owner to set an appointment. Too late! There was already an offer on the table and the sale was going through. I learned later that the buyer was Phil O'Connor, a former butcher from Hull in northern England. Over the ensuing years, we became good friends and I watched Phil develop a very successful operation. He had a boyish charm and, although a heavy drinker, he was a hit with the ladies. He also had an uncanny knack with business, so I couldn't help feeling that Phil had something of a charmed life. Not only did he turn the marina into a profitable sales and service enterprise, but his waterfront property soared in value twenty times over. He had a lovely wife, and two daughters with her – not to mention a lithe young Cuban mistress, with whom he had a third daughter. Tragically, Phil was to die suddenly from a heart attack in 2005 at the age of 50.

Feeling a little disappointed that the marina had gone, I concentrated my attention on the second choice: The Executive Health Club. This was a two-year-old fitness club and spa located in one of the busier shopping plazas in town. Throughout my life I had always been involved with sports, so the idea of running the only health club in Naples sounded very appealing. We learned from the information that a manager, an assistant manager and four exercise instructors were currently employed there. The club consisted of a fully equipped exercise room, sauna, steam room, hot tub, massage rooms and a reception area offering retail sales. Men and women were using the facilities on alternate days. Feeling a twinge of excitement and optimism, I decided to surreptitiously check out the operation under the guise of a prospective member. Less than an hour later I was walking through the inviting reception area of a spacious spa. It was early evening and the place was filled with men of all ages, working out on all types of equipment and free weights. There was an almost deafening cacophony of rock music, clanging metal and the hissing and groaning of men pumping iron to the limits of their strength. A quick scan of the workout room told me this was definitely a different type of gym than I was used to. But, despite the noise, it appeared from its lavish decor to live up to the image its name implied. The Executive Health Club was carpeted and tiled throughout and floor to ceiling mirrors filled every wall. The Manager, Don Myers, freely answered my questions and gave me the full history of the place as we walked through. Don was 6ft 4in with a full beard and thinning hair. Judging by the bulging muscles, he clearly made full use of the weight room. He looked like a bodyguard, but in reality, as I was to discover, he was a gentle giant.

Don was a friend of the owner, a successful Naples builder named Richard Vetter, and he had helped open the spa and had worked there since the first day. Don explained that no expense had been spared and he seemed justifiably proud of what had been achieved. He came across as being very conscientious and I sensed that he was an asset worth keeping if I decided to buy the business.

Back at Gil Pooler's office the following day, we called Vetter and asked to review the company's books and tax returns since opening. He appreciated my tight deadline and was more than happy to move quickly. Vetter was another bearded guy of 6ft 4in – you get use to that size and look in Florida – and he turned up later in a blue Mercedes convertible with all the information I needed. He seemed straight and open and left everything with us. After spending an hour or so going through the books ourselves, Gil arranged for a CPA to scrutinize them in detail that evening and give us his recommendations the following day. To my joy, the accountant announced that everything appeared to be in order. He said the books showed a good profit for the past year and pointed out that the business had signed an attractive long-term lease on the building with an option to renew for a further five years. The spa was situated in a small but busy mall in an ideal location in a growing town, so I figured there was great potential to increase the membership. All of this appeared to me to justify the asking price of $155,000. After discussing the matter over the phone that evening with Mo, we made our offer, with $100,000 payable immediately and the rest paid over time. It concerned me that I was putting up so much, but this had to be done to satisfy the requirements for the investment visa. Besides, the whole deal was dependent on us gaining that visa. If that didn't materialize, then the deal was off. Vetter accepted our offer immediately. On reflection, maybe he took it a little too quickly, but I was pleased as I left Naples, thinking I had gotten a good deal. Everything was fitting neatly into place. Now to return home and appease the immigration officials.

The next day, I arrived back at our lovely home at Keston Park, near Bromley in Kent, to the excited welcoming committee of a wife and three young children. Mo and I hadn't mentioned our plans just in case it didn't happen, but the time was right to tell the children. Kirsty was too young to really understand what we were saying, but she quickly mirrored Kieran and Dominic who went into an instant spin of innocent excitement.

"Going to *live* in America!" exclaimed Dominic with wide eyes. "Are we really going to live with Mickey?"

Chapter Five

Twenty-one years ago and yet it is so easy to recall the very first day we arrived in Miami on that hot, sultry July afternoon…one wife, three young children, Kieran, Dominic and Kirsty, eight suitcases and a long-time friend's sixteen year-old daughter, Alison, who was going to be vacationing with us for a few months and help Mo with the kids.

The eight-hour flight had been uneventful; all three kids choosing to stay awake the entire time and then crashing just as we began our descent into Miami Airport and had to be carried off. As a parent, you sometimes wish you were built like an octopus.

How different everything was way back then. None of the major car rental companies had anything like the luxury family vans they have today. Our request for "the biggest vehicle you have," turned out to be one of those big, ugly station wagons like we used to see on the old TV shows. In its own day it may have been impressive, but not to us. The powder blue vehicle stood out on the car rental lot, not so much because of its attractive appearance and size, but more because it looked so much older and more used than any of the other shiny vehicles around it. As we began what was quickly developing into an exhausting pantomime of trying to load all the bags and still leave enough space for three grown ups and three children, I really started to believe we were competing to get into the Guinness Book of Records. You know what I mean. The record for the most suitcases and human bodies in one vehicle. It was probably about this stage that I also had this premonition that something was about to go awfully wrong. And it sure did.

We were less than thirty minutes out of the airport, and I was still losing the battle with the heavy suitcase that kept falling back off the pile and crushing my head, when a sudden thudding sound outside suggested we had a flat.

We had no other choice than to pull over and stop on what must have been one of the world's busiest highways. With a constant stream of noisy traffic roaring past in the background, out came the kids from the vehicle, out came the suitcases, and out came Mo and Alison as we began our desperate search for the spare wheel and tools. It would certainly have been a whole lot easier with an instructional manual but that had either been lost or thrown out long before this evening.

What a start to our new life I was thinking as we labored for over an hour in the hot, humid evening air, with our sweat-drenched clothes sticking to our tired bodies and the light now quickly disappearing. A couple of sore and bleeding knuckles certainly didn't help either. *'Welcome to America!'* Alison called out sarcastically as she herded the children off to the safety of a nearby ice cream store.

It was after midnight when we limped into Naples, tired, aching and bruised, and pulled into the driveway of the Lakewood home we had rented. With the help of our contact man, Gil Pooler, we had taken a year's lease on the property. We had only seen photos but knowing it had been used as a model and hearing Gil's comments (who had personally checked it out) we held no fears it wouldn't be suitable. We had decided that renting for a year would give us time to look around before making a commitment to buy.

Negotiating the lease had proven to be a battle. The $700 a month original price tag had been renegotiated to $1,000 by the owner over the phone after he discovered we had three children. At first he told us he had changed his mind about renting to us. Even with the offer of more money, we still had a difficult time convincing him we would leave the place in pristine condition. In the end he took our word but not before raising the deposit from five hundred dollars to a thousand. Had I felt we had an option, I certainly wouldn't have agreed to the agreement which Mo described as "blatant day-light robbery." But our hands were tied. Each inquiry Gil had made on our behalf brought back only responses of 'no pets' and 'no children.' Apparently these were rules very common for the newer homes up for rental in Naples in those early days.

Lakewood was certainly an attractive new development with two golf courses and two clubhouses, each with its own swimming pool. It was an open-landscaped community with no fences, no garden sheds and certainly no clotheslines. I mention these facts because I remember being amused one day, shortly after moving in, and while waiting to pick up some brochures in the model home U.S Homes used for its sales office. As I was waiting for some brochures to be pulled out of a new box, in walks what I assumed was another interested homebuyer, loudly announcing he was from New York. I couldn't help but overhear him questioning the salesman as they moved towards a corner desk, on which sat what appeared to be a site plan. In his booming voice, the customer was asking: "And where would be the best place to put my garden shed?"

By the look on the salesman's face I could tell he wasn't sure if the man was serious or not. "I'm sorry sir but this is a deed-restricted community which doesn't permit garden sheds."

The New Yorker clearly wasn't happy with that answer. "Mmm… So where can my wife hang her fresh laundry? On hearing that clotheslines weren't permitted either, nor were wooden fences, nor trucks in the driveway, nor basketball hoops, the New Yorker stormed out scowling, suggesting he wasn't too keen on this deed-restricted community living.

When we moved into Lakewood it was about three quarters completed, with a mixture of family homes, condos and villas. Our three bedroom, two-bathroom, ranch-style rental couldn't have been more different from the mock, five-bedroom Tudor-style house we had left in England. But no one in our family appeared the least bit unhappy about that. We all felt it was more than a fair exchange.

That first night, we all looked, and certainly felt, totally exhausted as we struggled out of the car and made our way into the house. We made no effort to unpack a single bag. Instead, each of us quickly found a soft spot where we could crash. Certainly no one had the energy to even think about making up a bed. We each grabbed a blanket and pillow and everyone was sound asleep within a few minutes. For some of us, sleep came even before our heads hit the pillow. It was an exhausting end to a very tiring day.

I'm pretty sure that everyone who travels from Europe to Florida wakes about the same time, that time being 4 am. Our entire family certainly proved to be no different! By five o'clock, and with the bright morning sun already rising out of the lake at the back of the house, the rooms were buzzing with activity. The children were excitingly investigating their new surroundings as they wandered from room to room, picking up on things that were new to them…light switches that worked in reverse…lamps that dimmed and brightened with a touch of the base…the huge double refrigerator that made its own ice. The list of exciting new discoveries seemed endless.

Our first morning in America, and it just happened to be the Fourth of July. None of us had appreciated the significance of the day until we were leaving the downtown restaurant with our stomachs full of pancakes, grits and hash browns. "Got to try these new foods", mother had argued as the rest of us searched the menu looking for the basic eggs, bacon and toast combinations. While we were busy inside eating, the scene outside in the nearby streets was taking on a carnival-type atmosphere. We came out to a splash of red, white and blue and honking car horns. It was still before 10:00 am and yet the digital temperature clock across the road, outside the Barnett Bank building on Fifth Avenue South, was already recording 84 degrees. The high summer humidity was causing the clothes to stick to our backs…but you didn't hear one of us complain; we all loved the feeling! Around us, families were beginning to line up on both sides of the street. Roadblocks were now diverting the traffic and we realized we were about to witness a parade.

Excited children were jumping up and down around us and waving their Stars and Stripes flags. In the distance we could hear the bands warming up. It was like the magic of Disney all over again.

"Look mummy", said five year-old Dominic as he surveyed the growing crowds. *"Everyone is so pleased to see us!"* Our laughing brought tears rolling down our faces. I think it was Alison who pointed out that Dominic was displaying the Union Jack flag on his t-shirt. Surely, I remember thinking at the time, life doesn't get any better than this.

Initially, we rented a car for the first week. But the large wagon that had got us here from Miami Airport was quickly replaced by something more modern and, hopefully, more reliable. From a more sensible financial perspective, we realized we needed to quickly buy our own car.

But, of course, we had absolutely no idea what to get or where to go, so once again we called on Gil's help. As with renting the house, we decided to be cautious over the purchase of a new vehicle, choosing instead to buy a used one so we could then take our time on checking the new models later. As we expected, Gil just happened to know someone in the business.

I often wondered, in later years, if Gil actually got a cut from all the people and services he recommended to us in those early days. He never let on that he did and I never asked. It seemed he knew just about everyone in town!

Buying the car became our third major purchase after the TV and barbecue grill. We had absolutely no intention when we first entered the car lot of buying a Cadillac, but that's what we ended up with an hour or so later when we walked out. Roy Stearn, the lot owner, had convinced us it was a good, reliable car for the money and would be ideal for transporting our family of six. With U.S. gas prices being almost two-thirds less than what we had been used to paying in England, the purchase of a gas-guzzling Cadillac didn't faze us.

Now, with our three important purchases, we all began to feel we were settling in nicely.

Both Mo and I warmed to Roy from the beginning. He didn't pressure us and insisted he would spend a day or two to go over the vehicle himself to check everything was ok. He even offered to loan us a vehicle so we could return our rental and save ourselves some money. We both felt we had secured a good deal as we drove off that morning in the loaner. I could sense by the look on Mo's face that she was sharing my thoughts. I was thinking, even though we had owned new and more expensive cars in England, the thought of owning a big Cadillac brought on a different type of excitement.

This was early July and we were beginning to experience what had been described to us as the familiar summer weather pattern. Each morning would start out clear and sunny, with the clouds building during the late morning, bringing in the heavy showers most afternoons. We were told we could set our watches by the afternoon thunderstorm and most days that proved true. For an hour or so, Naples would be deluged with terrific thunderstorms and lightening strikes. It wasn't difficult to accept, when watching the flash and fork lightening long into the summer evenings, that we were living in the lightening capital of the world. The rainfall was so heavy during these thunderstorms that low-lying streets would quickly become flooded as the storm drains became overloaded. The homeowners on Lakewood, just like those in most other communities, were forced to carry flood insurance and many times over the years we had to drive through flooded streets as the lakes overflowed. We still have pictures of kids in the neighborhood paddling their canoes down the streets.

After leaving the car lot, I dropped off Mo and the others at the shopping mall. I had an appointment with a local printer to order business cards and to pick up office supplies for the spa. I had no idea as I approached the building that I was about to experience a never-to-be-forgotten lesson about South Florida tropical weather.

I had parked the loaner car off the road on the vacant site next to the printers. I was moving quickly as the darkening clouds began to threaten rain. Sensibly I made sure all the windows were closed in the vehicle before heading towards the office. Fortunately I managed to get inside the front door just as the first raindrops began to pound the pavement.

"Just in time" smiled the lady in the front office. "Hope your car windows are up. You did park in the parking lot at the rear of the building I hope?"

"No! I didn't see the car park," I said. "I left the car on that vacant site next door."

"Not a good move. New to the area?"

I now sensed there was a problem afoot.

"That lot is real low ground and floods very quickly. The ditch in front fills up and overflows. Water gets as high as a foot or more in a matter of minutes."

I really didn't appreciate the full significance of what she was telling me as I took a look outside and watched the rain streaking down. I couldn't see the vehicle from the window and so I was unaware that it was already taking on the appearance of a submarine in a 'dive' mode.

It proved fortunate that it only took a few minutes to place my order for the business cards and pick up my supplies. I pulled up my shirt collar as I prepared for the run to the car. I could have stayed and waited for the storm to pass over but the news about flooding had already set off some alarm bells. At the first sign of the rain easing up I pushed open the door and bolted.

Oh no! The woman in the office certainly wasn't exaggerating about the speed of the flooding. The water had already poured over the sides of the low ditch and I could see water seeping under the bottom of the car's doorsills. I was literally panic-struck as I waded towards the vehicle and dragged open the driver's side door.

Already the floor was covered with water. What a mess!

I knew I had to get the car back on the road and solid ground as quickly as possible. I prayed the engine would start. The first time I turned the key the engine just barely turned, before spluttering dead. I didn't want to flood the engine so I patiently waited and counted to ten. I tried again. Another splutter as I slowly eased my foot down on the gas pedal. Suddenly a loud roar, a few coughs, and the engine burst to life. I quickly put the car into gear and very slowly edged forward. The last thing I needed now was to spin the wheels and lose traction. Very gently I turned the steering wheel and pointed the front of the car towards the road. Inch by inch we eased forward, causing a gentle wake as we gathered a little more speed.

I had no idea where the ditch was, as everywhere around me was under a foot or more of water. I knew I had to find the hard surface. If we hit the ditch, I knew it would be goodbye to one loaner vehicle. What was I going to tell Roy I was thinking just before we made it to the road and dry land.

The rain was easing off and all I could hear was water flushing its way out of the vehicle. The water that could escape, that is. There still remained a full inch of brown-colored liquid covering the floor. The car certainly wasn't new but that was hardly the point.

Happily, the drive home proved there was no damage to the car, other than water-soaked carpets. The next morning, all the carpeting was taken out of the vehicle and left to dry out in the hot sunshine. We put Roy off for a couple of days before exchanging vehicles. It was several years later when we confessed to Roy about the experience. He laughed the loudest!

In the early days we would try and make a couple of Disney trips each year. With the spa closed on Sundays and sufficient staff members to ensure adequate coverage on Saturdays, we would start out on our Orlando trip at around 4:30 am Saturday morning. The idea would be for us to arrive at Disney World as the gates opened and stay almost until the gates were closing for the night. Sometime during the day we would take a break and find ourselves an inexpensive motel, which hopefully meant not paying more than $30 for the night. The next morning would begin with an early breakfast and another busy day at the amusement park before leaving around 5 pm for the four-hour drive back to Naples.

Of course, while I drove, everyone else got comfortable with pillow and blankets and slept for most of the journey. Then they couldn't understand why I was so exhausted by the time we got home late Sunday night.

The first time we made the trip, about six months after arriving in Naples everyone was just too excited to sleep. The three children were in the back playing games as we made our way through the back roads that led through the central part of the state. We chose this scenic route, as opposed to the interstate highway, because it threaded through the picturesque orange groves. At that time, rows upon rows of orange-laden trees lined up like soldiers on a battlefield as far as the eye could see. With the sun rising above the light mist and lightening up a clear blue sky, we all breathed in the pungent orange smell that wafted through the open windows.

We were on a stretch of road somewhere between Immokalee and La Belle, about forty miles from home, when I first spotted the police car approaching us. I easily recognized the vehicle from a distance by the light panel on the roof. We were the only two vehicles on the road for as far as the eye could see. I didn't even bother to check my speed because I knew we weren't going fast enough to get into any sort of trouble.

It didn't concern me one bit when I noticed in my rear view mirror the police vehicle was making a U-turn and following us several hundred yards back. Dominic was peering out of the rear window, saw the car turn, and was excitedly summoning his brother to take a look. With the two of them playing some type of cops and robbers game, we continued driving for another mile or so before the blue and red lights started to flash and a siren began to wail. I smiled to myself, thinking the pursuing cop had seen the two children peering out of the window and was amusing them, which, judging by their hooting and hollowing, they were really enjoying.

We drove for another half mile or so before the call for me to pull over blasted from the radio hailer. It stunned me for a moment as I tried to reason what was going on. The voice sounded anything but friendly. What could possibly be wrong I wondered as I slowed down and drove up on the grass verge. Although confused, I still really believed this was going to prove to be some sort of joke. But that feeling quickly changed when the police officer walked up to my vehicle and, in a brusque voice, asked to see my driving license. There was certainly no smile on his face as he peered over the top of his shades. It was like a scene out of a classic cops' movie.

"Do you realize you were doing eighty-five miles an hour when I passed you on the other side of the road, and seventy-five miles an hour when I was following you?" the cop was scolding me in a deep southern drawl. My *'Good morning officer'* was left trailing off in the breeze.

Mo and I looked at each other in disbelief. "I'm sorry officer but you must be mistaken. I'm fully aware the speed limit is fifty-five along this stretch of road, and there was absolutely no way I was doing much more than that."

My response brought absolutely no reaction from the cop. He merely turned his back and strode back to his own vehicle with my license in his hand.

Mo and I could only look at each other wondering what to do next. I truly felt we were being set up for some type of pay-off you read about in fictional novels. Was this cop looking for me to pass him a twenty-dollar bill? We all sat there in silence. The attitude of the cop had clearly intimidated the children and they sat there in the back seat with open mouths, clearly wondering what was going on.

When the traffic cop returned a few minutes later he was writing out a yellow ticket. His face was expressionless as he said. "I'm booking you for the lesser speed of seventy-five miles an hour. Consider yourself lucky."

"But there was no way I was ever doing seventy-five miles an hour, not with you on my tail and my kids waving from the back window. Do you think I'm stupid?"

My logical offering was clearly having no effect. He continued writing without looking up. When he finished, he simply thrust the pad through the window for me to sign. "You can contest this in traffic court if you wish," and walked away. Mo and I shook our heads in disbelief and continued the next hour of the journey in silence.

Back in Naples, I was told that what we had encountered through La Belle was not uncommon. It was a poor agricultural town, and it was well known that speeding tickets provided a much-needed boost to City Hall coffers. There were some who clearly believed that the traffic cops had a quota of speeding tickets to meet.

The more I heard these stories, the angrier I became. I decided not to heed the warning of some who told me not to fight it. "If you do, your car will become a marked vehicle every time you drive through the town," they said.

But I didn't listen. I informed the court that I wanted to contest the ticket and my wife would also attend the hearing as my witness.

I immediately began to work on my courtroom strategy and planned to get a head start by composing a detailed report of the situation and sending it off to the traffic court a week or so prior to our hearing. I figured a well-written letter would indicate I was not someone who would be intimidated and play dead to a bogus ticket.

I guess we should have realized that the eighty-mile round trip was going to be a complete waste of time as soon as we entered the courthouse and saw our traffic cop seemingly having a friendly chat over coffee and donuts with the elderly, white-haired man we were told was going to conduct the 'informal hearing'. Their raucous laughter filled the stately courthouse and their friendly 'good old buddy' pats on the back didn't go unnoticed by both my wife and I.

Inside the chamber, the atmosphere was very relaxed. Court staff was coming and going as doors opened and banged shut. Even as the magistrate ordered the proceedings to begin, little groups continued with their chatting. No one seemed to mind.

The first activity involved requests for bail. By the appearance of each individual who rose to stand before the magistrate, they were still suffering the affects of some hard drinking the night before. The smell of thick alcohol odor filled the room. Two of the men could hardly stand and swayed precariously in front of the magistrate's bench. Clearly both had to prop themselves up with the help of the desk behind them.

My name was called after about fifteen minutes and I rose from the hard wooden seat. My bottom was numb, but I quickly forgot about that as I moved to a seat at the table as directed by the official with the huge potbelly hanging over his belt. I was suddenly aware that I was feeling nervous and I grasped my manila folder tightly with both hands in an effort to control my shaking.

I looked up towards the magistrate but could barely see more than the top half of his head from where I was sitting. As I sat upright in my chair I noticed he had sunk low in his own chair, with his head resting in his hand. I sensed it wouldn't be long before he would find the proceedings boring and would take a nap. I hoped he would stay awake at least long enough to hear my side of the story.

The room actually quieted as the cop read his report. I half expected everyone to clap and cheer when he finished. He smiled smugly, placed his report book back into his jacket and stood waiting.

The silence was broken by the lean, tall man standing in front of the magistrate's bench who turned to me and asked if I had any questions to ask the traffic cop.

"I do," I said in a strong voice. "But first I would like to know if the court has received the letter I sent several weeks ago?"

Now that I was standing I had a clear view of the magistrate. He had slumped even further into his seat so his head was barely visible above the oak bench. He looked like a Mr. Magoo cartoon character, cupping his hand to his ear to hear what I was saying. I was wondering if he had ever heard a British accent in his courtroom before.

Blank stares suggested that no one seemed to know what I was talking about so I repeated my question. I asked the magistrate again if he had seen the letter I had written to the court. I should have guessed his answer long before he spoke. His words came out in a slow, familiar southern drawl.

"Can't say that I have son...why don't you just go ahead and tell me what you wrote."

I cleared my throat and thanked the magistrate and asked if I could first ask the police officer a couple of questions. A flick of the finger and a nod of the head indicated I could proceed.

I took my time, now beginning to relish my day in court, going over the details in the report with the traffic stop. I really wanted to establish the fact that the cop had seen my children waving to him out of the back window. I believed the basis of my argument depended on this single point. *What father would speed when their kids are waving at a cop!*

But clearly the witness realized the significance of this point too because he wasn't going to admit to anything. He said repeatedly that he couldn't see who was at the back window and his mind was more focused on watching his radar screen. He smiled confidently at smiling faces dotted around the room. I knew I wasn't going to get a Perry Mason confession out of this cop and eventually decided to move on with my defense.

Fortunately I had brought a copy of the letter with me and went ahead and read it to the court. I got the impression from the chatter that had started up around me that no one was really interested in what I was reading. I battled the noise.

The talking did pause for a moment when Mo got up on the witness stand and in her most posh, eloquent English voice said she agreed with everything I had put in the letter. After a couple of questions from me I began to sense the amusement of seeing a couple of strange people in the dock was over and everyone was beginning to become agitated by a foreign couple taking up so much time in this court. The novelty effect was gone. I decided to close quickly.

I left the magistrate with what I felt was the most compelling, if now all too familiar, argument. "Do you honestly think sir that I would be speeding with the full awareness of an officer on my back?"

I sat down and waited, like everyone else in the courtroom, for the magistrate to respond.

"Well son." The slow drawl was even more accentuated. "I hear what you are saying but I think it was more kinda like this." The courtroom had suddenly become completely quiet. There was a long pause while the magistrate shuffled in his seat. He ruffled the papers on the bench in front of him and proceeded in a voice barely above a whisper.

"As I see it, you were out with your family going on vacation. You're driving that big ol' Cadillac with the ol' air and radio going full blast. The foot presses down on that little ol' gas pedal and before you know it, you are driving a little too fast. I know how it is son. Done it myself."

He was like a friendly grandpa up from Hicksville reading a story to an infant grandchild. His voice had become a gentle drone. "I really don't think you intended to speed son…it just happened."

I realized there was no point protesting. Justice had been served. I was just feeling angry that he didn't believe my story… Or had he?

I was led down the hallway to an office where the ticket fines were paid. The court officer showing me the way, handed my docket over to someone seated behind a desk. The man peered over his bifocals and scratched his head. "That's strange!" the man said to himself.

"Is there a problem?" I asked.

"Not for you," he said. "The magistrate hasn't ordered you to pay court costs, nor is he putting points on your license. You just have to pay a $40 fine. Very unusual."

I quickly handed over the money and grabbed the receipt. Mo and I walked quickly from the courthouse before anything could be changed. We both felt we had won a minor victory as we drove ever so slowly through La Belle and back to Naples.

Chapter Six

The off-shore breeze has now dropped, and despite the late hour, a muggy warmth has returned. I'm looking towards Mo and asking her if she's ready to leave the beach and go back home. "Not just now," she answers with a warm smile. "I really am enjoying remembering it all...now that it's all behind us."

We snuggle in closer and I make a special effort to be the romantic she's always claiming I never am. I follow her gaze as we tilt our heads towards the darkening eastern sky that's beginning to fill with brightly twinkling stars. The passing seconds of silence tells me she is deep in thought. I wait for her to tell me what she's thinking. Casually she drops her head and nestles affectionately into my shoulder "No one can ever say we've had boring lives," she continues in her soft voice. "Look at yours. Seems to me your adventures started way back, the moment you left high school."

I hadn't really thought about that before. Had no reason to. I just accepted my early experiences were no more, or less, exciting than everyone else's. But now, being asked to think about it all these years later, my wife may well be right. Maybe I did seek a little more than those around me. At sixteen my father thought he was doing me a favor by suggesting I follow him into a job of manning the large newspaper presses; just a step up from mundane factory assembly line work was how I viewed it. The work paid good money but who would want to do that all their lives? I respectfully declined and chose to stay on at school with an eye for college and possibly a career in architecture. My brother Frank, four years older than me, had a different attitude. He hated every day he was at school and couldn't wait to grab the opportunity to join the workforce when it came along. I suspected later he regretted that decision from day one. Perhaps school didn't look quite so bad the day after he left it.

He once shared a silly secret with us during one of his visits to Naples. He explained it would prove fatal during his nighttime shift if he looked at his watch before midnight, triggering the unconscious behavior of checking the time every fifteen minutes and making the long night drag. I thought that both sad and funny. During one of his early trips to Naples he made the point of taking off his watch as he lay down on the towel at the beach and placing it on the sand in front of him. With us all looking on he would stare down at the gold watch and smile. *"Now tick away as slow as you like, you bastard..."* It seems that every family photograph taken with Frank during that and subsequent visits has everyone looking down at their watches. Our kids never forgot about Uncle Frank's crazy watch incident.

With darkness closing in around us, my mind is searching back into the stockpile of memories, trying to remember it all. I'm back to the time in the mid sixties when I'm eighteen and I have left school in our hometown of Catford in southeast London and facing the first identifiable crossroad in my life. I remember the occasion clearly, and the advice I was getting from my older soccer buddy Robin McGibbon, four years older but many years wiser. He was encouraging me to follow in his footsteps and look into the possibilities of taking up a career in journalism. His encouragement coming during a depressing, if short, period in my life when I was accepting that I simply wasn't good enough to accomplish my dream of becoming a professional soccer player and any strong thoughts about going into architecture had softened. Rob and I were discussing what I should do next and his journalism suggestion was offered as we trained together at the local running track. With Robin's enthusiastic encouragement, I decided I had nothing to lose by giving it a try. After all, as an eighteen year-old at the time, I was out of high school and only working a summer job as a lifeguard in a local outdoor pool. That employment would be ending soon, as the dipping, outside daily temperatures served to remind me. The days of summer frolicking were sadly coming to an end.

That evening, the news I took home to my parents that I was thinking about pursing a proper career was well received. My father especially had been showing signs of anxiety these past weeks after hearing I had given up on the pursuits of both soccer and college. He had mentioned to mom he felt I was looking "too comfortable" working as a lifeguard and spending my days 'gawking,' as he put it, at all the young women in their skimpy bikinis. He said he was concerned I would start looking for another lifeguard job when this one ended. I sensed a pang of jealousy there but decided not to mention it.

This was now September and I was about to discover that my timing to get into journalism was badly off. Newspapers throughout the country, or at least the ones I picked out of the hat, had already taken on their quota of summer-school-leavers. Of the fifty or so resumes I mailed out, each one accompanied with a personal note I laboriously typed out on an old, beat-up portable typewriter, I received back just two responses inviting me to job interviews. So I really felt very fortunate, a couple of weeks later, when my second interview at an East London weekly newspaper actually ended with a job offer as a cub reporter. The salary offered to me by Mr. Huddleston, the little, weasel looking editor with cigarette ash speckling his blue pin-stripe suit and making it look like a bad dandruff day, was a mere pittance. Maybe reason enough, I thought as I drove home, why no one else had accepted the position before me. But at least it was a firm job offer and an opportunity to test out a new career. I figured I would be able to survive financially by continuing to live at home. Not the ideal situation I had to agree, but a start at least.

The East London Advertiser's run down, rat-infested offices, beside the Grand Canal was probably another good reason why they had trouble filling the starter position. But I had to look on the bright side. It was located in the colorful dockland area; "a young reporter's dream territory," my experienced journalist buddy assured me. And he was right. I soon discovered on my own that it was where tough families and, most times, non law-abiding "salt of the earth' citizens as they described each other, provided enough human interest stories to fill a dozen weekly newspapers. I quickly appreciated this job provided a great learning experience, but I was a fresh, young apprentice learning the craft and even with my doctored, inflated expenses, I could barely survive on the meager wages. From the very beginning it was a worrying situation that kind of affected my attitude towards the job. No one likes to feel they are working as slave labor.

Under these somewhat stressful circumstances I was always open to any ideas that offered an opportunity to earn me more money, even like the stupid one that nearly got me involved with one of London's most notorious crime gangs.

The three Kray brothers were ex-professional boxers with broad, powerful shoulders but with fight-scarred faces that suggested they probably weren't that good at defending themselves in the ring where they had to adhere to the Marquis of Queensbury rules of boxing. Outside the ring it was a different story, of course, where, it was widely rumored, they enjoyed more success beating down opponents with an axe or sword or anything else they could lay their hands on. Other times they would have someone else in the firm doing the dirty work for them. They were ruthless thugs who gained a unique kind of respect by wielding enormous power and fear within the East London business community. But despite their well-publicized questionable activities, there were still many local families who were fooled into believing they were really kind-hearted modern day Robin Hoods. They were often pictured in the newspaper sharing their ill-gotten gains with their poorer neighbors. They did a good con job. For the longest time their notoriety had bought them a kind of respectability, even outside of the close-knit local community. There were many celebrities who seemed to enjoy being in their company. I witnessed that situation time and time again. There had been countless occasions when a show biz personality, or a sporting star, visited the area and at least one of the three brothers would be seen in the forefront of the publicity photograph, most times even escorting the celebrity to the event. In my naivety I was sucked in a little too, but my main defense for agreeing to meet the brothers to discuss a business idea was that it happened several years prior to seeing the proof of their crimes. That came when the twins, Ronnie and Reggie, were both convicted of murdering a rival gang leader in a pub shooting and were sent off to prison to serve life-long sentences.

But let me back up. Ron Newson was both the newspaper's Sports Editor and Entertainment Editor at The East London Advertiser. He had been around long enough to know everyone of prominence in the area…and that most certainly included the infamous Kray brothers.

Ron and I became close buddies over time, taking some comfort I suppose in the fact we were both in the same depressing situation of being constantly broke. It seemed this problem always became the main topic of conversation between us each time we splashed out to share a pint or two every Friday payday. The same conversation would inevitably continue a couple of times each week when lunching out at the pie and mash café next door, a welcome change of cuisine I might add to the dried out sandwiches we both brought in from our homes on the other days. Our café chats, without the effects of beer, wouldn't be quite so depressing and usually developed into positive ideas on how we could make some extra money. Even with his dual role on the paper, Ron, with a wife, two children and another "surprise' one on the way, was finding it difficult to scrape together a living wage.

It was during one of our reflective lunches when Ron came up with the idea of the two of us combining our talents, whatever they may be, to open up a jazz club at the abandoned Jewish Theatre in nearby Whitechapel Road. Ron had recently been involved in organizing a couple of successful Advertiser-sponsored music events, which had proven quite successful. He had already convinced himself that a fairly sophisticated jazz club could do well in an area seriously lacking anything other than the familiar loud and raucous pub entertainment. I didn't need much convincing. If his idea could be made to work I was certainly up for cashing in on the rewards, or as Ron put it, a chance of sharing the ladder to get us out of our deep financial shithole we were in. I was convinced he was only inviting me on-board just for the moral support, but that was fine with me.

On a used paper napkin, soiled a little by the gravy from the eel pie meal, we drew up our 'to do' list. Top of that list, and certainly the most important item according to Ron, was seeking the blessing of the brothers. I am not kidding here, or overplaying the situation. These brothers were like lords of the manor and they definitely decided which new business could or could not operate in this part of dockland. Looking back, I was either too young or too stupid, or both, to realize what I was getting into. Maybe Ron, a lot older than me, should have known better but he had been around the brothers at sports and entertainment assignments too many times and clearly didn't view them as evil people, nor as any type of threat to his well-being, providing of course, he, like everyone else, followed the unwritten, but clearly established, rules.

Our meeting with just Reggie Kray was brief and to the point. I had been in his company a few times at various functions, but that was when there were lots of people around and he was on his best and smoothest behavior. On those occasions there was no reason for me to feel threatened, unlike the way I was beginning to feel right now with just the three of us sitting in the dark corner of the pub. Incidentally, this pub, The Blind Beggar, would later be the location where the brothers committed the murder and blasted away a rival gang leader Mac 'the hat' McVitie.

My feeling of nervousness was growing. Maybe remembering that many have spoken about the twins having violent tempers that could blow up anytime for no apparent reason was causing the uneasiness. Now you can appreciate why I wanted to get this business meeting over as quickly as possible.

Across from me, Ron, in a pretty impressive eloquent manner I thought, was outlining his idea. He was speaking without displaying any real hint of suffering the nervousness I was feeling, or was he? Did I detect the occasional quivering in his voice? But overall he was doing real well. All the time he spoke, Reggie just sat there, arms folded, taking the occasional sip of beer. He was showing not the slightest hint of whether he was interested or not. Although fascinated by the bulldog of a man sitting just a few inches to the left of me, I tried desperately not to stare, choosing to look down at my hands that were clasped tightly and sweating in my lap. When Ron finished speaking there was that moment of uneasy silence around the table. I sensed Ron was now feeling just as nervous as me at this point as we both waited for a reaction. I silently prayed it wouldn't come with a choke hold.

The silence was eventually broken by a throaty, deep growl, followed by a nod of the head, which I translated as an indication that Reggie liked the idea and was actually giving his approval. Those feelings were gratefully confirmed a few seconds later when he proposed – not sure if that was the right word – that for a small cut, he and his business associates as he referred to them, would not only provide the security but would also take the empty space above the club to run a small gambling operation. I didn't want to know what type of security service he was thinking about, nor anything about the gambling come to that.

The next day, Ron and I went back to working on our list. We didn't like the idea of an illegal gambling operation going on above the club, but we knew there was nothing we could do about it. For a long list of reasons we just knew the importance of keeping ourselves as far distant as possible. Our revenue would be generated from club membership, entry fees and bar sales and we would make sure our side of the business would be run nice and clean.

Ron got on the phone and chatted with one of his police buddies. Among a list of things, he learned that we would have to acquire a membership club license from the local magistrate's court to serve alcohol.

From the forms we picked up from the courthouse that same afternoon, we learned that acquiring this type of license shouldn't be that difficult for law-abiding citizens like us. In essence, our business would be no different from a regular type of social club, and there were plenty of those operating throughout the area. Of course it may have been considered prudent of us to get a lawyer to take care of this application, but we both agreed we simply didn't have the funds to splash out on what seemed like an unnecessary service. The application only required our signatures, a fifty-pound application fee and the names of a dozen elected committee members.

Ok, maybe we should have been smart enough to realize that any application to serve alcohol in a private club with the name 'Kray' on it was going to raise some eyebrows, but at the risk of repeating myself, this was way before the brothers were indicted and they really did carry an aura of celebrity type status, even if only truly recognized in this tough area of London. I will even admit we actually believed the Kray name on the application would carry some extra weight and prove to be a benefit. So alongside the names of Ronnie and Reggie Kray, we added Ron and my name, plus the names of Ron's wife and his parents, and my brother Frank and his wife, and my parents. A nice family list we reasoned. *Definitely not so.*

It was about two weeks later when all hell broke loose and I faced my brother screaming at me down the phone. His voice was so loud I could hardly understand what he was ranting about. "What the hell have you got me into?" he was shouting. "I've just had the Superintendent from the local police station here questioning my involvement with the Kray brothers. It was like a bloody ninety-minute interrogation, going over and over the same stupid questions. Why the hell didn't you warn me?"

While he paused to suck in breath, I grabbed the opportunity to try and give some type of explanation. But clearly my brother didn't hear me or, more likely, chose not to.

"I'm sure this cop has gone away thinking I'm involved in opening up some type of gangster hangout," he blasted. "He's just left here wagging his finger at me and promising me I haven't heard the last of it."

It took only one phone call and a one-minute discussion with my newly acquired business partner to accept that maybe the jazz club in this part of London wasn't such a great idea after all. By a vote of two to none we decided to withdraw our liquor application the next morning and drop the jazz club idea before anyone else on the list got questioned. Happily, brother Frank and I quickly patched things up and have laughed about it many times since. It's nice to have a brother that doesn't hold grudges – even like the time I cut his forehead open by throwing a rock, but that's a different story for later.

I managed to hold out in my impoverished state for almost three years before deciding, out of sheer necessity, that it was time to move on and find a better paying position – wherever that may be. Although I gained a wealth of experience and, for the most part, I enjoyed my first reporting job in this unique location, it also proved to be a long and unpleasant game of survival, a situation of living from paycheck to paycheck, or more specifically, from loan to loan.

Although I had taken on extra part-time jobs, one was working at the local bread factory where I worked an eighteen-hour shift every Friday night, I still found myself borrowing from my mother every Monday morning to pay for gas to get to work. Regular as clockwork, every weekend, after cashing my meager paychecks, I would pay her back the loans I had taken out the previous week and the whole cycle would start over again.

I simply was left with no choice. I had to change newspapers and find a better paying position. A high-paying reporter's job on Fleet Street, the longtime, recognized hub of the national daily newspaper industry, could provide the solution I decided. But, after making some initial inquiries, I had to accept the fact no one was hiring young reporters at that time and, worse still, at any time in the foreseeable future. But I was motivated. I simply couldn't afford to give up on my survival plans. I just needed to be more imaginative. I certainly didn't want to move to a small town newspaper in some remote part of England, which was my most likely alternative, so what about going overseas? The idea quickly became a no-brainer. It would be so much more fun working abroad where I could take up a kind of new identity and more easily lie about my age and experience to earn more money. Overseas, I would face a smaller risk of detection. The idea sounded more appealing each time I thought about it. The only problem I could see, and not a minor one, was that I had absolutely no idea of where I wanted to go. Unable to pick up even schoolboy French, I realized my choices were limited, accepting the obvious fact that it had to be an English speaking country.

Checking out the local library I quickly found a heavyweight book listing hundreds of daily newspapers scattered throughout the world. That same day I began pounding out – that was still my typing style - a batch of personal letters to newspaper editors in Canada, Australia and New Zealand. With the last one stamped and mailed I sat back to wait for all the encouraging responses.

Even exaggerating my talents, I wasn't exactly swamped with offers. In fact, from all the letters I mailed, I received back just three replies. But I tried not to feel too despondent as I recalled a similar situation when I sought my first reporting job. I have always tried to look on the brighter side, so I simply accepted that three responses were much better than none at all. I just wished the replies in my hand had been a little more positive. Two said they didn't have any openings but would keep my letter on file and get back to me while the third, the one giving any hope at all, stated they would be pleased to see me if I was ever in their area. The letter was mailed from a place I had never heard of before; a town named Winnipeg, in Manitoba, central Canada and, I estimated from looking at my atlas, a mere five thousand miles away. Hey, small blessings. It sounded like a strong lead to me at the time and definitely a proposal worthy of a follow up!

One of my closest buddies during the previous ten years had been Ernie Collins. Some people find Jesus; Ernie and I found The Beatles, Buddy Holly and some fun party girls. We had gone through secondary school together, double-dated on numerous occasions and we had worked several part-time jobs together. We had become very close friends.

At the same time I was making plans to go off to Canada, Ernie was meeting up with a girl at a party who was visiting London on some type of work exchange program. Coincidentally she just happened to be from Winnipeg. Can you believe that! They dated a few times, enough time for him to fall in love, before she had to leave and return home. Soon after, a besotted Ernie decided he couldn't settle, was now totally bored with his job working in an architect's office and decided it was time to move on. It was an obvious choice where that destination should be. He flew off to Winnipeg just a few weeks before me.

Following a couple of visits to the Canadian Embassy in London's Trafalgar Square, where I was interviewed and asked to sign some basic documents, I was informed I would acquire landed immigrant status once I arrived on Canadian soil. It really was as easy as that. I figured these Canadians really seem to appreciate talent when they see it! Now I was ready, if not fully prepared, to leave the English shores. With a one-way air ticket and a treasure trove of fifty pounds in my pocket, the money from selling my car and paying off my debts, the time was finally here to kiss my confused looking mother on the cheek and to leave her standing in the doorway of our suburban London home, trying unsuccessfully to hide the fact she was wiping away a tear. I seem to vaguely recall my dad calling out something like "see you son," as he left for work earlier that morning. No one could ever describe us as an emotional family who displayed too much of their true feelings.

Maybe I was growing up differently. I did have some mixed emotions. After all, it was just a week before Christmas, 1966 and I was leaving my family to travel the world, or at least the Canadian part of it, not knowing when or if I would return.

I will confess that among my emotions I was suffering growing pangs of guilt, which were bubbling to the surface as I struggled along the sidewalk with my two heavy, old-fashioned suitcases, towards the local train station. I knew that my mother especially enjoyed me living at home with her and dad, even though I was now twenty-one years old. She would never admit to it, of course. My brother Frank was already married at my age and with his wife Diane and young daughter Julie, was living just a few minutes away. At least that made me feel a little easier knowing my parents had family close by.

Gripping the two battered suitcases containing most of my worldly possessions I entered the train station with sweat running down my face. During the two-mile walk I had plenty of time to examine the question of whether I was making the right decision. Those pangs of guilt were growing more intense as I rode the train and, from my window seat, watched the familiar suburban landscape flash by. Was it guilt or shame I was feeling knowing that I had lied to my mother? Not wanting to worry her, I had told her there was a definite job offer waiting for me in Winnipeg and it was just too good of an opportunity to turn down. Was I also lying to myself? I began to wonder.

The uneventful flight from London's Heathrow took me first to Toronto where I transferred to a smaller jet prop plane for the second leg of the journey to the Canadian prairies. From the bits and pieces I had read about my destination, I knew my final location was going to be a little on the chilly side.

What I didn't realize was just how cold is the Canada cold. Because of flight delays due to bad weather, it was after midnight when I, with just two other passengers, stepped outside of the warm comfort of the small commuter plane and gingerly climbed down the metal steps that had been wheeled alongside the plane. It felt like someone had opened the door to an icebox and I had stepped inside. Pausing for a moment halfway down the steps, the hairs inside my nose immediately froze and a pain shot up through my forehead. This was brain freeze, the type you sometimes get from eating ice cream too quickly. Peering into the darkness, a long way in the distance, I could just make out the illuminated sign spelling out Winnipeg International Airport, the red letters fading in and out of focus as the snowflakes swirled across the desolate runways. International Airport! A slight overstatement, I thought, as I counted just two other planes parked somewhere out there on the bleak horizon. The only sound around me, now that the engines had shut down, came from the howling prairie wind. But for that red sign I would have believed we had somehow got lost on route and had landed in Siberia!

Carefully dismounting the remaining steps, I followed closely behind the other two passengers across the slippery tarmac as the wind kicked up a few more knots, causing my face to burn with the intense cold. My ears were already numb. I quickly realized that my light raincoat, more suited to the London drizzle, wasn't going to help me much in this Arctic climate. Even with the coat lapels pulled up high, the now tingling sensation in the tips of my ears was beginning to turn to a piercing pain. Inside my kid-leather gloves, my hands were beginning to freeze, as were the toes inside my thin nylon socks and fashionable, soft-leather, pointed-toe shoes. My clothing selection, I was quickly realizing, was proving to be a little 'off'.

I had already been informed in a phone call that in the few weeks Ernie had been in Winnipeg he had broken up with *"this is the one"* girlfriend he followed out, and had taken up with a new one. The replacement was Grace who did become 'the one,' and they remain together today, partners in their own very successful Vancouver based architect and design business. As I made my way inside the single story terminal building, it was comforting to know that even at this late hour there was going to be a friendly face to meet me. Not only that, Ernie and Grace would prove to be great hosts, even offering me first option on the much sought-after, small luxury condo unit Ernie was vacating. The three of us enjoyed Christmas and a few days after together, exploring an excitingly and totally different environment. This was all so new to me. Everything was an adventure. Learning to ski, riding a snowmobile and cutting down a Christmas tree were just a few of the experiences there for me to enjoy.

But with the Christmas holidays over it was now time for me to get serious and find employment. But before calling the Winnipeg Free Press I decided to check out my options first by contacting a rival daily newspaper in town. I had met the paper's News Editor at a Christmas party hosted by Grace's parents. He admitted he wasn't too sure of the paper's current staffing situation but suggested I go ahead and contact his Editor. That interview, a couple of days later, didn't go well. Not that the Editor wasn't interested in hiring me but, as he explained or maybe it was just an excuse, the newspaper was simply overstaffed at this time and was not taking on any more editorial staff. He promised, however, he would keep my name on file.

I didn't think too much about the situation as I left the newspaper building or else I may have become a little nervous. If I had given it any serious thought then I would have come to a rather startling conclusion that I had just lost fifty percent of any journalism job opportunity here in this remote region which, and I didn't need reminding, was thousands of miles from home. It hadn't fully registered either that I didn't have enough money to pay for the fare back home should things not work out for me.

You could say I was feeling a little pressure two days later when I was sitting in the office of Albert Booth, the Editor of the Winnipeg Free Press. Before him on the desk sat the letter which I had mailed him several months before. Leaning up against the desk was a walking cane; its purpose, I was immediately informed, helped the editor to get about following extensive and painful knee surgery. I thought it prudent to pretend I was very interested in hearing about every minute detail of the operation procedure.

We sat there chatting for about twenty minutes, most of the time being taken up with the surgical details, and I was beginning to feel a lot more comfortable. But that comfort level was to be short-lived. I was brought back to paying full attention when the editor suddenly pushed back his seat, clasped his hands behind his head and delivered what was almost a repetition of what I had heard just two days before "I have to tell you this is not a good time for you to be here," he was saying.

Before I could show any reaction he quickly went on. "I'm overstaffed with reporters at this time and management has asked to me to adopt a hiring freeze."

My jaw dropped and my heart missed a beat as I began to realize the significance of what I was hearing. No job. No money... and I was a very long way from home.

"But..." a very long pause before he went on. "Looking through this letter of yours I have to admit you have a lot of experience for someone who is only 25 years old...." Yes, I had lied about my age, hoping the newly-grown, full beard successfully hid my boyish looks. And yes, I had also lied about much of my experience. But this was certainly not the time to come clean I thought.

I tried to suppress my excitement as I began to feel from the expression on the Editor's face that he was about to change his mind. Clearing his throat he went on. "I really feel we could use someone like you with your law courts experience..." Again I froze in my seat. This was definitely not the right moment to tell him that I had drastically over-exaggerated that experience in my letter and, in truth, I had never been inside a courtroom in my life, except once in juvenile court for stealing a couple of newspapers out of a rack. Forget all that, I decided. I think I'm about to be offered a job.

My air-punching enthusiasm as I entered the elevator on the way out of the building brought some inquisitive stares. Oh, I forgot to mention the salary. It went from the equivalent of roughly twenty-five dollars a week I had been earning in London to more than one hundred dollars. Not a bad raise I thought, as I strolled down Portage Avenue and into the Hudson Bay Company to purchase some more appropriate winter clothing with a newly acquired store credit card.

I quickly learned the reason I was being handed the Law Courts beat was because the reporter before me had screwed up. I never got to hear the full details but he was quietly moved from law courts to metro. I thought it reassuring to hear that reporters weren't fired on the spot for making mistakes. I couldn't help but wonder how long I could survive in the position.

If I thought I was going to enjoy some extensive training then I was dead wrong. That training consisted of being told the location of the Law Courts and where I would find the press office on the second floor. I was fearful of asking too many questions, just in case I blew my cover; the cover being that I was calling myself law courts reporter. Do I hear the word *fraud?* But good fortune was with me the first day I entered the huge, impressive-looking building and strolled over into the marble halls, which housed no fewer than fourteen courts. My assignment, as described to me, was to keep tabs on everything that was happening in those courts and file my daily reports before the two-thirty deadline.

My good fortune came after entering the small press office and coming face to face with an elderly ex-Brit, Les Rutherford. Working for the Winnipeg Tribune, Les should have been considered a rival but fortunately for me it didn't turn out to be that way.

I took a step towards the gray-haired figure, throwing out my hand in a friendly gesture and looking him squarely in the eyes. I guessed Les was in his sixties, although his doddery manner as he stepped forward to shake my hand did make him appear a lot older. I was soon to learn that Les had been around these courts for almost twenty years and was not only regarded as a bit of a character but was also very much liked and respected by everyone from the judges down. And here I was, a twenty-one year old, sorry, make that twenty-five year old, still wet behind the ears reporter who had been put in this position of competing with this seasoned professional for exclusive courtroom stories.

After our initial jovial introductions and references about the 'old country' Les became a little more serious. Stroking his chin and running his hand down to a puffy neck, he leaned forward in his wooden chair as if confiding in me with some major secret. "Well son, it's like this," pausing for effect it seemed. "There have been many before you and I will say to you as I have said to them…we can compete for stories …or we can help each other…."

Of course I knew what my response to his offer would be the same moment he presented it. But as he sank back into his chair I decided it was only polite to wait a second or two and give the impression his proposal was worthy of my professional consideration. A few seconds later the deal was struck and made official with another warm handshake. I can't begin to count the number of times Les got me out of trouble during the next few months by suggesting I go and check on what was happening in a certain courtroom. It wasn't that I wasn't trying to perform my duties with utmost diligence; it was more a situation of it taking time for me to become accepted within this close-knit environment. It wasn't so much working with the information listed on the daily docket sheet, but more about being aware of what wasn't there, like important background information on cases that would indicate if a hearing was worthy of a reporter's attention. I quickly realized I would only get that type information, be it from court clerks, secretaries and lawyers, after a period of time, and only then when I became accepted.

That unexpected day, or weekend as it turned out to be, came after about two months of working at the courthouse and I was told by my News Editor to prepare myself to attend a weekend Manitoba Bar Convention at an out-of-town luxury lakeside lodge. As I was handed the keys to a smart looking company car and a five hundred dollars entertainment allowance, I couldn't help but compare this situation to my days working in East London. My buddy Les, sitting beside me as we drove to the Minakki Lodge, was asking me what I was smiling about as I recalled those days of poverty again.

After watching over the completion of the convention's formal business, and taking care of my duties of phoning in several articles, which took up most of Saturday morning and the early part of the afternoon, I was caught up in a completely different and informal atmosphere around me. The mood suddenly became very social and relaxing and it was amazing to witness the change. At dinner that evening, Les and I were invited to sit with a group of Queens Bench judges, prominent lawyers, various law courts personnel as well as the wives or husbands who had accompanied their spouses to the event. I sensed I had been invited to the table on the coat-tails of Les but that was ok. It was a pleasant feeling to notice, as the wine flowed during the meal, that I was being brought more and more into the conversations around me. I hoped it wasn't just the wine, but more the fact I hadn't screwed up in my two months of working at the courthouse, that was getting me closer to earning my wings.

Long before the dinner was over the atmosphere had become loud and boisterous. It was like a New Year's Eve celebration. I think there were some formal speeches but no one seemed to be paying much attention. As dessert was being served, our table joined in with all the other tables in the joke telling and limerick contests. My fifteen seconds of fame came when I was awarded the first place plaque and a bottle of whiskey for my old and trusty limerick winning entry, *"There was a man from Kent..."* I won't go into any more detail here, just in case there are children around.

By eleven o'clock, just about every one of the two hundred or so remaining delegates appeared nicely, or in some cases overly, lubricated with alcohol. A few had already disappeared to their rooms. In this raucous atmosphere, I was suddenly aware of being in the spotlight, surrounded by several judges and three or four celebrity lawyers.

"Well John, you are the youngest one here," announced one of the judges with a certain degree of authority. I felt honored that he remembered my name. Although thinking about it now, perhaps my name tag helped. "What are we going to do to finish off the evening?" I was lost for words and certainly lost for any ideas. What could I possible suggest to this formidable group?

"Personally I was planning on going out to the pool for a late night swim," I offered, thinking that this would present an activity considered unsuitable by my elderly, inebriated friends. "Then let's go for it!" came back the slurred response from another voice in the group. Now try and picture a conga line of perhaps seven or eight men in formal wear, swaying drunkenly out of the ballroom, and you will be rightly focused on this Kodak moment.

To this day my memory is still a little foggy as to how we ended up scaling the mesh fence to gain access to the locked up pool. I do remember clearly, however, an alarm sounding and two bright searchlights blinding us as half the group, myself included, had somehow managed to reach three-quarters the way up the fence. The fact that this group had already discarded most of its clothes in preparation for the climb and swim only added to the hilarious sight. No one made it to the summit, which, thinking about it soberly the next day, may well have been a blessing. I feel pretty sure no one had noticed in the shadowy darkness the razor wire that ringed the top. *Ooouch!*

After we all carefully climbed back down, I left it to one of the lawyers to explain to the two security guards, standing there scratching their heads in bewilderment, exactly what we were attempting to do. Surprisingly the incident was discussed and joked about in the halls of the Law Courts for many days after. It was also about the time I got fully accepted into the courthouse fraternity.

I came across many characters during my time working on the Winnipeg Free Press. There was Scotty Jones, then over eighty, who had left the Scottish shores more than sixty years before. When he first joined the paper, no one was quite sure when, he was the only one who knew anything about soccer. When the sport found its way to this prairie town, Scotty naturally became the soccer writer. I never learned whether Scotty had ever reported on any other topic during his time at the paper, or even if he had learned how to type. When I met him he would write out his reports in almost illegible longhand on small sheets of white paper that resembled toilet tissue. He actually died at his desk with pencil in hand while I was working at the newspaper, at the age of eighty-three.

Then there was Don Johnson. I promised myself I will write a book just on the exploits of this man. He was also an ex-Scot, the younger of two sons born to wealthy parents who owned an estate on one of the Scottish islands. Maybe they even owned the whole island, I'm not sure. I soon realized, after hearing Don's stories, that the entire family was a little different. The eccentric father chose to drive in his Rolls Royce around the island checking on his flocks of sheep.

Don came to Canada to hide from a second wife and the Inland Revenue. At the age of twenty-four his older brother was reputed to be the youngest editor ever to work on Fleet Street while Don himself had earned the reputation of being one of the youngest reporters working on a national newspaper, while still attending classes at Edinburgh University.

Don arrived on Canada's eastern shores four years before with very little money and barely more than the clothes he was wearing. His first task was to find work, and because there didn't seem to be any in the area where he first landed, he took up being a railway hobo, hitching train rides from one side of the country to the other. Stopping off at different towns along the way, he apparently had little trouble finding jobs; the problem seemed to be in keeping them. His questionable legal status demanded he worked for cash, which kept him away from newspaper offices.

In his broad Scottish accent which for most people was difficult to understand and certainly made worse when he drank, he could easily relate fascinating stories about working in lumber camps and west coast seaports. His face, now dotted with small fighting scars, was testimony to the fact there was little else for him to do in the isolated lumber camps after work but to drink and fight. I cannot prove his claim that he won a fifty-dollar bet playing Russian roulette with a Canadian lumberjack - his opponent apparently giving up when there were three bullets in the pistol chamber. But, knowing Don, I strongly suspect it was all true.

Don was an admitted alcoholic or, in his terms, someone who enjoyed to drink socially every single day. When I arrived at the newspaper I was warned about Don, but I chose not to listen. He was a fun person to be around, and as Business Editor he carried a lot of prestige around the office, especially in the eyes of a younger reporter like me. Despite having a drinking problem, which was never witnessed around the office, he obviously had tremendous writing talents that were clearly acknowledged by everyone working on the paper. I guess I felt a little honored when he suggested during my first week we go out after work for a *'wee get-to-know-you drinky.'*

Of course it didn't stop at one drink, or one social evening. It wasn't long before we were hitting the bars two or three evenings a week, until I soon began realizing the error of my ways and decided drinking myself into alcoholic oblivion wasn't the healthiest form of sport. Actually, Don was very understanding when I explained I needed to cut back on my drinking so I could get fit again for local soccer, and I would therefore be limiting my drinking sessions to the once-a-week pay day.

About a month after my arrival at the newspaper I was invited, along with the entire editorial staff, to the annual Oyster Eating Competition organized by Labatts, the local brewery. In the days leading up to the event I learned that huge quantities of fresh oysters were flown up from New Orleans on the day of the competition. The competition rules were very simple, with a prize being awarded to the person eating the greatest number of raw oysters in a ten minutes session. And while this non-Olympic sport was going on in one area of the room, the brewery employees were working to ensure there was no down time anywhere else. Around the large room they had set up on the floor what appeared to be amusing giant board games. On closer inspection of the boards we noticed that mugs of beer had replaced the familiar checker type pieces. Clearly the purpose of the games was to get everyone as drunk as possible before loading them into cabs waiting outside and sending them off with a *'bon voyage'*.

I lasted about two hours before deciding now was the appropriate time to leave. With my whimpish effort of consuming just a dozen or so oysters, now doing cartwheels in a stomach full of beer (the winner, by the way, ate 173), I staggered towards the cab line.

For most of us the evening ended there or soon after, but not for Alcoholic Don. The party for him, apparently, was just warming up. There was still a vat or two of beer to finish!

We picked up the story the following morning when we learned that cleaners had come into the newspaper building around six to find Don slumped over his typewriter. Beside the machine and neatly stacked were six pages of perfectly written business page copy. Everything looked fine, except for the fact that Don was sitting there in his underwear, his lips had turned blue and his body was shaking. Medics were called and Don was hauled off to the hospital where he was treated for exposure. It turns out that Don had lost the last three checker games, and despite noble efforts, he just couldn't consume all the beer that was required of him...so he traded his clothes instead. No one was quite sure why he chose not to use a cab, instead deciding to walk in the fresh late night air the three miles to the newspaper offices. It wouldn't have been such a bad decision, had not the temperature that night dropped to fifteen degrees below zero. Apparently the alcohol in Don's body attributed to saving his life. Who could possibly convince Don after that incident that alcohol was bad for him.

At some time in my life, and I can't quite remember when, I learned the practice of never saying "no." I don't mean that literally, but certainly when I felt a negative response could jeopardize an opportunity to get ahead. So when the Sports Editor at the Winnipeg Free Press approached me at my desk a few weeks after my arrival and asked me if I played hockey, I just had this strong intuition to say 'yes.'

"Then I will put you down for Smocky Night" he said, quickly adding my name to the list on the clipboard he was carrying.

There had been several occasions back in England when I was asked to play on various newspaper soccer teams in friendly rivalry matches. They had always been low profile affairs. A bunch of wannabies kicking a ball around on a park pitch somewhere and watched only by the odd girlfriend, wife or maybe one or two from the office.

This was how I conceived this charity hockey game to be. A group of guys from the two newspapers in town combining to play a team made up of local radio and television news crews. Apparently, this short, twenty-minute game would be played at the end of the touring Ice Capades annual event out at the Winnipeg Arena.

I guess I should have known it was going to be a lot more serious than what I had first imagined when I started to hear the promotions for the event blasting out every few minutes from the car radio. Because of work duties I was unable to attend the two practices. As game day drew closer, I began to sense I was being viewed as the team's secret weapon. For which team I wasn't quite sure.

Oh my god! The Winnipeg Arena was filled to the rafters when I arrived sometime during the show's halftime interval. A couple of weeks before, the Canadian national hockey team had won a memorable game against the Russians to take the world championship title. It was reported the game had attracted an arena record audience of nearly eleven thousand people. As I made my way through the tunnel to the dressing room I heard the announcement that tonight's crowd had beaten that by several hundred. *Did I mention I had been on skates only twice in my life and both times had trouble standing?*

Inside the dressing room, cases of beer were stacked from floor to ceiling, again compliments of Labatts Brewery. My first reaction was to open a case and drink to ease away my nerves, but there was no time for that. I was being pushed and shoved as I was bound in padding and adorned in a smart looking hockey uniform, if only I could skate I would really look the part, I thought.

Of course this was not a serious game, just a light-hearted conclusion to this big charity event. It was pleasing to hear from the coach as we gathered around that we were here to have fun. "Don't try to be funny out there on the ice," he was saying. "It will happen on its own." Why was he staring at me? I wondered.

The next twenty minutes or so was just a blur. I can report I was on the ice for the entire game but not because of my skills. When I fell down in the middle of the ice in the first minute, I found it impossible to get up again, at least until someone came to assist when the game was over. During the entire game I just sat there as skaters sped around me. Although I sat there embarrassed and fearing for my life, eleven thousand fans seemed to think it was hilarious. I don't know how, but I managed to survive without injury and that night I made a promise to myself that next time, if asked I will definitely say "no".

If I related all the coincidences that happened to me surrounding the trip to Canada you would think I was making them up, but honestly I'm not.

For a year or so before going off to Winnipeg I had been dating Helen, a law firm secretary I had met on vacation in the West Country. We had talked a lot about me going off to Canada and we decided that if things worked out for me then she would join me for a vacation. We were both happy with our relationship and agreed to let things happen at their own pace.

A couple of days before my departure I was at Helen's home when she was visited by one of her former school friends. They hadn't spoken for over a year and her friend had no knowledge that I was going off to Canada in a few days time. It turns out that the friend was sharing an apartment with two Canadian girlfriends who were planning to return home in a few weeks time...home being Winnipeg!

Now that in itself seemed like a big coincidence to me, especially coming off the back of Ernie meeting up with that girl at the party...but stay with me on this one. This incident was going to get a lot more unbelievable before the evening was over.

Helen's friend asked me if I knew where I would be staying, suggesting she could pass on the address to her roommates so we could all meet up. I wrote down Ernie's Winnipeg address on a piece of paper and left it on the coffee table as she went over to the phone. I could hear her relating the situation to one of the roommates. "Give me your address," she was asking, "and I will hand it over to John." After finishing the conversation she came back to the coffee table and put down her notepad with the address. I could read the writing clearly: *Apartment 304, 33 Kennedy Street*. The notepad was lined up against my own slip of paper with Ernie's address which read: *Apartment 204, 33 Kennedy Street!* The two girls rented an apartment directly above!

About two years after returning to England I was working for the Mecca organization, a major entertainment company. My office was in the heart of the capital's entertainment area, just off Piccadilly Circus. I was in a cab on my way to a meeting and we were caught up in traffic, driving very slowly past the nearby Regent Hotel. I guess I was kind of daydreaming as I was looking out of the window. Imagine my shock when I suddenly focused on the face of my former editor, Albert Booth. There he was, half a world away from Winnipeg, still leaning on that familiar walking stick, in the front of the hotel lobby. I jumped from the cab, shouting my greetings as I made my way through the revolving doors. It was so hard to accept that here we were, all those miles from his home, and we had come face to face in one of the busiest areas of London.

After recovering from the initial shock, Albert explained he was on a brief group vacation with his wife and was waiting for the rest of his party before moving off to the next location. We barely had time for a cup of coffee and a quick update on what had been happening in our lives the past two years. His knee surgery had not gone well, hence the continuing need of a walking stick, and there hadn't been too many staff changes since I left. It was heartbreaking to hear that Don Johnson had been sent away to prison for several years for his part in trafficking drugs. Many years later I learned he had been released early from prison and returned to England where he was back working on a London newspaper. In my mind I wished him well and after some thoughts about contacting him, decided to let sleeping dogs lay.

You just can't make up these types of coincidences. How about this one? A week before leaving Winnipeg to return to London I was attending a boring law firm party and talking to an equally boring attorney who had just finished writing a law book. He was explaining, as though I was interested, that he was planning a trip to London in about a month's time to meet with possible publishers. He was an arrogant type, so it was with some reluctance I agreed to hand over my parents' phone number, which I immediately regretted doing, where he could reach me.

Well, it turns out he loses that phone number and arrives in London knowing only from our conversation at the party, that because I had missed out on a planned holiday camp job, I was thinking about taking a temporary reporting job for the summer before going off to South Africa. The same afternoon he checked into his hotel he started calling around to different newspapers in an effort to locate me.

I was to learn later that after an hour or so of this fruitless searching he decided on another idea. Instead of phoning, he went off to find the hotel concierge to ask him for directions to 'downtown London'. The concierge had difficulty explaining that downtown was not a word often used in the UK. Under what seemed like some type of interrogation, the hotel employee, scratching his head and surely wondering if he was on Candid Camera, suggested that Trafalgar Square could possibly be considered by some to be a downtown area and likely as good a place as any to begin a search for someone.

At this time in my life it was a rare occasion to find me visiting London's touristy West End. But this day I found myself there, but for what reason I can't remember. All I can tell you is when I strolled into the Lyons Corner House coffee shop, the first person I noticed was my Canadian attorney friend sitting there with his back to the counter, casually raising his head from the pages of his guide book and exclaiming with a broad smile. *"John. So good to see you. I've been looking for you."* He seemed completely unaware of the odds against this chance meeting.

My list of Canadian coincidences doesn't end there. Two more unfolded years later, long after we arrived in Naples and when I was employed at The Ritz Carlton hotel.

One afternoon I was driving out of Ft Myers Airport with my two passengers who had arrived on a flight from Toronto. We soon began to chit chat and they seemed interested in hearing about my Canadian ties;

my working in Winnipeg and learning that my son's in-laws came from that area too.

"Fascinating," said the husband. "My wife here Jean was the curling champion of Manitoba."

"That's interesting," I said "I wonder if she knows my son's mother-in-law. I hear she played a lot of curling. Her married name is Bridgett."

In my rear mirror I could see the wife sit up, take notice and smile broadly. "You remind Sandra next time you see her that she never once beat me, Jenny the twin."

Less than a month later I was driving back from the same airport with an attractive lady passenger sitting in the back of the Lincoln town car. She was explaining it had been a long and tiring day, with a three-hour stop over in Detroit. "I left my home in Vancouver at four this morning."

"Nice town Vancouver," I said. "Been there a couple of times.....still have an old school buddy, Ernie Collins, living there."

I have to tell you that I haven't been in contact with Ernie for nearly twenty-five years. Not since the time when he got into an argument with his mother and I somehow got in the middle of it. Then Grace decided to interfere and the whole mess just got messier. I've sent Ernie a couple of e-mails over the years in an effort to patch up the relationship but they somehow got intercepted by Grace who took it upon herself to reply, claiming Ernie had chosen not to speak to me again.

"You mean Ernie Collins, the architect?" screamed the women, leaning forward in her seat. "Wow, isn't that just incredible. Grace is my very best friend!"

After dropping off The Ritz Carlton guest at the hotel front door and pocketing a nice tip, I made my way slowly back to the transportation offices with a very strong suspicion that my excited passenger wouldn't be able to honor my request for silence in this matter. I sensed she was already dialing Grace's number from her room.

Looking back now as we lay looking up at the twinkling stars, I recalled I had survived quite happily the bitter Canadian winters for over two years. Maybe that sounds strange after hearing my passionate liking for the hot Florida climate. Possibly the younger years helped. I certainly enjoyed some wonderful new experiences before accepting that my life in Winnipeg was already becoming a little too repetitious. It was uncanny how Winnipeg locals could tell you the exact day of when to expect the first snow fall and they were absolutely on the button both winters I was there. Just like the first snow flurries, the social events seemed to follow a strict schedule. I realized the time had come to move on. But not back to England. Hopefully not yet.

I decided to find a job in a more hospitable climate. I had written to several newspapers in South Africa, and the Editor of a newspaper in Durban (on the south coast) seemed more than a little interested in my journalistic talents. On this occasion, a little older and a little wiser, I had been more truthful in my letter about my professional experience. We had agreed to meet later in the year, sometime around October.

With money saved and high hopes for the future I decided to stay in England for a few months, working the summer as a local reporter, before taking the trip down to Durban. I would also be able to spend some time with my family.

It was a pity that, because of a short delay in flying back, I had missed out on what could have been a fun summer experience.

Len Walley, a reporter who I had met while working at the East London Advertiser had long ago given me the idea of working in the public relations office at one of the Butlin's Holiday Camps which, at the time, were sprinkled around the English coast. These camps were popular with both families and youngsters alike who seemed to enjoy the all-inclusive, entertainment-packaged vacations. He claimed he was only able to survive the job for one season, proclaiming, or perhaps merely boasting, that he had no problem dating most of the winners of the camp's weekly beauty pageant. Len appeared to revel in explaining to an enthusiastic male audience that his first call of duty every Saturday evening, as the PR officer, was to crown and interview the pageant winner! We each drew our own conclusion as to what his crowning duty implied.

Lenny was a tall, good-looking, athletic type of guy. I tended to believe that most of what he was telling me was probably true. Apparently his downfall came when all the weekly winners were invited back for an end of season gala party and Lenny was called up to host the event.

"It was like facing a herd of wild stampeding horses," he explained with a broad smile, "And all with the same idea of trying to run me down!"

I had to assume that the young beauties had probably been comparing notes during the evening and came to the same conclusion that Casanova Lenny was responsible for more than a few broken promises. I would like for readers to know that my reasons for applying for the job was for more sincere, respectful reasons. But it was never going to be put to the test. Albert Booth had asked me to stay on for two extra weeks at the Winnipeg Free Press while they found a replacement for my law courts beat, and the delay caused me to lose the camp job.

I had been back in England less than a week when I caught up with my buddy Robin at the local outdoor pool where I worked, and where this part of the story began six summers before. He was still in journalism and recently was promoted to the paper's Night Editor. He still enjoyed the work and pay was good, but with four young children he was looking to the future and accepted he needed to get into something more profitable. He began telling me about a restaurant promotion idea he come across while on a recent assignment in California.

"We can both work on the project part-time," he said excitedly. "I'll continue working nights and you can continue with your reporting job."

Robin's enthusiasm was contagious, and I was already sensing that my intended plans to work in South Africa were going to be shelved for the time being.

"Wouldn't you rather travel as a millionaire!" was Robin's parting comment as we left the pool together and walked to our cars. I realized at that moment that I was definitely committed to my first business venture.

I wish I could say that making our first million proved to be easy but it turned out that we barely made enough money to pay our expenses that first year. Despite the difficulties though, both of us continued to have confidence we could make the project work. We teamed up with another sports buddy, our friend Dennis Fowle, who had recently resigned as Managing Editor of a local Kent newspaper and was looking for a new interest.

But again, after a few more months and despite all our extra efforts, we came to accept the scheme was hardly moving forward. Although we expanded the operation from the mid-Kent area to a coastal town, we knew the project required some serious financial backing if it was ever going to become the financial success we all dreamed of.

In retrospect I'm not sure who came up with the idea of going to the Mecca organization, but we all agreed that it should be Robin who made the connection. With a reputation among fellow journalists of being able to get his foot in the door, he was quickly assigned the job of making contact with the hugely successful company at their headquarters in south London.

But the challenge was proving to be a daunting task even for Robin. A week of phone calls brought no results and he admitted he was getting the run-around. Finally he decided there was no alternative but to go directly to the top.

Eric Morley was the charismatic CEO and Chairman of the rapidly expanding company, which was now into nightclubs, casinos and bingo halls throughout the UK. The jewel in their crown was that, under Morley, Mecca had become the much-publicized organizers of various beauty contests, including the hugely successful Miss World beauty pageant.

Another week passed, and Robin reported back that still he had made little progress and was unable to get an appointment to see the chairman. Calls left with his secretary were not returned and we were all growing frustrated and concerned over our immediate future. I had given up my reporting job to work the coastal resort project on a full time basis, and Dennis was definitely looking to the project for some much needed income, if not now, then certainly sometime very soon. Mecca seemed so perfect for what we were looking for. Someone in our group joked that we could make the company famous!

It was Robin who suggested he would be more aggressive and go to see Morley personally the next day. He outlined his simple but ballsy plan, which in reality was no plan at all. He would simply be waiting in the chairman's office the next morning when he walked in.

This was long before the need for increased security spread into every area of our lives, so Robin had no problem walking freely into the building with the cleaning staff around 7:00 a.m. He made his way to the third-floor executive offices and into the unlocked chairman's suite. He made himself comfortable in the large leather winged-back chair that sat in front of the heavy dark-oak desk, opened up his newspaper, and waited.

When he later filled us in on all the details, Robin said he tried to appear as casual as possible when the office door opened and Eric Morley entered the room. "I was hoping he wouldn't notice my whole body shaking as I held out my hand to say 'good morning.'"

Needless to say there was a look of complete surprise and bewilderment on the chairman's face as he stopped, looked Robin up and down, and posed the rather obvious question, "Who the hell are you?"

Sensing he had very little time before Eric Morley would raise the alarm and have him thrown out, Robin reeled off his story of how he had tried everything to get an appointment and how nothing had worked. There was silence for a full minute before the chairman spoke. "You have just five minutes to tell me why you are so desperate to see me. I have to admit though, I kinda like your resourcefulness."

An hour later, Robin left the building with an offer for the three of us to join the Mecca organization to operate our idea in cooperation with other promotional plans the firm had been considering. The projects would come together under a subsidiary company and, listen to this, we would be the well-paid directors in charge!

We all worked hard over the next two years as we pursued our mutual dream of becoming successful directors within the Mecca organization. We heard later that Eric Morley had been anxious to bring "new young blood" into the organization and viewed us as suitable candidates for injecting some fresh thinking. Sadly though, his expectations and our dreams never became a reality. We had a few notable successes in selling our promotional ideas to the likes of British Airways, but they weren't profitable enough to satisfy the aggressive and profit-conscious Mecca board. We knew that Eric Morley pleaded our case at every board meeting, asking for continued patience from the senior directors, but eventually our time ran out. His voice sounded genuinely sad when he called to say we had to go.

In September 1971 we returned our company cars and handed back the office keys and walked away from the building. We had enjoyed the experience, learned much, and decided the three of us would remain together as business partners.

....

Suddenly my memories are interrupted by Mo's soft whisper as she walks barefoot into the falling darkness, across the cooling sand towards several sail boat hulls lying upside down and secured by chains to a palm tree at the edge of the beach. She sits down on one of the fiber glass hulls and gestures for me to sit down beside her. "Do you realize we have been married thirty-four years this year?" How could I not know. There seemed to be a landmark for every year we had spent together. So many years…so many experiences…

We had met in January, 1971 when I was still working for Mecca. Our matchmaker was her cousin Charles, who handed me her phone number as we sat in the bar after playing one of our weekly games of squash. He said he hadn't seen his cousin for a few months, but had heard she'd recently broken up with her boyfriend. He seemed to think the two of us would get along fine. His suggestion came at a time when I wasn't seeing anyone special either. Charles's enthusiasm about his cousin's great personality and looks made me eager to try and set up a date.

Mo had been teaching elementary school for several years and was ready for a change. She was planning to become a flight attendant and travel the world. We spent our first date in a quiet country pub near her home in Epsom. It was easy to understand what Charles meant about her warm and vivacious personality. She was so easy to talk to that, even before the evening was over, I had made what could only be described as a crazy decision. As strange as it may sound, I really felt a premonition that I would end up marrying this woman.

From that first date we went on to enjoy an incredible, fun-filled summer, seeing each other as much as possible in between her hectic flying schedule. Working for a big entertainment company brings some exciting perks, and we went to top-quality shows and major sporting events. We even had a box at London's Albert Hall during the Miss World contest, later joining a group of show business guests at the celebrity party afterwards. During my employment at Mecca, I, along with Robin and Dennis, was even called in to help judge the Miss Great Britain beauty contest where I felt excited and important, as well as something of an impostor, sitting alongside a host of celebrity judges.

Mo and I had made plans to get married in October, just nine months after our first meeting. We both wanted a simple wedding ceremony we could enjoy with just our immediate family. The ceremony was to be held at Epsom Registry Office on a Friday, with a party for friends at our apartment the next evening. In those days, most airline companies wouldn't allow married women to fly, so Mo was about to lose her job. Then came that phone call from Mr. Morley and I was unemployed too...just one month before the wedding.

Our meager savings barely got us through the weeks leading up to the wedding. Mo's car had died and my company vehicle was back in the Mecca garage. The money Mo had saved to cover her income taxes was used to pay for the simple wedding ceremony and a lunch reception for our thirteen family guests. Beverages for the party arrived via duty-free supplies and bottle donations from airline crew colleagues. The only thing still needed was a rental car to get me to Epsom for the wedding ceremony and to bring the two of us back to our apartment after the reception. With such limited funds available, we agreed a one-day rental would have to be sufficient. We would make sure we had the car back to the rental office which was located just around the corner from the apartment, by midnight.

The excitement of our wedding day had exhausted both of us. We could barely stay awake as we drove back to the apartment in the late afternoon. Without taking off our clothes, we both collapsed on the bed and it was just after 11:30 when Mo sat right up and screamed; "The car! It has to be back by midnight or else we have to pay another day's rental!"

Still dressed in our wedding clothes we ran to the elevator, rode down to the garage and hopped into the rental car. With the sound of screeching tires, that surely must have woken up everyone living in the apartment block, we raced out of the lot. A few minutes later we were hurriedly punching the rental agreement into the time clock outside the rental car office. We were both laughing with relief as we noticed we had clocked in with just a few minutes to spare.

As we dropped the keys through the letterbox I can recall an awareness of feeling hungry. I realized neither of us had eaten since the reception. With stomachs growling, our attention was drawn to the noise of several young couples climbing out of their cars and running to the nearby fish and chip shop that was looking to close, just a few yards down the street. We both caught a whiff of frying fish batter in the cool night air. It drew us like magnets to the little white building.

Mo and I were smiling at each other as I quickly dug deep into my pockets for change. Our laughter caught the curiosity from the other young couples as we excitedly counted out the coins. We had just enough money to buy ourselves our first meal as husband and wife!

With our fish and chips doused in salt and vinegar and wrapped in newspaper, we sat down wearily on the curb. Under the soft glow of the streetlight, Mo snuggled into my side. We looked into each other's eyes and knew we didn't have to say anything. We could never be happier, or as broke, as we were that night.

Chapter Seven

Even before the discovery of the books we were beginning to sense a major problem as early as the second month of owning the spa. Although these were the quieter summer months and we accepted business would be slow, the income simply wasn't matching the figures we had been given. In fact, it just wasn't making any sense at all.

It had become very clear that all our members were extremely appreciative of the changes we had made and were giving us very positive feedback on the way we were operating the business. We had installed new carpeting throughout and purchased additional exercise equipment. We had asked members for suggestions for improving the club and we were working hard at trying to meet just about every reasonable request. The increased number of hourly aerobic classes for the women, which ran throughout the day, was proving extremely popular.

Although Mo had openly expressed a strong dislike of exercise, she decided she wanted to be fully involved in this new business and would take charge on ladies days. On top of everything else, she even became one of the three aerobic instructors. Being used to teaching, she quickly picked up the techniques and with her bubbly personality it wasn't long before she became a favorite with the ladies.

As the number of classes increased, she would be seen bouncing around out front of the Jane Fonda workout classes, three and four times a day. Not bad for someone who hated even the thought of exercising!

So with all these improvements, we were both surprised and concerned that we had so few new members signing up. We even turned to our manager Don for some type of explanation, but all we got back was a shaking of his head and a puzzled expression. When we pushed him for comparisons with the membership enrollment we were seeing now, compared to what they had been under the former owner, he claimed all the financial data was recorded in the company's business books. He was adamant he had no real knowledge of what the true profits of the club had been. He was also adamant that the former owner and his accountant had handled all the bookkeeping and they were the only ones who knew the full financial picture.

Looking back, there was absolutely no reason for me to move the large sheet of plywood leaning against the wall in the storage closet. Maybe I was thinking at the time about making the area look a little tidier. The three receipt books fell down from the narrow shelf as I eased the heavy sheet to one side. I immediately recognized the books as being similar to the ones we were currently using and those the seller had given to our accountant for scrutiny. I was curious as to why these books appeared to have been hidden away and so, for the next two hours, I ploughed through the books with a calculator in my hand. The more I turned the pages, the more frightening became the emerging picture. According to these membership receipts there was absolutely no way the spa was making the income that had been reported to us. Even scarier was the fact it was probably suffering heavy losses!

By the end of the afternoon I was left believing that instead of a $60,000 annual profit, the number claimed by the former owner, these hidden books were indicating the spa could be losing up to $30,000! The difference was made up, as we later proved in court, by including income from the sale of some building land. We learned a long time later that the tax return we had been shown, and we passed to immigration, had been amended with the land sale income deleted. All of this without our knowledge.

After several unsuccessful attempts to contact the previous owner in a desperate search for some type of explanation, I began to believe I was left with no other option but to find myself a lawyer. I realized that to take any legal action to sort out the mess was going to take money we didn't have, but what else could we do? This situation as it stood was going to ruin us financially anyway. My first action was to stop payment on the balance we owed the seller.

It wasn't a pleasant meeting with my wife at home that evening. I explained how we had been duped, and for several hours we mulled over the problem. Eventually we reached the decision that we would have to keep the spa open and try and cut our losses by finding ourselves a buyer. We both knew it wasn't going to be easy to sell a business that was losing money and, at the very least, we were going to be forced to drop the price considerably. Mo agreed we should meet with a lawyer as soon as possible to discuss our legal options.

I reasoned that it wasn't Gil Pooler's fault that he had put us in contact with a crooked businessman. Neither was it his fault that he also recommended the attorney we hired to handle our case who decided to run off with our $3,000 deposit. The deposit was up-front money the lawyer wanted before he would even start on our case. With our savings now down to zero, we had no other choice but to start using our credit cards and when they became maxed out, to begin the embarrassing scenario of borrowing from family and friends.

That first attorney, Art MacDonnell, came across as a likable, affable sort at our first meeting. He had grown up in Naples and supposedly was a partner in several successful local businesses. After hearing our story he expressed confidence that we had a strong case, and advised us to pursue the spa owner for fraud in civil court. The up-front money he required would cover his initial expenses.

We could no longer afford to pay Mo any salary out of the spa account and she was forced to take on extra work on the days the spa was closed to the ladies. This included running private workout classes in the nearby luxury high rise condos, as well as embarking on a career of substitute teaching.

Weeks, then months went by, and despite several meetings with our lawyer, we still didn't have a court date set. We were getting more desperate as each Friday came around and salaries and other expenses had to be met. We were trying to keep the place operating while we found ourselves a buyer. We were using some of Mo's earnings, together with the small monthly payment I was getting from selling off my business back in England, to help pay the wages for the two remaining instructors. Hardly anything was left to meet our personal needs. Our credit cards were well past their limits as we tried to survive from one depleted paycheck to the next.

As the situation worsened, the phone would ring at both home and office with creditors chasing down late payments. We would listen to the television and radio financial experts giving advice to people in credit card debt, and just shake our heads as they admonished people for not controlling their buying. We often wondered if these experts were in touch with the real world, a place where a lot of families like us were using these cards at the grocery store just to survive. You wouldn't see a purchase for a luxury item on any one of our cards, only for food and household necessities.

With no credit left it didn't take long to be back to writing checks at the local grocery store. We would leave the store praying that some money would come to us the next day so we could cover each written check. Each new visit to the checkout line would bring a hope that the number "11" wouldn't appear on the cash register screen. That number, we quickly learned, indicated that the store was holding a bounced check and the store manager would be called over. That embarrassing scenario happened twice to us!

It proved impossible to keep the seriousness of the situation away from our children. Our eldest son, Kieran, offered us money from his Christmas gifts, while Dominic went off one Friday evening to buy food from money he had earned finding and selling golf balls. Our ride to the land of opportunity had somehow derailed, and yet above it all our close family bond remained strongly intact.

With Mo's income from teaching and private workout classes, together with the money I earned from refereeing evening and weekend soccer games, we were able to keep going for a time. I began taking on any odd jobs I could find when I wasn't at the spa, no matter what it was. It could be painting or yard work. Anything to help us make ends meet. But I soon realized this was only temporary survival. Unless something happened soon we would be virtually destitute.

The months were slipping by and we were now into our second year of owning the spa. But instead of enjoying prosperity, we found ourselves slowly drowning in debt. We needed to get into court in a hurry. But far from seeing progress, we were hearing only excuses for delays. My first suspicion that something was wrong with Art MacDonnell came when I couldn't reach him on the phone any more. A disconnected line has a certain ring about it. I wasn't at all surprised when I biked down to pay him a visit and found that his office was locked and empty. Peering through the window I could see that the office furniture had been removed. Not a good sight. The newspaper report the following morning filled in some more details. In short, there was an arrest warrant out on Art MacDonnell who, it appeared, had been enjoying a lavish lifestyle with his client's money!

It was now December, 1982 and we had wasted more than a year with McDonnell. Could our situation get any worse, we began asking ourselves. We hoped not, but we were living on false hope. Before this matter was anywhere close to reaching a conclusion, the immigration authorities were already bombarding us with questions now that our two-year investment visa was coming up for renewal. They had begun conducting an interim review of our situation and more times than not we sensed the bureaucratic minions at the department were viewing our answers as being evasive and suspicious.

As bad as our situation appeared with the disappearance of our lawyer, it took us no longer than one evening of mourning over a bottle of cheap wine to find our resolve to continue the fight. Before going off to bed, Mo and I came up with a game plan, or at least the idea that we would contact the Collier County Bar Association the next day to discuss our options and to see what help they could offer us. After all, we reasoned, it was one of their members who had screwed us and didn't they have some type of responsibility?

Apparently not. We would soon discover that we were out of luck where any real help was concerned. While the association president Nelson Faerber did lend a sympathetic ear when I related the full story, he immediately made it perfectly clear there was nothing his association could offer in terms of free representation or any other type of financial compensation. "Our association simply doesn't have the means to do so," he explained.

Nelson appeared sincere when he said he was disgusted with MacDonnell's behavior and his association would certainly be going after the man on ethical grounds. "But I'm fully aware that does nothing to help you," he said. His message was loud and clear. If we still wanted to go after the rogue spa owner we would have to hire and pay for a new attorney ourselves.

I was feeling a little numb, and was not fully tuned in during the rest of the conversation. I do remember asking Nelson if he could recommend a lawyer.

In fairness, Nelson never stated he was the best. He merely said he felt confident in ranking himself in the top half dozen or so trial lawyers in town. I didn't know about that. But I did feel if he was elected president of The Collier Bar Association then he must be regarded by his peers as an honest sort of guy, and that's what we needed right now. I left his office promising him that I would find the money to hire him, despite having not the slightest idea where I would find those funds. I felt pretty low as I took the elevator down to the street. I was also feeling guilty that I had let down my family.

I walked outside the building to find that my bicycle had been stolen.

I walked the four miles home, shaken to the core by what had transpired. I did not understand how our dream could have turned into such a nightmare.

Despite the fact we were making every possible cut at the spa, we were barely hanging on from week to week. We could only hope our economic disaster didn't appear too obvious to our members. I desperately wanted to keep the spa open until I could find a buyer, knowing full well that if the word of our problems got out then we couldn't expect any new members to join. Just as it had been for us, we would insist the new owner would honor all current memberships.

Although the spa had been the first in town, now there was some serious competition. Several new spas and workout places had opened up which were diluting the membership base. The competition had become fierce and we could understand that people would be selective, maybe choosing a spa more conveniently located to their home or work, and certainly influenced by that ever present 'special discount offer of the week'. Our frustration mounted because I still believed we were operating the best spa in town.

We had wasted many months as a result of MacDonnell's charade, and now our new lawyer was trying to pick up the mess he had left behind. Nelson virtually had to start from scratch. Court papers either hadn't been filed or had been misfiled. Nelson commiserated with our situation, and knowing just how desperate we were, he promised to do all he could to get a speedy trial date. But nothing was moving quickly or quickly enough for us. Weeks moved into months. Mo and I had stopped speculating about when the court date would be set. The situation was making us irritable with each other. We had become short-tempered but, fortunately, we both realized what was happening, so we adopted a kind of truce policy. If one of us felt a need to take out our frustration on the other, we would take a 'time-out,' just like we would impose on our kids. We would go outside to the patio area and cool off for a few minutes before coming back inside. It seemed to work... for most of the time.

Eventually we were given the news we had been waiting for. Nelson's office phoned to say a court date had been set. At first we were ecstatic with the good news but the initial joy soon turned to one of disappointment when the secretary said that the date was three months down the road. How the heck were we going to survive until then? We had already cut the spa staff from seven to three. Now I was wondering how patient the landlord was going to be when we stopped paying the rent?

Somehow we were holding on by a thread. Time has since wiped out the memories of just how bad it was at that time, but Mo and I can still remember certain bouts of desperation of trying to make ends meet both at home and at the spa. Many nights I would be awoken by Mo's stifled sobs. I would lay there feeling completely helpless as I took her into my arms, wondering what I could possibly do to make the emotional pain she was suffering go away.

Then, with just a few weeks to go before the trial, we were hit with yet another bombshell. Judge Hugh Hayes, who was going to preside in our case and himself a spa member, contacted Nelson to say he was excusing himself from the case. The situation was getting worse every time we turned our heads. Here we were, both putting in long hours at the spa and financing a project from funds we didn't have; for what? It was a miserable feeling for both Mo and I every time we walked into the spa building.

Finally the inevitable happened. It was just after 7:00 pm one Saturday evening and we were just five weeks away from our new court date. Despite placing ads in the newspaper and meeting with potential buyers, we had no firm offers on the spa. I had been working since five that morning and I felt totally exhausted. I realized it wasn't the work that was proving exhausting, but more from the mental anguish of feeling that this was all a waste of time. It was all for nothing!

My head was pounding as I turned off the main lights and headed towards the front glass doors. In one hand I was holding a letter addressed to the landlord while in the other hand I was holding a sign I had just written with a thick black marker pen. I had already placed scotch tape on the four corners of the white card so I could attach the message to the front door. The sign read simply: CLOSED UNTIL FURTHER NOTICE.

It was strange. I felt no sadness, just a great sense of relief. It was as though a huge weight had been lifted from my body and I was able to breathe again. I walked around the building in the warm night air and noticed for the first time in a long while, the clear, starry sky. I suddenly felt good. I took my bike, a cheap replacement I bought at a local thrift store, from the storage area and headed home.

As soon as I walked through the front door I knew that Mo had guessed that something had changed. Maybe it was my smiling face. She was standing at the table, clearing away dishes and I could see the three children playing games on the living room carpet. "What have you done?" she asked in a suspicious tone.

"I've closed the spa," I said.

I could sense Mo being overcome with the same type of relief that had washed over me earlier. She didn't ask any more questions. We both accepted we had no other choice. We had severed the ties that had been slowly strangling us!

As darkness fell we both enjoyed the best night's sleep in ages. It was mid-morning when we were both awakened by the bright sunshine bursting through the bedroom windows. We jumped out of bed, eager to spend some quality time with the children. For a long time now we had both been feeling guilty that we had been neglecting them. That was certainly now going to change.

We spent all day at the beach enjoying one of the pleasures that had brought us to Naples in the first place. We all had a great time.

We had just arrived home and I was still unpacking the car when the telephone rang. I picked up the receiver to hear, "Good evening sir. This is The Naples Daily News here. May we ask you a few questions regarding the closing of The Executive Health Spa?"

The male voice seemed young and a little hesitant and I was reminded of my earlier reporting days back in London when I would often make similar calls.

"Sure," I said in a friendly tone. "What do you want to know?"

I was on the phone for about thirty minutes, answering every question as honestly and thoroughly as I could. I felt I had nothing to hide. As I replaced the receiver, I was a little curious about how they would handle the story.

There was no way I could have expected the headline that appeared the next day as the lead story on page three. Above a picture of members peering through the front glass door was the bold headline. "OWNER CLOSES SPA. SAYS NO REFUNDS ON MEMBERSHIPS." The copy underneath was less than complimentary to say the least.

I felt this was a grossly unfair headline. What I had told the reporter was that I was unable to pay refunds at this time because we simply had run out of money. I said that there was a court case pending and I had every intention of using any money we received from the case to pay off our debts. That night we received four calls from irate members who blasted us over the phone. Two days later we started to receive the first of several pieces of hate mail accusing us of every conceivable sin. One letter was especially spiteful. The writer claimed she knew us. She further expounded that she despised the fact that we had been permitted to come to America, and in return, we had shown our gratitude by robbing good hard-working people.

The letter ended: "You live in a nice house with a big car parked in the driveway, and then you try to cheat people out of their money. You should be kicked back from where you came from."

At first I felt anger towards the letter writer, but then I began to realize she was only reacting to what she had read in the newspaper. I felt horrible that someone would have this impression of my family and me. During the next day and that evening the contents of that letter remained in my mind, eating away at me. Without saying anything to Mo I knew what I had to do. I was able to track down the woman's phone number and I went ahead and called her house. She answered the phone but made it perfectly clear she didn't want to speak to me, instead handing me over to her husband.

Not surprisingly, he was very cool towards me. I had thought this all through before making the call and I was determined not to let whatever anger they were feeling get to me. I reasoned the man, like his wife, was only reacting to the newspaper article. At first he made it clear he didn't want to hear anything about what I had to say and I could sense he was about to cut me off.

"Please. Just give me a couple of minutes to give you my side of the story," I pleaded. I still don't know why it was so important to convince a couple of total strangers that I had done no wrong.

I didn't hear a click or the dialing tone so I quickly started to explain. There was silence at the other end of the line as I continued to talk. When he did eventually respond, I could sense a changing attitude. I wouldn't go as far as saying I was winning over a new friend with my explanation, but clearly he was accepting that the situation wasn't as malicious as had been suggested in the paper. I let him know that we were behind with our mortgage payments on what could be described, at best, as a modest family home in need of some desperate TLC. As for the big car in the driveway, that was a rusty ten year old, in need of new tires and an air conditioner that worked. We couldn't afford to replace either.

By the end of our conversation the angry husband had come around to wishing me luck with the court case, perhaps hoping this would be a way his wife would get reimbursed for her membership fee. I felt a lot better as I went outside and threw his wife's letter in the trash.

Chapter Eight

While the anger we felt over the jury's verdict has softened over the years, the feeling of complete bewilderment certainly hasn't. Even to this day, on the rare occasion we think about it, we can easily recall our feelings at the time. We were left numb, wondering why?

And yet everything appeared to be going according to plan as we sat there waiting to be called back into court. A few hours earlier, we had been summoned from the coffee shop in the Collier County Courthouse complex and told that the jury was asking the judge for direction on awarding damages. What clearer message could we get than that? Seemingly we had won a guilty verdict and now it was simply a matter of determining how much money the jury was going to award us.

It's funny how you remember the strangest of things and places. That coffee shop is still deeply implanted in my memory. Even today I can easily recall the feeling hitting me within the first few minutes of being there that this wasn't the sort of establishment one wanted to hang around in. By any standard it was very basic, lacked any type of cozy atmosphere, and provided chairs so uncomfortable that I figured they had been carefully chosen with the deliberate intent of keeping customers from loitering for too long.

But there was something else in the place that left me with a more lasting and positive impression. Forgetting the menu, the ambiance, even the chairs, it was the picture of the incredible blind man who appeared to be running the place. I was totally fascinated as I watched him work with an easy efficiency, clearing the tables, bringing out the food, and working the cash register. As I sat there with Mo and our attorney Nelson, I recalled reading a feature article some months prior about this inspirational figure. According to the article the man had become recognized within the Naples community as someone who had triumphed over adversity and had inspired many others suffering with physical disabilities to return to the workplace. I suddenly felt very humble. All my problems up to this point seemed very minor compared to what I could only imagine this man had faced.

Those thoughts were suddenly interrupted with the hushed tone of our attorney. "We want to stay here for as long as possible," Nelson was saying. I guessed he was assuming we were growing impatient with the waiting. "The longer the wait, the higher the damages!"

Nelson was a young, ambitious lawyer who had become a celebrity himself as a result of successfully defending a couple of notorious criminals in recent months. Their stories had made newspaper headlines throughout Florida and Nelson gained a reputation for not only being a successful trial lawyer, but for also achieving high profile status, be it some years later, as Chairman of Collier County Public Schools.

As we sat there chatting, I inferred from Nelson's casual manner that these stark and somewhat shabby surroundings didn't strike him as the worst place in the world. At least, not when one is waiting for the next directive from the jury. Then again, perhaps he had simply become accustomed to being there. There was little doubt in my mind he had spent many waiting hours within these walls.

And wait we did. The cafe clock reminded us we had already been sitting there for more than an hour. "If they've found him guilty it's been my experience that for every hour the jury is out we will get an additional $100,000 in damages," Nelson whispered, clearly not wanting others around to hear.

But, even with this new show of confidence, it was difficult for Mo and I to accept that after nearly two years of waiting we were now about to see justice. Even though we were totally convinced the man we were facing in court was guilty, proven beyond any reasonable doubt by the amended tax form among other things, we still needed to hear that conviction decision from the jury.

If a long wait was what our attorney wanted, he wasn't to be disappointed. We sat there for over three hours before being called back into the dark-paneled courtroom to hear the long awaited jury's decision.

The courtroom was still half-filled with a few of our loyal friends, as well as several of the twenty or so witnesses we had called to testify during the two-day trial. The rest was made up of court staff looking completely disinterested in what was unfolding around them. The jury filed in for the last time and immediately I felt my stomach begin to knot. Mo reached across and we squeezed hands, giving each other a confident smile. This was it. Time to be financially solvent again.

We had been poor for too long. Spending the money to buy the spa, combined with two years of trying to keep it afloat as well as funding the improvements, had used up half our savings. The other half of our money was lost quickly in real estate investments we made shortly after arriving in Naples. Those investments went sour when mortgage rates reached the unbelievable high rate of nineteen percent. Our carefully researched plans of flipping pre-construction Marco Island beachfront properties in partnership with two friends from England went belly up. Virtually overnight, because of the high mortgage rates, buyers disappeared and we were left holding the units and the killer, non-fixed mortgages.

With no buyers and rapidly dwindling resources, our investment group of three was left with no option but to hand the properties back to the lenders. For my friends Chris and Mel, our two partners in the deal, it wasn't so bad. They both had very successful businesses back in England. But for Mo and me, this unexpected turn of events completely drained a major chunk of our resources and helped in contributing to our current desperate position. To add insult to injury, we knew we might even have survived this overall financial disaster if the value of the British pound hadn't fallen so drastically before we had the chance of exchanging our money. From the time we had set our course for American shores until the time came when we were able to transfer our savings, the exchange rate of the pound dropped almost twenty-five percent. The last of our reserves had dried up ages ago and we were left with absolutely no fat left in the piggy bank. We had been battered on every possible front.

Flashes of what our lives had become appeared in my mind as the jury forewoman rose. Mo, clasping my hand tightly, looked exhausted from working two jobs and from the emotional effects of working the spa. Our once cozy lifestyle had been wrecked. The children had long ago been pulled from private school, and one of the two family cars had found its way to the auction block a long time ago. With Mo requiring the one car to ferry our children to school and for work, I was left with the rusty old replacement bike as my only source of transportation.

In the months leading up to closing the spa we had reduced the staff to the bare necessity, and that certainly didn't include keeping on a cleaning service. Without any objection I was immediately promoted to the head janitor. It all seems a little funny now, remembering that each morning at five I would take off in the dark on my bike for the thirty minute ride to the spa and my pre-dawn cleaning duties. Thankfully it was all behind us. We were about to get back into the game.

All these strange thoughts were running through my mind as the jury foreman prepared to read the verdict.

I looked across for the umpteenth time at the man we were suing. He gave no indication of how he was feeling other than the fact his head was bowed and he was looking down at his hands clasped in his lap. Around us, the courtroom was silent, broken only by the elderly lady who rose and nervously thumbed the piece of paper in her hands.

Before the woman had a chance to speak, the judge lifted his head and looked at the woman. In a warm and friendly voice he asked her if the jury had reached a verdict. The woman paused before giving her answer. "We have Your Honor" her voice was soft and barely audible. The forewoman gave a gentle cough to clear her throat. Raising both her voice and her head she read out the verdict.

The jury having found for the Plaintiffs, Defendants, RICHARD VETTER and ROYAL COVE OF NAPLES, INC., on his claim of fraud and the jury having awarded the Plaintiff the sum of $49,000.00 as damages for the said claim, Judgment is hereby ordered in the amount of $49,000.00 against the Defendants, RICHARD VETTER and ROYAL COVE OF NAPLES, INC., jointly and severally in favor of the Plaintiff, JOHN W. FRESHWATER.

The jury having determined that the Plaintiff did execute a promissory note in favor of the Defendant, ROYAL COVE OF NAPLES, INC., as partial consideration of the subject contract for the sale and purchase of the subject business pursuant to the allegations of the Counterclaim and the evidence as presented the jury during the course of the trial, and the jury having awarded the Defendant, ROYAL COVE OF NAPLES, INC., the amount of monies testified to be due and owing, Judgment is hereby ordered in the principal amount of $39,536.22, plus interest in the amount of $8,723.92 to April 2, 1984, for a total of $48,260.14 against Plaintiff, JOHN W. FRESHWATER, and in favor of the Defendant, ROYAL COVE OF NAPLES, INC.

The Court, having considered the Motion for Directed Verdict argued on the Defendant's Counterclaim allegations of fraud against Plaintiff and the Defendants having no argument on the Motion, the Motion for Directed Verdict as to Count 111 of the Defendants Counterclaim alleging fraud against the Plaintiff be the same and is granted.

The Court, having considered the Motion for Attorney's Fees of Plaintiff and Defendants, it is ordered that the Plaintiff obligated to the Defendants in the sum of $9,662.50 in attorney's fees; and that the Defendants are obligated to the Plaintiff in the sum of $2,500 in attorney's fees.

The Court herewith consolidates all of the foregoing awards and Judgment is hereby entered in favor of Defendants and against Plaintiff in the sum of $7,903.00 for which let execution issue."

Nelson's arm came over my shoulder. "I'm sorry," he whispered. "I just don't understand it."

Chapter Nine

Our memories of the spa are certainly not all bad. We built great relationships with both our loyal staff and many of the members. There was a great deal of camaraderie and there were occasions when we just had a blast. Swamp Buggy Days quickly comes to mind.

Did you know that Naples is home of the World Swamp Buggy Races? The word "world" in the title may sound impressive, but you have to know Naples is the *only* place in the world that holds swamp buggy races.

Talk about the two extremes. On one side, you have a town that boasts of the most millionaires per capita on the planet, while on the other side you have this crazy event, which encourages just about every good ol' boy around to come out of the woods to either race or watch these strange looking machines race through deep mud. What other event anywhere in the world is witness to a beauty queen, dressed in a full-length gown and adorned with her crown and finery, being dumped unceremoniously into a six foot deep mud pit! That's the fate of the Swamp Buggy Queen at the conclusion of the races.

We first came across the event when Don, the spa manager, suggested it might be a good promotional idea to enter a float in the upcoming annual Swamp Buggy Parade which serves as a warm up to the two-day racing event. It usually attracts several thousand onlookers as it winds its way to downtown Naples. Mo and I had to agree it sounded like a positive idea and could be a lot of fun.

At this time, The Executive Health Spa, was still the only spa in town and enjoyed a lot of influential business people among its members. One of these was Henry Kreiling, owner of Kreiling Industries, a large local cement operation. Henry's company had prospered as Naples developed. His large fleet of white cement trucks could be seen at the majority of construction sites, as well as on roads all over town. Don suggested we ask "Hank" if we could use one of his flat bed trucks for the parade.

Henry gave one of his good ol' boy chuckles when he heard that we wanted to dress up one of his trucks and load it with hot-looking women and muscular men. "Never thought I would ever see one of my trucks being used for that," he smiled in his southern drawl. "I have a brand new one you can use."

The week before the parade, we had every spa employee working at dressing up the showroom-clean truck. Our three children were included too, and thought it was great fun. We lined both sides of the huge flatbed with chicken wire and poked the holes with blue and white tissue paper. The final affect was something like what you see on the floats at the famous Rose Bowl Parade in Pasadena, California. Only there they use real flower blooms, not boxes and boxes of tissue paper.

Our one concern was that it might rain and ruin our hard work but the rain gods proved to be kind to us and it stayed dry all week as we dressed the truck. On parade day we awoke early to another gorgeous, sunny day.

Apart from Mo and the other instructors all neatly dressed in their powder blue leotards, we invited several of the regular members to come aboard. We had no trouble recruiting as many as we felt we could comfortably fit on the truck. They all thought it would be fun posing on the exercise equipment and to throw candy out to the kids who lined the route. Up front with the driver were three very excited people, Kieran, Dominic and Kirsty. We weren't quite sure how many pieces of candy Dominic threw out to the crowds and how many pieces he kept for himself!

The parade went smoothly and the hot-looking, female members we had on board in skimpy workout clothes, certainly attracted plenty of attention. We actually received a lot of membership inquiries during the following week and signed up quite a few, which clearly proved our decision to participate was a sound choice.

After the parade, we all helped to strip down the truck before heading off to the races on the east side of town. As we sat in one of the long lines waiting to enter the swamp buggy grounds, Mo and I were amazed to see the popularity of the event. It seemed to us, judging by the numbers, that just about every one who owned a truck in Naples and surrounding areas must be here today to enjoy the races.

It would be difficult for me to describe a swamp buggy. It is like nothing else I had ever seen. I can only tell you my first impression was that it is something very basic, no more than a frame with a big powerful noisy engine and two huge wheels at the back. It soon became obvious why the vehicles have those big wheels. Much of the figure eight course comprises of deep mud holes. But even with such big wheels we would soon be seeing many of the buggies falling victim of the muddy trenches before the afternoon was over.

It seems that the event is all about noise. The louder the better. The roar of the engines was deafening as eight buggies lined up for the first race. Under the fierce afternoon sun, we squashed ourselves into the crowded, uncovered bleachers. It was hot, it was sticky, it was loud…it was the swamp buggy races.

It certainly proved to be something different, watching these strange looking vehicles blasting through the mud with engines screaming and the crowds roaring. It was as noisy an event I can ever remember attending and the children loved every minute. They hooted and hollered with the rest of the crowd when the buggies got stuck in the mud pits, watching them slowly sink deeper and deeper into the murky waters.

Both Mo and I got as much amusement from watching the spectators as we did from the races. While the majority appeared to be locals, there were also an easily recognizable number of tourists. The first thing we both noticed was that the group of locals around us didn't stop eating or drinking. As one hot dog was flushed down with slug of soda or beer, someone in the group immediately got up to go to purchase another supply. This scenario seemed to go on all afternoon. I did mention quietly to Mo, I wondered if anyone in the heavy-set group had ever heard the word 'anorexia"

Then there were the names of their kids. The calls to Billyjo, Homer and MaryLou cut through the noise and made us feel that we really were in the Deep South. So these were the 'rednecks' we had been hearing about. They certainly knew how to have a good time.

We had been told that rednecks were mostly poorer, uneducated white folk, who were now being forced to share their land with the prosperous families moving down from the north. Some held resentment, we discovered, but mostly they continued with their own way of life, enjoying their six-packs with friends on the back porch and accepting that development was bringing some benefits in the form of jobs, mainly in the construction and service industry. And there were those who had hit it big and were sitting on large tracks of 'desirable' land that their forefathers had purchased many years back for a few dollars and was now worth many thousands.

As the afternoon wore on, the noise seemed to get louder, if that was at all possible, as even larger vehicles were wheeled out to the starting line. Everyone seemed to have a favorite buggy and driver and the roar of the crowd became ear-splitting as the drivers came under starter's orders. Long before the races ended, both Mo and I confessed to having pounding headaches. There was no shade anywhere and the sun shone relentlessly throughout the afternoon. We would have left sooner if the kids, caked in sun-screen, hadn't begged us to stay until the end,

This was the swamp buggy races. It held a fascination of its own. Everything about it was unique to us and we enjoyed the experience...not so much, mind you, that we ever wanted to go again.

Chapter Ten

Easter bonnets and cucumber sandwiches hold a special place in our memories. It happened as a result of The British American Club we helped to set up shortly after arriving in Naples.

It should be made clear that we have never been a family to overly brag about our British heritage, at least not anywhere near a level, we hope, where it could be considered annoying, offensive, and boring. But we have come across many couples that do. Anyone who has traveled abroad will know what I'm talking about. There are those people that choose to immigrate to another country, only to continually bad-mouth their new homeland, or compare it unfavorably with the one they have just left. I recall hearing this went on a lot way back in the sixties when families emigrated from Britain to Australia on what was labeled "the ten pounds assisted passage program." Instead of being grateful for their new opportunities, large numbers of the new immigrants continually berated their new homeland. It seems hardly surprising to me that the Aussies turned their backs and coldly declared. *"If you don't like it here, why the hell don't you go back?"*

But let me start at the very beginning of how this patriotic thing first started. Please bear with me for a moment because the story meanders a little along the way.

Shortly after arriving in Naples, we enrolled our three children in the summer camp programs at the YMCA. This was a great help in those early days, when both Mo and I had to work long hours and our babysitter, Alison, here for just a few months, needed some vacation time by herself. It also led us innocently into our first bit of notoriety in town.

The swimming activities quickly proved to be the favorite of all three children. Every day, during that first summer we would drop off the boys at the 'Y' and for much of the day they would enjoy playing with newfound friends in the pool. After a couple of weeks, both Kieran and Dominic were swimming so well that they were asked if they would like to join the YMCA swim team. They jumped at the opportunity, and we suddenly found ourselves committed to an extended daily routine, involving swim training classes.

The swim coach, Fran, was a friendly and energetic woman about our age who quickly revealed she was bouncing back from a recent divorce. She had two young children of her own who both swam on the team. One evening, when we went to pick up the boys from practice, Fran came over and asked if we would like to come to a party at her house the following Saturday. "There will be a lot of the swim team parents there and it will give you an opportunity of meeting them," she said.

Of course we agreed to go. We were always keen to meet new friends and Alison was around to look after the children. As we stood there chatting, I couldn't help but notice that Fran seemed to be moving nervously from one leg to the other, making it appear she wanted to add something. Her expression seemed to be indicating she was feeling a little awkward and embarrassed.

"Something you want to tell us, Fran?" I asked.

My question appeared to provide the opening she was looking for. "I have to warn you that a couple of the parents decided to do some…well, skinny dipping last year," she finally blurted out. "You won't be offended if it happens on Saturday?"

Mo laughed. "We are from Europe you know. We are used to topless beaches. I really don't think there's any chance of us being offended." We could see Fran's body relax.

The party turned out to be really nice. There were about 30 adults and, as Fran had indicated, many of them were parents of the team swimmers. We noticed immediately, from looking around at the groups of people busily engaging in conversation, that everyone had respected Fran's request to leave the children at home. Grabbing ourselves a drink from the kitchen bar, we moved from group to group, happy to mingle and introduce ourselves to the various groups of couples. Everyone seemed very friendly, and curious to hear how we had come to be in Naples. The wine flowed freely during the evening and the candles on the pool deck provided a relaxing setting. It was a warm and muggy night so it seemed inevitable that someone would eventually suggest it was time to cool off in the pool.

Certainly the illuminated pool looked very inviting as we noticed several couples grabbing towels from the pile stacked on top of one of the patio tables. Mo looked at me and gave a nod that suggested she was keen to join in. Remembering what Fran had told us, we made our way over to one of the sun beds in a darker corner of the patio and undressed. As we stood there folding our clothes, the first naked man appeared from the shadows and ran diving into the pool. Mo and I quickly followed. The water felt great.

The first hint that this wasn't going to turn out quite as we expected was when we noticed the five or six other couples walking towards the pool and all wearing bathing suits. Furthermore, the wife of our naked swimmer was now frantically jumping up and down and screaming for her husband to get out of the pool and go back inside the house to get his bathing suit. "Don't be so disgusting," she was screaming. Clearly this wasn't the same group that was here last year.

Oh dear, we thought. All these people and we are the only naked couple. Mo and I looked at each other and burst out laughing as we edged our way towards the side of the pool as others were jumping in around us. Was it just our imagination or were the pool lights getting brighter as we waited for the right moment to haul ourselves out of the water and back into the shadows to gather our clothes?

The following Monday we were reminded we were living in a small town community, still with somewhat of a bible-belt mentality. The word had gotten out about our naked exploits and while we sensed that several members were giving us a kind of disapproving look, there were others, with broad smiles and knowing winks, asking in hush tones, for a full report on our scandalous behavior.

About three weeks after becoming members of the swim team, the boys participated in their first competition. The YMCA was hosting its second swim meet of the season. Five swim teams from the southwest Florida region were invited along. The Naples parents were encouraged to volunteer to help in the serving of food and drinks, as well as helping with a wide variety of tasks, including timekeeping and keeping stats. For us, it seemed a little less intimidating to help with turning hot dogs and burgers, rather than getting involved with the more official type duties. And that's how we came to meet up with Andrew and Jo Johnston.

Andrew was one of those people who is never lost for words or a colorful story to relate. We were reminded many times during the years we were friends that Andrew would never spoil a good story by incorporating only true facts. We quickly accepted that the substance of a story we may have heard several times would certainly change each time we heard it. But this was Andrew, and with his charismatic personality, he was able to get away with it.

If his resume could be believed, he had risen to senior management in a British pharmaceutical company. He and his wife had lived in Hastings on the south coast of England and came to Naples with their two young children just a few weeks before us.

Jo's mother had married an American serviceman after the Second World War and so Andrew and Jo were able to move over with very little immigration hassle. Andrew didn't have a job waiting for him so he had taken temporary employment as a chauffeur to a wealthy family living in Port Royal, one of Naples' wealthiest communities. His demeanor fitted the job perfectly. In fact, you really couldn't imagine Andrew doing anything else but driving a wealthy, older couple, around the streets of Naples in a gleaming, tan Rolls Royce. His new employers truly believed his story that he was a Rolls Royce-trained chauffeur!

The idea of a British American Club was borne as we flipped our umpteenth burger and turned, what we hoped, was the last of the hot dogs in the energy-draining, baking-hot midday sun.

It was Andrew's idea and we continued discussing it as we moved from the grills over to where we could watch the children race. It soon became apparent that neither of us had any set ideas on how the club should be run, but we both agreed we should test the waters by getting something published in the newspaper. That evening, I sat down and wrote a short press release, giving our phone numbers and a few basic details. We would now wait and see what sort of response it would bring.

Both Kieran and Dominic had become stylish swimmers in the couple of weeks they had been training with the team. Both looked pretty good as they ploughed freestyle up and down their lanes. The only ingredient that was missing, noted their doting mother, was the unfair, much faster speeds demonstrated by their competition. Neither of them won too many races during that first year on the team, but they certainly had fun and made many new friends.

Kirsty followed her two older brothers into the YMCA Swim Team before she was even five years old. We will never forget her first race.

Actually, she wasn't supposed to race this particular hot afternoon. After all, she was still only three and had been on the team only for a couple of weeks. Fran had already told us she didn't want to push Kirsty and planned to have her wait a few more weeks before putting her into her first race.

But this was before the B Team Medley Relay Squad came up one girl short. Several girls had called off sick and only three showed up for the race. The team members were clearly disappointed that, without a forth member, they wouldn't be able to compete.

It must have been about then that Fran saw Kirsty's angelic-looking face peering up from under a towel as she lay beside us on the bleachers. Kirsty was about to take a nap.

"Wanna race?" Fran called over. Kirsty was up on her feet immediately, nap time forgotten, and with a grin from ear to ear.

Fran came over. "You can start off with backstroke. I think that's your strongest stroke, but remember, it's two lengths of the pool."

Kirsty didn't appear fazed by the thought of her first race, nor by the size of the other girls, all of which were a lot older and towered over her as they moved to the side of the pool and dived in to take up their starting positions.

At the sound of the gun, all six girls pushed off from the wall and stroked their way down their individual lanes. Kirsty was neck and neck with all the competition, for the first couple of yards at least. But then the inevitable started to happen... and she began to lose ground. By the time she reached half-way down the pool, all the other swimmers were already turning for their second length. Our hearts went out to our young daughter trying desperately to stay in the race. By the time she reached the end of the first length, nearly all the other girls had finished their leg and were handing over to the next swimmer.

Kirsty hit the wall at the far end of the pool and stopped. We weren't sure if she was confused and thought her part of the race was over or she was just too exhausted to go on. We both felt helpless as we watched. I could sense Mo wanted to rush down and scoop her up into her arms.

But suddenly we could see that she wasn't giving up. Meeting the cries of encouragement from her teammates and the hundreds of spectators around the pool, Kirsty gave a big smile and started her overhead stroke once more. Yard by yard, she slowly made her way down the lane as the second swimmers on the other teams were now beginning to overtake her. To the emotional cheering of the crowd, she eventually finished her stage and handed over to the next member of the team. She scrambled out of the pool, completely exhausted, but smiling at the continuing cheers and applause.

The response we received from the two paragraphs appearing in the newspaper about the planned British American Club was quite amazing. More than twenty people phoned us over the next few days and expressed a desire to get involved with the club. What was surprising to us was the fact that only about half the inquiries came from what we could discern as being 'True Brits.' The other half claimed some ambiguous connection through ancestry. One young man admitted his connection came via once having a college roommate who happened to be British. But of course we didn't care. We decided it would be fun just getting the club off the ground with a group of enthusiastic members and watching it develop from there.

Around that time, Brian and Viv arrived from London to take over The English Pub, located in one of the rare poorer areas of town. Brian had been a professional musician and was once a member of a group called Pickettywitch, which had enjoyed some fame in the UK with a couple of hit records. Viv's family, we later learned, operated a very successful carpet company back in my old journalism haunt in the East End of London. The first impression you got of Viv was that she could handle herself in any situation.

Like so many other foreign couples, Brian and Viv had fallen in love with Naples during a vacation and decided to come back and stay. They did it the same way as us. They also went through a business broker and checked out several different businesses before deciding on the pub. The only problem about The English Pub was that it didn't look anything like an English pub! The previous American female owner had moved down to Naples several years before from North Carolina, and apparently had visited England for a few days many years before that. She seemed to think a couple of posters of the Tower of London and Big Ben provided sufficient décor to entitle her to advertise the pub as being a *"little bit of England away from home."* Before Brian and Viv took possession, the only beer sold in the The English Pub was Bud!

Poor Brian and Viv quickly learned they were going to have to change more than the décor and the beer they served. On their first Saturday evening, a fight broke out in the bar resulting in one of the patrons having part of his nose bitten off. Viv took one look at the mess, rolled up her sleeves and ordered everyone to leave. The bar was closed for a couple of weeks as the couple made changes.

Both Viv and Brian, as well as some family members who mistakenly believed they were over on a relaxing vacation, worked feverishly. The hammering of nails could be heard late into the night, so it was fortunate that the pub was situated in an industrial part of town with few residents around to complain about the noise. When the bar opened a couple of weeks later, there were now several British ales on tap and mock oak timber beams covering the ceiling and walls. There was still a lot of work for the couple to do, but almost over night, the bar had taken on an authentic English pub flavor. Posters had been ripped down and replaced with framed pictures of English country scenes. A new dress code was introduced which proved effective in keeping out unwanted patrons. With Viv taking on more of the front of the house duties, it was soon known around this part of town that you didn't mess with these new owners.

The English Pub now became the unofficial headquarters of the British American Club and hosted the first couple of social gatherings.

The club gained more popularity when the Naples Daily News ran several articles about its members. By the middle of October we had acquired the names of more than fifty people who wanted to be included in forthcoming events.

It was Andrew who decided it would be fun to hold a November 5th Bonfire Night, the historical English fireworks event which celebrates an unsuccessful attempt at blowing up the Houses of Parliament. The idea was well received by all the members, although we felt there were some in the group who had no strong ties with British history and were possibly left wondering if we were celebrating the right result. Being a non–political group we chose to ignore their good-natured jibes. As the weeks passed, several members stepped forward to donate fireworks.

Even back then, most fireworks had been outlawed in the State of Florida, but not so in other states. Several families purchased boxes of rockets and firecrackers when driving through Georgia where, just across state line, huge firework stores were open year round.

We may not have faced a huge problem if we hadn't advertised the upcoming bonfire event with a brief press release. But the Miami Herald picked up on the story and after interviewing Andrew at length, ran a large article on the front page of its regional section. The article proved to be a firecracker itself, bringing an immediate response from the local fire chief who phoned Andrew at home to scold him, tersely reminding him it was unlawful to set off fireworks without a permit.

"So how do I go about getting a permit?" inquired an unflappable Andrew. "You need to check that out with the local police," came back the reply.

This was Friday, just one day before the planned event. Fortunately, Andrew's employers were out of town, so he was able to take time off to drive the Rolls Royce to his local police station.

"You wanna do what?" asked the young duty corporal scratching his head, trying to make some sense out of a story about a guy who held such a prominent position in British history. Andrew soon realized he wasn't getting anywhere slowly and was obviously making the whole matter much too complicated. "We just want a permit to let off a few rockets," he finally pleaded.

"Not as easy as that, sir," said the uncompromising police officer now swinging back in his chair behind the desk. "You first have to get the fire department to come down and check out the area where you plan to launch the rockets. If they think everything is ok and not a fire hazard then we'll consider issuing a permit, providing you have a licensed firework expert in charge of course."

"But it was the fire department who sent me to you," said Andrew getting a little agitated at the way this was going, or not going.

"Sorry sir, that's they way it has to be."

Andrew's house was located in the heart of Golden Gate Estates, an area that had been targeted originally to provide homes for the working class employed in the local service industries. Although construction was going on at a feverish pace, the area was still viewed as rather remote with large, two and five acre plots providing a lot of space between the scattered homes. Andrew's house was newly constructed and was still lacking any real landscaping. There was a little sod in the front and back of the house and most of the site had been cleared of shrubs and trees. The closest house was nearly two hundred yards away so we felt there was very little chance of our fireworks setting fire to anything of value!

Over at the fire station, Andrew enjoyed no better success. Once again he was told the decision on issuing a permit rested at the police station. The stocky, red-faced fireman sitting in the office admitted he had never been asked for a permit before. "Any fireworks set off in this town always takes place downtown and is handled by the downtown offices. I really don't know what to tell you...."

With Andrew shaking his head in disbelief, the fireman rose from his chair and walked over to close the office door. He dropped his voice to a whisper. "Look, you are not hearing this from me. But you are so far out in the boonies that most likely no one is ever going to know you are letting off a few fireworks. If we get a complaint it's going to take us ten minutes to get out there and you will see our lights and hear our sirens long before we arrive. If we are called out, you just make sure we don't find anything when we get there.... and be very careful." And with that, he looked back down at the pile of paperwork sitting on his desk, indicating the discussion was now over.

The following evening, under clear starry skies, The British American Club celebrated Guy Fawkes Night by sending off rockets and igniting a hundred or so roman candles. Although the firecrackers must have sounded like gunfire, we had no complaints and no appearance of any fire trucks or police cars. We realized, as the twenty-minute show came to an end and everyone cheered that we were probably the only ones in the entire country honoring such an important event.

With such a rousing success under our belts – more than one hundred and fifty people came out to witness the firework display - we were eager to plan more events. That Christmas, we held a party on Boxing Day, a traditional UK holiday celebrated the day after Christmas. We invited all the children from a nearby foster care center to an afternoon party at The English Pub and then later, when they were sent on their way with gifts and boxes of food, we enjoyed a party ourselves. With British ales flowing freely, we all stood around the piano belting out old favorite tunes until the wee hours of the morning. Our pianist that night was another newcomer to town, Eric Easton, the first manager of the Rolling Stones! In all the years I knew Eric I couldn't bring my self to tell him that our publishing company back in England had published the book, *"The Ups and Downs of the Rolling Stones,"* which the group didn't like one bit and successfully got banned in England. The book did, however, enjoy some success in America and was serialized in newspapers throughout the world.

But as good as these two events proved to be; perhaps our most notable success was an Easter Garden Party we set up in the beautiful home of an English couple, Carol and James.

Back in Bath, in western England where he lived until coming to America two years before, James was viewed as a kind of lord of the manor. He owned a large country estate with horse paddocks and cattle herds. Sadly his long-time wife had died several years back, leaving him alone to enjoy his wealthy lifestyle.

He told us he found his large home extremely lonely and he hated the evenings and eating alone. After a short time, he started taking his evening meal at the nearby hotel and that's where he met Carol, the hotel barmaid. A year later, a picture appeared in the local newspaper of the happy couple getting married. The accompanying article was all about the fairytale story of the barmaid marrying her wealthy lord!

The Easter Garden Party was causing a lot of interest. Locals seemed fascinated to hear about these strange Brits planning an Easter Bonnet competition, eating cucumber sandwiches with the crust removed and coconut shies where, for a dollar, you had the chance of winning a coconut if you could knock it out of the cup with the throw of a baseball. A local radio station planned a live remote for the event. The station executives obviously thinking it would be amusing to interview a group of crazy Englishmen and their ladies planning to enjoy too much fun in the Florida noonday sun.

A few weeks before the event, I had sent a letter to the Queen at Buckingham Palace congratulating her on her forthcoming birthday. This was simply a ploy to get a letter back from the Queen *'thanking The British American Club for its kind thoughts and wishes.'* The reply was framed and still hangs proudly in The English Pub.

While the Easter Garden Party was a little off the wall, it wasn't quite as crazy in the eyes of some locals as the British American Club's first cricket match!

It had been agreed in the early days of forming the club that we would try and show our American neighbors all the quaint British customs...and, of course, that had to include a game of cricket.

Fortunately for the club, one of the members was friendly with a member associated with one of the English county cricket teams. The member said he was confident he could persuade the team officials to provide us with a couple of pieces of essential equipment – the main items being two bats. We never dreamed just how generous the club would be in meeting our request. They shipped over, not only the bats, but new sets of pads, gloves and wooden wickets; everything in fact that was required to play this gentlemanly game.

Try explaining the rules of cricket to anyone who has never seen the game being played. Of course, all our new American friends wanted to compare the game with baseball, figuring it would be easier to comprehend. I'm sure they kind of gave up comparing when we told them a test game between two countries could last for five days and still end in a tie. This was beyond any American comprehension. We know they think a baseball game going into a couple of extra innings is something special!

We handed out copies of the rules of the game prior to match day but I can assure you that anyone who was relying on reading the rules to understand the game arrived at the field completely confused. It was decided it would be better to start playing and allow the confused players to learn as they went along.

A Caribbean team from Ft. Myers was going to be our first match opponents but when we heard that several of the players had played at a professional level back home, we decided we needed some serious practice first. We quickly rearranged our first game to be a make-up game between members within our own club.

On match day the weather was hot – unusual setting for English cricket, unless it is played abroad - and I have to admit that a considerable amount of alcohol was consumed before the start of the game in an attempt to beat off hydration and to relax the players.

The teams were evenly divided, mixing up those who had played before with those who had absolutely no idea of what the game was all about. It has to be said that those who had no idea on how the game should be played, left the field five hours later still with absolutely no better understanding. Even with a few more practice games under our belt, we never did feel competent enough to take up the challenge and play the team from Ft. Myers.

Chapter Eleven

Following the trial, both Mo and I went into bouts of depression, even though our friends rallied around us, offering wonderful emotional support. We experienced so many acts of kindness that Mo and I both felt guilty that we were feeling so sorry for ourselves.

One day we came home to find an envelope pinned to the front door with twenty dollars inside and a brief note with no name, simply saying the money was to help buy groceries. Another time we came out of the house in the morning to find a new charcoal grill sitting there. Someone close, we never discovered who, had to know that our old grill had recently burned out and we had no money to fix it. Looking back now, we can accept we didn't fully appreciate what we still had. All we could see was our mountain, rising ever taller before our eyes, and a feeling we were slipping way down the slopes and floundering about in the scrabble below. It was a selfish attitude when there were many more people so much worse off.

Someone handed me a book to read; Robert Schuler's *"When Times Get Tough, The Tough Get Going."* I had never heard of the author, or the book, and it lay unopened on the coffee table for several days before I casually picked it up and skimmed through the pages. I was immediately hooked, quickly reading the book from cover to cover and finding it both inspirational and helpful. It was a book I couldn't put down.

Schuler's words made me think, and I quickly attempted to adapt and apply some of his suggestions into my life. I came up with my own ten-point positive plan, which started with number one on my list of simply getting out of bed in the morning and taking a shower, whether I was leaving the house or not. The other 'must dos' included simple tasks like writing ten letters and making ten phone calls. Schuler's doctoring also inspired me to be more active in trying to find work, any legal work that is, both in the short, as well as in the long term.

But even though I now had a plan, it didn't mean I was going to enjoy an immediate reversal of fortune. I had put the word out that I was looking for painting and wallpaper work, a couple of skills I had picked up over the years and felt comfortable performing for others.

Carl and Dee Jones had become two of our closest friends. Mo had met the couple when selling them advertising at their Maaco car-painting franchise. Sadly, just a couple of years later, both the business and their marriage failed.

After their divorce, Dee moved back to Pennsylvania and Carl stayed around Naples to take a course in hanging wallpaper. Despite the failed Maaco operation, he was quite an astute businessman, and very quickly developed his wallpaper business enough to hire me to assist with some of his bigger jobs. It didn't take long for me to grasp sufficient skills to work alongside Carl, as well as taking on smaller jobs on my own. Admittedly, I made my fair share of mistakes in the early days, most of which we were somehow able to cover up.

Probably the worst experience I faced was when I was working my own job and was hired to hang some very expensive, hand-painted wallpaper for a very fussy lady customer who had recently moved into a new condo. I should have known this wasn't going to be an easy job the first time I ran my hand over the paper. I felt a texture like no other I had experienced. It was thick and heavy like cardboard, and I kept asking myself if it would stay up on the wall. The fact that the concerned customer kept reminding me that the wall covering cost nearly two hundred dollars a roll didn't help calm my nerves one bit.

By the end of the first day I had hung seven rolls and finished the kitchen area and part of the breakfast room. It looked good to me as I stood back to admire my day's handiwork. Fortunately I had been left alone while the fussing client went off to do her long list of chores and didn't see her again before I left to go home. I slept much better that night than any previous night leading up to starting the job. I had truly suffered nightmares; seeing clear images of the paper falling off the walls, and me drowning in expensive wall covering piles, growing larger at every turn.

The next morning I was just about to leave our house when the phone rang and my customer's voice boomed from the earpiece. "YOU have a big problem with my wall covering," she was screaming. Immediately, the nightmares flooded my brain. I closed my eyes, trying to shut out the problem. She gave me no time to respond before yelling, *"You've hung it upside down!"*

My body was shaking and my stomach was churning as I drove to the woman's condo. All I could think about was doing my math; seven times two hundred dollars. I just wanted to run away and hide, hoping this latest nightmare really wasn't happening.

At the condo, the woman didn't want to hear that she had watched me hang the first couple of sheets and should have noticed what I was doing. To me, the apples and leaves looked perfectly fine sweeping upwards, but this lady was determined to see her fruit hanging down. We looked at each other in a standoff mode. Neither one of us was sure what to do next. I moved over to the kitchen wall closest to the door and ran my hand gently over the paper. I was playing for time, desperately thinking of a practical solution.

Fortunately, this was to be one of those occasions when good luck was on my side. On inspection of the first sheet I'd hung the previous morning, I found I could easily peel it back from the wall. The fact that the paper was so heavy and thick meant the heavy coating of paste still hadn't fully dried. Almost miraculously, I was able to peel off each sheet and lay them out on the kitchen floor. In just a few minutes I had paper lying throughout the condo. The woman stood back and said nothing. I really think she was in a state of shock. Amazingly, I was able to re-hang the wall covering without wasting more than a couple of sheets. After a very careful inspection when I completed the job, my client seemed satisfied enough to pay me. I couldn't get out of that condo quickly enough.

But it was still summer and responses to my calls for work were few and far between. The only job offer I received was to help rebuild a seawall on Marco Island. Of course I had never rebuilt a sea wall before, but a little lack of knowledge was not about to stop me from earning some much needed money.

In reality, I wasn't required to actually rebuild the wall. Over the years, heavy summer rains had washed away the earth behind the concrete barrier, and several sections were left without earth support. The entire structure was in danger of breaking up. My job was to haul ballast, which the property owner had arranged to be dropped near the front of the house, across the yard to the sea wall, and to fill in the open trenches. To me it sounded like half a day's work as we discussed it on the phone and the offer of a $200 payment sounded generous.

It was around mid-morning when I pulled up at the large house which sat on a huge, beautifully landscaped lot. The owners were out of town, but they had arranged to leave me a wheelbarrow so I could do the hauling. At first glance, the pile of ballast didn't appear too high, and I estimated that the job shouldn't take more than three to four hours. Wrong! I should have known better!

On the way to Marco Island I had driven through a typical, heavy summer rainstorm. As I climbed out of the car, it was like walking into a sauna. The air was hot and heavy, and within minutes the humidity had soaked my clothes. Worse still. I looked down to see that my uncovered legs and arms were now feeding areas for scores of mosquitoes.

I suddenly felt very down. What had I set myself up for? It really did take a lot of will power for me not to climb back in the car and drive off. But of course I didn't. I needed the money and there was always Mo to face.

Pulling a shovel from the trunk of the car, I moved towards the pile of stones. I peeled off my soaking shirt, threw it to the ground and took up the challenge. The sooner I got into this, I reasoned, the sooner I could get away.

I quickly shoveled the first load into the wheelbarrow and with a burst of energy I grabbed the handles and started pushing. I had barely covered half the distance to the sea wall when the wheelbarrow lurched to one side and almost toppled over. I held on desperately and with a supreme, back-breaking effort, managed to righten the contraption.

It was only when I tried to push off again that I noticed the cause of the wobble. Looking down, I saw that the wheel was hanging loose, making the wheelbarrow lurch from side to side. A brighter person would have stopped right there and gone off to find a new barrow. But I didn't. I chose not to waste time and to stay with the one I had. With fresh determination to get the job finished as quickly as possible, I heaved the first load forward.

This proved to be the hardest and longest day's work of my life. Work gloves would have been a blessing. Instead my hands were soon covered with open blisters. But that was good. The pain in my hands took my mind away from the itching mosquito bites, now covering at least a third of my body. I soon gave up counting the number of trips I took from the rock pile to the sea wall. I truly believe, looking back now, that with the sun beating down on my aching body, my mind had gone into a semi-conscious state.

The mountain of stones seemed to stay the same height for the longest time and it was almost six o'clock when I dumped my last load and propped the wheelbarrow up against the side of the house. I slumped into the car totally exhausted. It seemed every muscle in my body was sore and aching, and yet I was also aware I was almost enjoying a sense of achievement. Is 'masochistic' the right word to describe my feelings? I couldn't help smiling as I recalled the title of the Schuler book I had recently read.

The next morning I got a call from Gil Pooler. I hadn't spoken to him since he gave evidence during the court case. He said he was with Phil, the owner of that marina I was interested in buying when we first came over. Phil was discussing opening another outlet for his boat rentals and was looking for someone to run the new operation. "Was I interested?" Gil asked.

The rest of that summer was spent painting and cleaning up an old ship store at the City Dock. It provided gas and supplies, along with the boat rentals. I really enjoyed working there, and for the next year some sanity returned to my life. It was pleasant work that gave me time to catch my breath while thinking about my next business project. Unfortunately Phil was only able to sign a short lease on the property and the landlords were unwilling to extend the lease when the time was up. He lost his profitable little business and I was again out of a job.

When Mo and I were both working we were not only able to cover our current bills but we could also make some inroads into our credit card debts. While this was a much improved situation we still believed that we had to find a way back into owning our own business if we ever wanted to have a real chance of getting out of our financial mess. Although Mo enjoyed teaching, the substitute work paid poorly and offered her no benefits. Not surprisingly the time came when she decided to look for better paying employment.

Now out of a job myself, I was anxious to find new work to bring in a regular pay check. We just couldn't afford to slip back. I did my best to make sure the word was still out there that I was available for painting and wallpapering jobs. One day, out of the blue, I received a phone call which led to some contract painting work on Marco Island. Friends knew someone who ran a condo management company, and they in turn knew of several condo owners who wanted their condos painted before the coming winter season. Some owners would be returning to Marco Island and staying in the condos themselves, while others planned on renting them out. The deal was a sweet one for me. I would paint the condos and pay a 20% commission to the management company.

For a couple of months I was moving from one condo job to the next. I had set up a simple routine, which had me in and out of the condo in around thirty hours. Often I worked 15-hours at a stretch, striving to finish each condo in two days as new work orders began flowing in. For the first time in ages there was a little money in our bank account and with it, a feeling of great relief all round.

But of course, it wasn't to last. All too soon the busy winter season was upon us and none of the condo owners wanted a painter disrupting their organized lives. "Come around after season," was a common expression I came to dread hearing.

When you are looking at bare condo walls you get plenty of time to think and plan. One day it occurred to me that the huge condo block was almost empty during the summer months. Here were these beautiful homes just begging to be rented out. In between rolling gallons of "white linen" and "traditional gray" I came up with a business idea. I would contact the owners and suggest renting out their apartments to foreign visitors who, I knew, would be interested in short-term summer rentals.

The Brits, as I knew from personal experience, enjoy traveling to Florida in the summer months. How about suggesting they take a week in Orlando to enjoy the major touristy attractions, before traveling down to Marco Island for a second week of lazing on a beautiful tropical-style sandy beach? I would set up the arrangements with travel agents in Britain. The condo owners would earn a rental fee that would cover the high condo maintenance charges they were always complaining about, as well as covering any other related condo expenses. In addition, I would arrange for their apartments to be freshly painted and cleaned for the start of the winter season. To me it seemed like a win-win situation all round.

I contacted several condo owners who expressed a positive interest, sufficient for me to contact several of the larger travel agents in England. Two were receptive to the proposal, but warned it could take as long as a couple of years to set up. First would come the required 'site inspection' of the condos, and then contracts with the owners would have to be signed. I was told it would take up to a full year for this travel package to get into the agents' vacation brochures, and then probably another six months before clients would start coming out to use the properties.

This two-year time lag was too long for the impatient owners. Many were already thinking about selling for a profit and moving into more expensive units. Over the next few weeks my plan to involve hundreds of condos throughout the island fell apart. A rough draft of the travel brochure still sits in my desk drawer, alongside a dozen or so other business ideas.

But the painting work was not entirely dead. I moved to a new, higher level of business when a neighbor's son contacted me. He had recently become president of the resident's association where he lived and had been asked by the association's board members to obtain quotes for painting the three large buildings. Each stilt wooden structure comprised of eight apartments, with parking spaces underneath.

I had absolutely no experience of quoting for this size of a job. I wasn't even sure I could handle all the labor work myself. Still, the opportunity was just too good to turn down. I took a little comfort in the thought I probably wouldn't get the job anyway. After all, they were also looking for estimates from major painting contractors too. The son warned me that the quote would have to look professional on company letterhead. Rummaging through the Yellow Pages and picking out different pieces of artwork easily overcame that first obstacle. With the help of a photocopier, "Freshwater Painting" was born and we now had the company letterhead on which we could submit our quote. I would figure out later what to do if I was asked if I was insured and bonded. My next challenge was to come up with a price!

I walked around the trio of buildings once, twice, three times. It was hard to overcome my nervousness and apprehension. Was I setting myself up for something way over my head, I wondered. A couple of times I almost got back into the car before deciding it would be even harder to face you know who if I backed out now. I continued my walk around the property, estimating how long it would take to paint each section of the building. Then, with my final total scrawled on a piece of yellow paper, I doubled the estimate and then doubled it again. I figured it would be safer not to get the job than to find out later I had underestimated time and cost of materials. The last thing I needed or wanted was to end up losing money I didn't have.

As it turned out, my quote of $5,800 was just two hundred and fifty dollars less than the next lowest figure and thankfully, without further inquiries, I was given the job.

Throughout our time in America, my parents, until my father died in 2000, would come to visit every eighteen months or so. Just a week before I was due to start the painting job my mom and dad arrived for a two-month vacation. Now, my father was 73 years of age at this time, but he was one of those workaholics you hear about but rarely meet. He said he would like to come along and help me. He thought it would be fun!

I'm a little embarrassed to admit that it was my aged father who climbed the tallest ladder to paint the higher spots. The truth was, he was up the ladder before I could stop him. Together, we had the job completed in just over two weeks and everyone seemed delighted with our work. The only real problem we encountered was when paint from my roller blew onto a car parked underneath one of the buildings one windy day. Fortunately, the owner was very understanding about the situation and was satisfied when I had the car professionally detailed and all the paint spots removed. I realized I was very lucky, and got away with what could have been a costly blunder.

With the money we received from the job I decided to splurge a bit on a much needed family trip to Orlando. This would serve as a gesture of thanks to my father, who refused to take any money for all his hard work in the blistering heat. It would also be a wonderful tonic for Mo. For the first time in ages we were able to put memories of the court case and financial problems aside. For a couple of days, we were able to experience a little of what we had come to America to enjoy. *"Let's drive to Orlando and find Mickey!"*

The family trip to Disney world would not only help to recharge our batteries, but also gave us time to think in a more positive way about what we had and what was happening in our lives. Mo and I could now talk about the court case without a cloud of depression appearing over our heads. Maybe we still couldn't understand how the jury had arrived at their decision, but we no longer felt the same level of anger and resentment. I can't remember which one of us raised the question of filing an appeal, but we both felt we had nothing to lose in checking it out.

Back in Naples, I made an appointment to see Nelson to discuss our idea. It was interesting that, when I explained at our meeting what Mo and I had been discussing, Nelson smiled and said he was planning to call us later that week to suggest the same course of action. He said he felt strongly we had grounds on which to appeal, but also pointed out it was still a risky call with no guarantee of getting a change of decision. And there would be more legal costs involved; fees we would have to find if we didn't win the appeal.

Jointly we decided it was worth taking the gamble. Mo and I accepted that if we didn't take this one final step it would haunt us for the rest of our lives. I guess we were looking for that final closure, one way or the other.

This time there was no work for us to do. Everything was left in the hands of our attorney. It was a completely unemotional exercise from our standpoint. The paperwork was filed with the Appeal Courts in Lakeland in central Florida and there was nothing left to do but to get on with our lives and wait for the decision to be handed down.

It was many weeks later when the phone call came through from Nelson's office. As soon as I recognized the secretary's voice I knew it had to be about our appeal. I have to admit my chest tightened and my knuckles turned white as I gripped the phone and waited for Nelson to come on the phone. I knew straight away, the moment he first spoke, what the decision was. His voice was flat and unemotional. "It's not good news, I'm sorry to say. The appeal has been turned down."

Once again I felt like someone had just kicked me in the stomach. My legs felt weak and I had to lean across the kitchen counter top to stop myself from falling. I can still remember clearly the long silence, eventually broken by Nelson's soft voice saying he would call back later with more details.

We later learned that the appeal court had stated in its written judgment that, while they were *"sympathetic to the Plaintiff's situation,"* they were not prepared to reverse a jury's decision. So that was that. Case finally over. Closure. Well, almost!

There were just a couple more incidents to add to our legal saga. The next winter Nelson and his family were on a skiing trip in Colorado when he met up with Judge Carlton, the judge who presided in our case. Nelson said he was hesitant to mention it to us now, but Judge Carlton had raised the topic of our case over a social drink one evening. He openly admitted he had found the jury's decision in our case a surprising one, and clearly gave Nelson the impression that had the decision been left to him, he would have awarded us substantial damages. As Nelson was telling me this, my mind was racing back to a pre-trial meeting in Nelson's office when he suggested we should take the option of bringing the case before a judge, but I was insistent on having a jury trial. My thinking at the time was that it was less likely that six people would make a bad decision.

And finally, remember our first attorney, Art MacDonnell, the one who fled town with our money? He would receive his comeuppance. One evening, about a year after our court case, we received another phone call from Nelson, this time saying he was sitting in a restaurant in Miami. Of all people, MacDonnell was sitting across the room. Nelson, speaking in a hushed tone, was telling us he had already called the police and was waiting for them to arrive and pick up the fugitive.

That story certainly made us smile!

Chapter Twelve

In the spring of 1984, Mo had taken a job selling advertising for a local shopper publication. This was a free paper, available from pick up points located all around Naples. For Mo, time had now clearly eased the hurt she had felt over the court case. On the surface it appeared she was moving on with her life.

She had never sold advertising before, but I knew, with her outward confident appearance and warm personality, she would do well. Within a few weeks she was pulling in the most revenue among the four sales people. Her salary, based entirely on commission, was proving to be more than she could ever earn from substitute teaching. She would have enjoyed her new job more if not for her boss, a cranky older woman who seemed to take pleasure in upsetting or annoying everyone around her.

Fortunately Mo took a stand early on, and this surly lady went on to harass those among her staff with weaker characters. Each week, Mo increased her commission, and with me still picking up odd jobs on a daily basis, I began to sense that the financial side of our life was slowly taking a turn for the better. There was even talk of fixing the air conditioner in the car Mo was driving. I learned much later that my wife was making as many calls as possible early in the day, before the temperature soared into the nineties. This schedule, which she kept private from me, prevented her having to go into client's businesses clad in a sweat-soaked outfit. When the heat got too much she would drive back to the air-conditioned office to make phone calls. Throughout our married life we've held back few secrets, but this was a time when we both wanted to protect each other. She knew there was nothing I could do about fixing the air in her car, so she reasoned it was best I didn't know about the problem. She accepted the car would be fixed as soon as we had the money to do it. That time came some weeks later, and well past the hottest part of the summer.

Summertime in Naples not only brought the heat and high humidity, it also brought the slow time for most businesses. Mo's list of advertisers was cut in half. To compensate, she had to put in longer hours and make lots of cold calls to find new business to meet her quota. It was hard and tiring work, walking down the shopping streets and industrial areas of Naples seeking out new clients.

Unlike the daily newspaper in town, with its many regular advertisers, a freebie publication attracted a different type of clientele.

Most were already committed to long-term contracts with either the Naples Daily News or local radio and television companies, and they would only advertise with *The Shopper* on an irregular basis. This meant always having to find a constant flow of new advertisers every week. But Mo never complained. She learned to take the rejection that came with the job.

One day when she was in the office she overheard a conversation between the publisher and her long-suffering husband about retiring. In essence, they were talking about selling the publication. Later that evening when Mo was telling me about this conversation, I realized it brought up an interesting possibility. With my own background in publishing, and Mo's ability to sell advertising, perhaps we could propose some type of deal to take over the operation. We decided it was certainly worth checking out.

I made the call the following morning and after determining that there was an interest to sell, I set up an appointment to meet with Mo's boss. There were many questions I wanted to ask. With our unfortunate spa experience behind us, there was no way any business owner was going to be able to hide the truth from us this time.

Seated across from her in the dark and gloomy, cigarette-smoke filled office, I immediately got the feeling that this obnoxious boss lady was trying to assess if I was a genuine buyer. I felt like I was involved in a game of poker with a lizard. She sat behind her untidy desk in the corner of this tiny room, mostly devoid of furniture and with dirty, brown shag carpet covering the floor. A miniature poodle sat sleeping at the woman's feet. Her voice was deep and raspy, as if she had just finished smoking her third pack of cigarettes for the day. As the conversation proceeded it became clear that she was going to be very reluctant to reveal any real financial information. She kept repeating that while the books might not show handsome profits, she and her husband were able to enjoy a comfortable lifestyle from the business. It turned out that they were heavily involved in a bartering service, which allowed them to trade advertising space for personal goods and services.

That was certainly a nice arrangement for the two of them, but not one that would be acceptable to us. We required hard currency to pay for the likes of groceries, mortgage and everything else involved in our family life. Hearing her gloss over everything, I got the impression she really didn't know how much she was earning from the publication. It was soon obvious she was running the business in a haphazard manner.

I let her drone on for a few minutes longer before asking the most important question. How much was she asking for the business? There was a long pause as I waited for her to speak. I shuffled in my seat before making the mistake of leaning back so my chair leaned on the chair rail behind me. She stopped boasting about her publication just long enough to find her cigarettes amongst the cluttered pile of papers on her desk. Quickly I jumped in again to ask the selling price.

I really can't be sure whether it was my body reaction to hearing the figure of $150,000, or merely the smooth paint on the chair rail that caused the chair to slide and buckle under me, causing me to crash to the floor. Her facial expression clearly indicated she wasn't the least bit amused by what she assumed was my reaction to her price. She took a long drag on her cigarette, before blowing out the smoke my way in an obvious sign of disgust.

There was an embarrassing silence. I didn't want to offend the woman by telling her that I felt she had overpriced her product fivefold. After all, my wife was still employed there and we desperately needed that job...at least for the time being. I feigned a continuing interest and explained I would need to discuss the matter with Mo. Before leaving, I did have another thought, and asked if she would be interested in a partnership venture. The answer was a stern 'no'. Her mind was set on selling out so she and her husband could move to the Carolinas.

That evening, Mo and I sat down and discussed the meeting I had with her boss. Tears of laughter were soon running down Mo's face when I retold the story about falling off the chair. Each time we tried to get serious, one of us would start giggling, which would set off the other one. It took us a long time to be able to discuss the matter without cracking up.

Since working at the publication, Mo had formulated some of her own ideas on how improvements could be made on the advertising side. From my perspective, I had always believed that some editorial material would greatly improve the overall quality and appearance of the publication. The big question that came out of our discussion that evening was.... should we publish our own shopper publication?

We both shared the confidence that we could produce a superior type of publication. But the obvious question was how were we going to fund it? We certainly couldn't do it ourselves.

We racked our brains and came up a list of people we felt might be interested in listening to a business proposal. Although I hated the thought of trying to do this project on a shoestring budget, I quickly accepted it wasn't going to be easy to find a big financial backer. Our plan was to get our hands on $20,000 and, hopefully, avoid having to part with any of our meager savings.

Alan Boole and his wife Pat were ex-Brits too and we had become friends over the years. Alan had purchased a pool-cleaning route when they first came to America the same year as us and was continuing to do very well. He was planning on developing the business and getting into spa sales. Alan said he liked our publishing idea from the very beginning, and offered to put up $15,000 if we could find $5,000! There was no way he would shift from that proposal so we left the meeting to search for our portion of the funding.

Thank god for Uncle Norris and Auntie Marge! They were an elderly couple who lived just across from our house and had become 'auntie' and 'uncle' to our children. Their own family, including much-missed grandchildren, lived back in Cleveland, Ohio where Norris had retired as the city's Fire Chief. The couple had come to Florida to enjoy retirement, but Norris had soon grown bored and was now back in the fire service as the Naples Fire Chief.

They adored our children, who seemed to spend as much time with Marge and Norris as they did with us. Perhaps their pool was more than just a side attraction!

That same week we were invited over to the couple's home for dinner. During the evening we grabbed the opportunity to discuss our new business idea. I excitedly explained that we were planning to publish a completely new concept in shopper-style publications. It would include editorials about our advertisers, which would help to promote their businesses. Norris showed some concern with that policy, believing we would eventually run out of stories to write. It was amusing to remind him of his comments five years later when we were still publishing and using the same format. But despite his initial concerns, Norris said he wanted to help us and he and Marge agreed to loan us our share of the money, to be repaid with interest over two years.

We left their house in a joyful mood. At last we had an opportunity of getting into our own business. We were all set to go ahead with *The Collier Advertiser*, the name we both felt was appropriate for the type of publication we had in mind. Mo knew two women who had shown an interest in working as advertising reps, and with me taking care of the editorial side, we set ourselves up in a two-room office on Central Avenue in downtown Naples.

The printing of 40,000 copies with set-up charges was going to cost almost $2,000. We had already made the major decision of mailing out the publication rather than having it thrown onto driveways. We felt strongly that this would give the publication a certain level of prestige which was lacking in the free publication field. The mailing costs would add another $1,500 to the budget.

As one would expect, we encountered many obstacles in the early days. Naples was still a small town with limited services and we had difficulty in finding an experienced freelance typesetter. After a lot of searching, we had to settle on a young lady who had only a limited knowledge of design. Laura, being a single parent, was desperate for money and was prepared to work the crazy hours we knew we were going to demand. The downside to doing our own artwork was that every advertisement that appeared in the paper would have to be cut and pasted together by Mo and me. We estimated that each issue, with office overheads, would cost almost $5,000. We planned to publish every two weeks so it was obvious to everyone from the very beginning that we didn't have too much financial maneuverability. The publication had to be virtually profitable from the very first issue.

Mo brought a bright confidence into the mix. She had either forgotten that she really didn't enjoy selling advertising, or had successfully pushed the thought far back in her mind. The knowledge of knowing we were starting a business that could get us back on our financial feet was powerful motivation for both of us.

Mo had discussed our publishing plans with her former clients, and almost everyone agreed to give our publication a try. Even without the additional ads from our other sales people, we figured we had an excellent chance of doing better than breaking even on the very first issue. And so we all went to work.

We drew up our publishing schedule. The local printers required the finished artwork from us on Monday at noon, giving them time to print the publication and have it to the post office the following day. For us, that meant we had the weekend to build the ads and, along with the editorial copy, paste them to the art boards. We were quickly going to discover that this was going to prove to be a long and laborious process.

After making sure we had a babysitter at the house, Mo and I would start the production job Friday evening. She would leave around midnight to go back home to the children while I was left to drive between the office and the typesetter's home, collecting typesetting galleys as they came out of the developer. Then it was back to the office to build and paste-up another batch of ads. I would leave around five o'clock the next morning, and Mo would come in to relieve me and continue with the same process. This was how it worked for the first half a dozen or so issues until, thankfully, the printers decided to set up their own typesetting and production department and we were left with just a long Saturday work day.

At the end of the day we would take the boards home and proofread all the ads and editorial copy. On Sunday evenings, our living room floor looked like a huge jigsaw puzzle, with a dozen or more art boards scattered over the rug. We would return to the printers early Monday morning to take care of corrections, before the boards were sent out to the pre-press production department.

These were hectic times, but we really believed we were making progress. We received a lot of compliments on what we were doing. We had decided to use color in our very first issue, which went a long way in establishing a style that many conceded was above the usual format of shopper-style publications. Even today we have the first issue of The Collier Advertiser framed and hanging on the wall in our home. On the front cover, dated November 19, 1985, is a picture of a happy family in a spa, which was given as a prize in a free drawing by our partner Alan. We didn't have the funds to find ourselves professional models to pose for the pictures. *Our family all look a lot younger in that photo!*

During the busy winter months the paper continued to prosper. We not only streamlined production to make our lives a lot easier, but we also took on extra sales staff. With an established publication, we were able to attract experienced salespeople from other publications. By the following Easter we were up to five sales people and we were on a roll.

And then came summer and as predictable as the late afternoon rains, the advertising dried up almost overnight. Winter residents headed north and the tourist train stopped rolling.

As much as our advertisers had grown to like our publication, they always become fearful of slow summer business and were not prepared to risk money on advertising that wouldn't be seen by too many people. It didn't help to hear that we were still mailing into more than 20,000 homes. For most of our clients, it was time to be cautious and back off.

We made cutbacks ourselves, but still it was difficult to break even. We were forced to extend credit and allow receivables to grow. By the end of the summer we were almost back to square one. With $60,000 in accounts receivables, increasing printing and mailing charges were adding pressure to our cash flow situation.

But, even if finances were extremely tight, we could still take comfort that we had made some wonderful progress. We knew if we could just hang on until "season" then we would prosper again. Maybe then, as we got more established, the following summer wouldn't be quite as tough.

Ron Marr entered our lives when he came for an interview for a non-existent job. He had phoned earlier in the day to say he was working as an advertising rep for the Naples Daily News. He had just moved to Naples from Kansas City, and after just two days he decided he hated his new employer and was already planning to leave. Selling advertising was not for him. He was a writer. I promised him nothing more than a cup of coffee if he stopped by the office.

That afternoon we sat around casually chatting about ideas for improving the paper. We were using photographs to accompany the articles, and Ron claimed he was an accomplished photographer, to go along with his writing skills. He left that afternoon to go off and write a couple of advertorials, the style of writing we were using. A week later he was working full-time for The Collier Advertiser and being paid the meager salary of just $200 per week. Ron told me some years later, after he became a partner in the paper, that this was in fact his first professional writing job and that he had never shot photos before.

Although we didn't realize it at the time, Ron, who came across at our first meeting as very shy and nervous, had the potential of becoming a very talented writer. During our long and close relationship that continues to this day, we have seen him develop his talents into writing books, writing articles for national publications and even publishing (and later selling) his own successful weekly publication in Montana. When our second season rolled around, Ron was producing his own Page Three editorial pieces that became a favorite for many of our loyal readers. With so many improvements The Collier Advertiser was indeed growing in stature.

Following a successful second season with what had now become a weekly publication, we had to prepare ourselves for the slow summer ahead. A few months prior we had taken a calculated gamble by moving to larger premises, just a couple of blocks away. These offices, which had been used by a weekly newspaper that had gone out of business, were ideal for us. They provided the extra space we desperately needed. Now we had room to give our five advertising reps a makeshift desk each, comprising of painted doors placed on two filing cabinets, as well as offices for Ron and myself. We even had a small reception area, a necessity due to the increasing number of callers.

Probably the biggest improvement came when we set up our own art department and hired a full time graphic artist and typesetter. Now we were able to produce our own artwork. No longer would we have to use up valuable time constantly driving back and forth to the printers. The whole operation was running quite smoothly and we knew we were beginning to attract comments from several big publishers in the area. We had recently decided that our goal was to work for three to five years on the publication, build it up and then, hopefully sell it at a great profit.

Chapter Thirteen

October 29th, 2004; our thirty-third wedding anniversary and Mo and I are happily celebrating the occasion with a rare visit, thanks largely to a gift certificate handed to her by an appreciative group of parents at her school, to one of the newer plush restaurants recently opened in the downtown Fifth Avenue South area.

We are reveling in one of those beautiful, humid-free evenings that seem to remain in the memory forever. The digital temperature clock on the bank building across the street is recording seventy-eight degrees but a cooling breeze makes it feel very comfortable and we seize the opportunity to sit outside under one of the half-dozen or so large white umbrellas, soaking up the relaxing, tropical-style atmosphere. We order drinks and just as we begin discussing the menu, Mo silences the conversation by holding a finger to her ear, directing my attention to the orchestral background sound of a hundred swishing palms. Once again, we are reminded, as if we really need it, that this is truly our paradise.

Looking around at the pleasant hustle and bustle of the street, we wonder why it took so long for outside dining to become popular in this part of Florida. For many years, the older local eateries seemed reluctant to go al fresco, recalling that when we first arrived there were no more than a couple, now it seems just about every restaurant is jumping on the bandwagon and following the Miami South Beach style.

Late October, and the hectic tourist season is still to get into full stride. To most permanent residents this is definitely one of the better times of the year to be in Naples. The sweltering summer heat is behind us, while the crowded roadways are yet to happen.

Our young, smiling waiter returns with our drinks and when he leaves, we chink our glasses, quietly toasting each other. It feels so good, looking around at what has become just as much our town as anyone else's.

This is where the whole adventure started, or at least got into gear. A single street that sold me a lifestyle when I first drove it twenty three years ago. But even more than that, it has now become the new symbol of a town that has finally grown up and grown awake, not that everyone wanted it to develop that way of course.

It wasn't so long ago that this same thoroughfare was beginning to present a different symbol – an image that was beginning to show signs of exhaustion below the surface as its classy shopping heritage started to give ground to more youthful and more vibrant areas around town. This noble First Street of Naples was unquestionably beginning to die on its feet, at least from a shopping area perspective, as an influx of large corporations including banks and stock brokers began replacing the unique stores that had given Naples its original appealing character.

Fortunately, just in time, the few remaining merchants stepped up to the plate and decided something desperately needed to be done to stop the hemorrhaging. Fewer stores attracted fewer shoppers and the once affluent street was becoming more like a ghost town.

So the merchants banded together and formed an association. They hired the services of a trendy Miami town planner who came riding into the city with his band of young student followers. Within a couple of days they produced notebooks full of sketches and suggestions on ways to resurrect the ailing street. Everything was planned down to the minutest of details, including the design of benches, lampposts, even trash cans. Surprisingly, the locals thought the $60,000 fee was well spent and the city council concurred by giving its support to the project.

The basic, three-floor building concept that was presented by the design team called for an increase in the permitted building heights. The new Mediterranean style structures with their abundance of columns and open patios would provide retail only space on the first floor, offices on the second and, in an effort to revitalize and rekindle the 'village' spirit, residential apartments on the third floor.

With both the immediate and on-going backing of city council, the street was soon taking on a new design as construction work began. It has been a constant work-in-progress until now, five or six years down the road, a new downtown area has come into being. But sadly there have been losers too. Ironically, those few merchants who started the project are now unable to afford the new rents, and have been forced out of the street they so nobly saved.

On a night like this, it's inevitable we delve into our memories. Some good, some funny and certainly some we would sooner forget.

Just to the side of the dining tables stands one of the many sculptured alligators that you will see on display in various parts of downtown Naples. They were created last year as a fundraiser, purchased by business owners for several thousand dollars each to support local charities. Each alligator, standing regally on a pedestal, was designed as a different character. The one close to us is fitted out in a waiter's costume and carrying a tray. His name is *Alliwaiter*, of course.

"That gator reminds me of a couple of stories." I say to Mo. "Remember how a gator saved Dennis from getting a speeding ticket?"

It happened when our friend Dennis was driving back from Miami after picking up his wife Sybille, who works as a flight attendant for Continental Airlines. In those days, the sides of the Alligator Alley were unfenced. From the hard pavement ran a grassy bank, sweeping down towards the canal that ran on both sides of the road.

Dennis admits he was totally distracted with the conversation he was having with his wife he hadn't seen for over a week, and simply hadn't noticed the flashing red and blue lights getting closer in his rearview mirror. It was after midnight and the road was empty of traffic and it was just too easy to rest a heavy foot on the gas pedal. Cursing loudly at the thought of an expensive ticket, Dennis eased off the gas and steered the vehicle towards the side of the road. Just as he was about to drive onto the pavement he was forced to swerve to avoid hitting a large black object lying across almost half the highway. His first thought was that the large mass was a section of a tire from a truck that you often see lying in the roadway. But then it suddenly hit him. It wasn't a shredded tire at all, but a giant alligator, possibly as big as ten feet in length as best as he could make out. After successfully maneuvering around the creature and stopping a safe distance up the road, Dennis noticed that the police vehicle had also stopped, but on the other side of the alligator. In the moonlight it became clear to Dennis that the officer, now out of his car, was more interested in the obstruction that lay on the highway than a speeding motorist. Realizing that the cop had to take care of more dangerous business first, Dennis chose not to stay around to see how the officer handled the problem. He roared off......"That alligator saved me a ticket," joked Dennis when he told us the story in his thick New York accent.

We also had our own 'Alley experience' when driving home in the early morning hours after visiting friends in Ft. Lauderdale. It was soon after we had arrived in Florida and we were driving home in that first Cadillac. We had been warned by many that it was never wise to stop on the Alley, although no one could explain exactly what to do should your car break down. Of course, this was long before the appearance of cell phones, rest areas and roadside assistance services.

My first recollection of a car problem was noticing the needle on the temperature gauge hitting the red mark. It was around 3 am and Mo was beside me sleeping. Although I had driven this road several times, I wasn't completely sure where we were at the time but I sensed we were about half way, maybe just a few miles closer to Naples than Ft. Lauderdale. Hearing all the warning signs in my head, I still decided there was nothing for me to do but to pull over. As the car came to a stop somewhere in this vast wilderness, I saw steam spewing out from under the hood. It was an eerie scene in the bright moonlight. With Mo now awake and wondering what was going on, I opened the door and walked to the front of the vehicle to investigate the problem. I had barely popped the hood when a vehicle pulled up behind us. I had no time to warn a sleepy looking Mo to stay inside the car and lock the doors before two young men came up to the side of the vehicle.

From the stories we had heard, I was convinced I was about to be attacked and robbed. I even braced myself for what I thought was the inevitable, and then immediately felt a little stupid when the two young men offered nothing but warm smiles and concern as they asked what was wrong. Peering under the hood with their own flashlight, they quickly determined one of the rubber cooling hoses had split. As I stood back, it took them just a few minutes to cut back past the split in the hose, reattach it and declare everything was fine again. I wondered if they did this for a living; stopping to help motorists in distress. They offered only a token resistance when I handed them a few dollars to buy some beers. They seemed happy as they returned to their truck stuffing dollar bills into their pockets and I was left standing there, feeling happy myself that we could continue our journey home. To be honest, I was also feeling more than a little relieved that I hadn't been beaten and robbed.

But the story isn't quite over. It wasn't going to be that easy. Although the hose was made good, the radiator was now completely empty. It took only a few hundred yards of driving for the temperature needle to rise once more to a dangerous level. What were we to do now? I figured our good luck had just run out as, once again, I pulled over to the side of the highway. I had no time to think much before another vehicle pulled up behind us. Believing we couldn't be so fortunate twice in one evening, and again recalling the scary stories we had been told about nighttime robberies, I quickly looked around inside the car for an object that I could use for protection. There was nothing I could find except for a plastic coffee cup. A lot of good that was going to do me, I thought. Dropping the cup, I accepted it was now too late to do anything as the huge outline of a figure loomed over the side of the car. In a quite calming voice the stranger asked: "Need help?"

Sheepishly I pushed back the door while, at the same time, trying to prepare myself just in case I had misread the person behind the greeting and I was about to be assaulted. But again, my concerns were quickly proven to be unfounded and for a second time we found ourselves facing more roadside kindness. As I started to explain our problem, our six foot seven or so black traveler was already looking under the hood of the vehicle.

"It's the radiator" I explained. "We had a split hose and we've lost all our water. The engine keeps overheating."

Without speaking, our new found 'St. Christopher' smiled as he walked back towards his tow truck. When he returned a few minutes later he was holding two large plastic coke bottles. "Use these," he said. "They should do the trick." He explained that he couldn't stay around because he was on an emergency breakdown call. We thanked him warmly and offered a generous payment for his Coke but he refused. As our Good Samaritan disappeared into the night, we quickly filled the radiator and once again fired the engine.

It was about two miles down the road that we realized large engines require large radiators to keep them cool. Two bottles of Coke clearly were not sufficient to do the trick. Once again we were forced to stop and begin our search for more liquids. The Everglades was serenely quiet and beautiful in the moonlight but this was certainly not an appropriate time to enjoy the sights!

Was it just the bullfrogs we could hear coming from the canal? We peered into the darkness and realized the canals were our obvious solution; our source for water. But who was going to venture down there and draw from the canal, which we both knew was filled with alligators? It may have been that immediate sense of fear that brought on my need to pass my own water. As I made my way to a nearby roadside bush a thought occurred to me. Hold on, why waste it!

A moment later, with two feet on the front bumper and hanging on for dear life I proceeded to try and personally solve our dilemma. I was hoping no other traveler would come by for the next few seconds as I stood exposed. Climbing down from the front of the car, I looked towards Mo..."*don't even think about asking,*" she mouthed from inside the car, clearly reading my thoughts.

You would think the emptying of two large bottles of Coke and a full bladder would fill any radiator, but not this one. Another mile and another pinging sound of an overheated engine. I was left with no choice. I had to go down to the canal and fill the bottles. I'm not much into praying but that certainly changed that evening. I couldn't get out of my mind a vision of two large open alligator jaws jumping out of the dark water and tearing off my limbs. With my heart racing and beads of sweat running into my eyes I moved cautiously toward the bank. Very slowly I bent down and lowered one bottle into the shallow water's edge.

The eerie quietness was interrupted by the loud gurgling sound of the water filling up the bottle. Any minute now, the noise would awaken the monsters just lying there waiting for some tasty prey to come along. My back was beginning to ache and I needed to stand up. I lifted the bottle and held it up in the moonlight. It wasn't even a quarter full! I think my breathing stopped when I placed both bottles back into the water. I started to count quietly to myself, trying to forget about the imminent danger and the fear I was feeling. Eventually the two bottles were filled and I raced back to the car. I had hoped I would see the brackish water overflowing from the radiator before emptying the second bottle, but I didn't. Nor after the fourth, or the sixth, which was when I gave up. Enough water or not I had decided three trips were all my heart could stand. We were off and we wouldn't stop until we got home.

I couldn't hope to describe the horrible smell that emulated from the radiator the next day when I decided it would be prudent to flush it out with a garden hose. We told our neighbor who came over to chat that canal water and Coke just don't mix well. Mo thought it was best if we didn't mention the other component.

"That was so funny," says Mo. "Kind of puts the whole adventure into perspective. There were certainly as many good times as there were bad." I was left wondering if my coming face to face with danger was considered one of the 'good' times in her eyes. I let it go.

Looking around, as we sat there enjoying the ambiance of the street, everything seems so calm and peaceful. Even the very worst moments could be recounted now without causing a tightness of the stomach.

"Where are you now?" Mo asks, breaking the short pause in the conversation. Her head cocks to one side and she lifts her glass to her lips.

"Oh, just reminiscing," I respond. "One of the worst times…"

"Like when?" she asks.

"Mmmmm. Like that occasion I walked out of the American Embassy with that 'sonofabitch's' voice ringing in my ears. That uncaring bastard! I will always remember those words. *Four months. Four bloody months!*"

I really can't remember too much about walking away from the American Embassy to Victoria Station, nor indeed much of the train journey back to Epsom. My mind was in a haze. I felt totally beaten. For the first time in my life I had absolutely no idea of how to solve the problem before me. I know I must have been desperately trying to think of something, anything, that would give us hope when explaining to Mo everything that had happened.

Four months here in London! Everything we possessed was four thousand miles away. There was our house, our business, the school the kids attended. America was our home, and we were being stripped of our identity. We didn't exist anymore.

Poor Mo. Her dear mother was dying before her eyes and I was about to hit her with the news that we were about to lose everything we owned. I realized there were far deeper ramifications than just the problem I was enduring. If I couldn't get back into the country, then neither could she.

By the time I reached my sister-in-law's house, I had already decided I wasn't going to tell my wife about the four months waiting period. I would only tell her that we had to wait for the report coming back from St. Louis and let her believe it would come to the embassy a lot sooner. She had enough to worry about. I would go and meet with Gudeon, the attorney who got us our first visa, at the earliest opportunity.

That evening I phoned the president of Dominic's soccer club and explained that I wouldn't be back to help with taking the teams to Colorado. I'm not sure he believed the story I was telling him. I'm not sure I would have believed it myself if the situation had been reversed. I had also made the difficult phone call to Ron Marr to tell him he would have to publish the next issue of The Collier Advertiser without Mo and me.

Ron had never been involved with the graphic design of the paper, or anything to do with the business dealings with the printers. He was about to undergo baptism by fire, from creating a dummy for the paper and overseeing the production over the next twenty-four hours.

He told me later that our printers and suppliers didn't believe my story that I had been held up in England, thinking it was just an excuse for delaying payments. They even went as far as suggesting that Mo and I had skipped the country on a permanent basis to avoid our financial problems. Poor Ron had to beg and cajole to convince them to continuing printing the paper in our absence. I dreaded the fact that I would, at sometime, have to reveal to Ron that I may be gone for four months. Knowing Ron as well as I did I was fairly certain he would take the initial news of our delay in his stride, no matter how terrifying or frustrating it may strike him inside. It was fortunate, I thought, that by this time he had made a substantial monetary investment in the paper and was a true partner. Still, I also knew he was not as fond of Naples as we were and I did wonder if he would stick around if we weren't there to give our support.

With Mo's mother's health deteriorating further with each passing day, it seemed like a dark cloud was hanging over our heads. Sheila was now confined to her bed and her husband Tom was beginning to fall apart. The couple had been happily married for more than forty years and had never spent a day apart since the day Tom returned from war duties in Egypt. He was sent overseas less than twenty-four hours after they were first married and they didn't see each other for the next three years. On his return, Tom vowed he would never leave Sheila's side again, and he kept that promise until the day she died.

It took several phone calls to track down my immigration lawyer. He had changed offices and was now situated in Mayfair, one of the more expensive areas of London. Clearly business must be good I was thinking as I dialed his number and hoped that he could give me an early appointment.

It became clear within the first minute of speaking with Gudeon that he had indeed prospered since we last met. After some initial pleasantries, followed by my impassioned declaration that I needed his help desperately, he quickly explained that he no longer handled individual immigration applications. "All my immigration work now is for large corporations who require visas for their employees transferring to offices in the U.S." he said.

Perhaps sensing the utter desperation in my voice, he eventually agreed to meet with me. "After all, you are a former client," he said. I couldn't prevent myself from letting out a long sigh of relief which immediately changed to one of concern with the next piece of information coming over the phone.

"An initial consultation fee will cost five hundred pounds, and I would like that in cash."

I had no way of knowing where I would find that sort of money. All I knew was that I was in a life or death situation and I needed help. I agreed to the payment with a casual *'no problem'* and we set up a meeting for the following morning.

Not since my high school days had I found a need to borrow money from my parents. They live modestly and survive only because my mother follows rigidly to an old-fashioned budgetary discipline. She and Dad would never think of buying anything on credit. They would purchase an item only when they had the money saved. They had never opened a bank account and my mother still keeps various cans around the house with labels detailing what the money inside was for. No bills ever get paid late. In fact, come rain or shine, all bills are taken care of the same day they arrive at the house, which usually means the couple taking a daily walk to the local high street to pay anything that can be paid through local offices.

That evening I used Mo's sister's car to drive over to see my parents. We had visited them several times during our stay, but this time it would be for an entirely different reason. I desperately needed their help. I didn't want to alarm them by saying too much so I decided I would temper the situation by explaining I had come across some unexpected expenses involving our new visa and could they help? I asked for a thousand pounds with the promise that it would be repaid as soon as I got back to America.

Like most loving parents they were only too happy to help. Mom never had a problem lending my brother and me money when we were teenagers. A problem only arose if we ever forgot to repay. She left the room and came back a few minutes later holding a fistful of twenty-pound notes. I smiled to myself thinking their old bed was going to be a lot less lumpy that night.

The meeting with Gudeon the next day was not good. Instead of giving me confidence that we could resolve the matter far more quickly than the American embassy official had indicated, my attorney was actually suggesting that I may never be permitted to return to the States again.

"It's all about technicalities," he explained. "Your original investor visa automatically expired when you closed down the spa."

"But the reason we closed down the spa was because the seller had committed fraud", I countered. "We proved that, and don't forget the immigration officials were shown all the paperwork regarding the purchase, which included his phony tax filing, before giving their approval. Now we have the paper. Surely that helps." I realized I was sitting there pleading with him, as if he had control over government policies. Or was I just looking for his sympathy?

"I'm sorry," he sighed. "It may well appear unfair but nothing is going to change the current law. It really doesn't matter if your new business is making money and employing American citizens. That's not what your original visa was given to you for. You should have applied for a new visa when you decided to open the paper."

I couldn't believe what I was hearing. I was floundering to come up with some type of logic.

"So what you are saying is that the immigration people can insist on seeing all the paperwork and take three months to review it. Then, after giving approval, if it turns out to be a fraudulent deal they can just turn their heads and say thanks for investing your money and sorry to hear you have lost it all, but we can't do anything to help. And they won't give you the opportunity to get back on your feet. Worst still, they tell you, *"leave our country immediately."*

"A single word answer would be yes," he responded coldly.

With his elbows resting on the desk and his hands clasping the sides of his face Gudeon offered a hint of a compassionate smile. "I couldn't begin to tell you all the bureaucracy that goes on and the ineptitude of the American immigration and naturalization services. I face it daily. There have been so many headaches and heartbreaks and that situation is never going to change."

"So don't think you are alone. Let me tell you there have been couples who have gone ahead and purchased a business, only to see their application turned down and big deposits lost. Try getting that money back when you are living in a different country."

There was silence and, after a long pause as he collected his thoughts, Gudeon, went on. "I truly feel there's little point in you hanging around expecting anything good to come from the report coming from St.Louis. At best it will show that you weren't trying to get into the country illegally, but that is all. You will still be stuck here with no valid visa and unable to go back to your life in Florida. I realize that means giving up everything you have there, including your new publishing business. And let me warn you that if you do try and go back now you will definitely be breaking the law."

Gudeon's remarks were making me more depressed. A big black cloud hovered over our heads. Here I was, paying five hundred pounds to hear this man tell me just how desperate my situation was, and with no possible solution. The conversation was now beginning to repeat itself as I probed for answers. I began to think it was a good job for Gudeon that I had already paid him his fee.

Despite being summer, the weather outside as I left Gudeon's building was cool and damp. As I buttoned up my light jacket I was reminded of why we had left these shores in the first place. I was also reminded of why I so desperately wanted to get back to our Florida home.

I strolled around the West End of London with my mind in a foggy haze. Nothing seemed quite real anymore. I was beginning to feel like a prize fighter who had been knocked down one too many times.

Every time I tried to get back on my feet, my legs would buckle and I was back down on the canvas. There surely had to be a way out of this mess. I couldn't just give up....not for me and certainly not for my family.

I stopped off at a little coffee shop, taking in the sight of colorful window boxes full of summer flowers. I forced a smile, remembering how the usually wet English summer is so good for flowers. I needed to sit for awhile, catch my breath and think where I should go from here. Nothing Gudeon had told me had given me any hope. Nothing....except maybe for that one casual remark. What was it he said? *"You should have applied for a new investment visa."*

A new visa. That might just be the solution. Surely Gudeon would do it for a reduced fee to help. He must be feeling some compassion after hearing about all our woes. My brain was racing. We already had a company and a business. So why didn't he think of this solution during our meeting?

I quickly found a public phone and called Gudeon's office. His secretary answered and said he was just leaving for the day but she would see if she could catch him. I was surprised to hear his voice come back on the phone. As successful as he had become, I assumed he wouldn't be taking anymore calls so late on a Friday afternoon. Was it compassion or did he view me as a cash cow? I didn't try and guess the answer.

I didn't bother with any pleasantries as I blurted excitedly down the phone, "What about me applying for another investment visa? It can't take any longer than the four months I have to wait anyway, and I already have the company up and running?"

His voice didn't have the same excited ring to it as my own when he replied but he agreed it was certainly something worth considering. "Why don't you stop by the office on Monday. Let's say 9:30."

As I slipped the phone back into the cradle I allowed myself a moment to enjoy the feeling that there was now a glimmer of hope. Maybe, just maybe, we had found the solution.

If I believed for one moment that my status as a former client was going to give me any discounts on Gudeon's fees then I was quickly disappointed. Those thoughts were dispelled within a few minutes of being back in his office on Monday.

"I did tell you that I no longer do these types of applications because I find them too time consuming. I will, however, make an exception in your situation, but I have to tell you my fee is now three thousand pounds."

I looked across his desk with disbelief. A jump from twelve hundred to three thousand pounds in just a few years was a staggering amount. But then it could well have been a million pounds considering my present financial situation. I didn't know whether to laugh or cry as I sat rooted to the seat. I had absolutely no idea where I was going to raise that sort of money.

But for whatever reason it didn't matter. Somehow I would find it. "Let's go for it partner" I said in a corny western drawl. I think I detected the faintest of smiles on Gudeon's face before he reached across for a pad and pen.

Quickly writing down an extensive list, he explained that these were the things he needed from me as quickly as possible. "There is also the question of the investment money. Can you raise a substantial investment sum?"

I knew that one was coming. A substantial amount the last time was one hundred thousand dollars. In my mind I figured I had that one covered.

I chose not to get into specifics at this time so I merely shrugged my shoulders and nodded. I assume he accepted this as a positive reaction. Appearing satisfied he went on. "When you renewed your visa after the spa was closed what company did you put down on the form?"

He clearly liked my response. "I wrote down both companies. Freshwater Health and Leisure because I always felt I would do something with that company one day and Collier Advertising, Inc. because that was now my current business."

"That's good. Really good," he said, letting a second hint of a smile spread across his face. "That won't hurt us a bit. In fact it will help us. It's good to be truthful in these matters."

Gudeon went back to his list and continued writing for another fifteen minutes or so. He passed the pad towards me and said that the sooner I get all these things back to him, the sooner we can get going on the application.

"And what about my fee? I must insist that it's paid up front."

He couldn't help but notice all the embarrassing signs on my part. My shuffling in the chair, the nervous cough, and the biting of my lower lip. "Can you give me one week?" I asked. "I need to transfer some funds."

The hard stare softened as he leaned forward. "Sure. A week then." He held out his hand and I was embarrassed further that he could feel my clammy palm. I left his office and walked out into the crowded street thinking my mountain had just grown a little higher.

A week had gone by and it was now time for Mo and the children to try and return to America. Mo's mother was still gravely ill but we all felt there was little more we could do. Even Mo's father agreed that her time would be better spent back in Florida where there was a business to run. We had to wonder how Ron was making out. We made daily phone calls but were we hearing the truth?

Mo and I both had a restless night as we thought about her trip the next morning. We accepted it would have been too expensive to change the travel arrangements and return by a different route, so she was left still traveling with the original round-trip tickets and following my path back via St. Louis. Although we figured it was highly unlikely, we had to ask ourselves what would happen if she, with Dominic alongside, came face to face with the immigration officer who stopped the two of us before. That officer's face appeared in my mind most nights as I drifted into sleep...the same nightmare repeating itself over and over again...

There was absolutely nothing else we could do. This was a game with high stakes. We both knew it was imperative she got back to Naples, or we could quickly lose everything.

From the latest phone calls with Ron we felt he was successfully guarding the business fort, but both Mo and I both knew it was too much for one person to handle for too long. And who would be bringing in the advertising if Mo wasn't there? She had always consistently billed the most, week after week. Usually it was more than the combined total of the other sales people. Without her, even though Ron had embarked on something of a scorched-earth policy in collecting accounts receivable from a growing list of tardy clients, the paper couldn't survive. We would be in major trouble after one issue and it would quickly get worse from there. Again, we were at a time in our lives when the line between survival and failure appeared to be wearing very thin.

As Mo prepared to leave for the drive to London's Heathrow Airport, we sat down with the children and attempted to explain in simple terms the problem they could be facing when they arrived back in America. It would be Dominic's job to look for the immigration officer who had stopped him and me just a week before. And if he saw they were heading towards that man, then to let his mother know. A squeeze of the hand would be the secret code in this real life drama.

I drove back from the airport thinking about what lay ahead. Mo faced eight hours of sitting on the aircraft worrying about what was going to be there to greet her when she landed. I knew her nerves would be stretched razor-thin by the time she walked up to the barrier and presented her passport to the immigration officer.

I sat back at the house literally watching the time tick by on the large kitchen clock. Remembering one of my mother's favorite expressions about a watched kettle never boils, I tried to busy myself with reading and watching television. Neither diversion seemed to work and very quickly I was back staring into space. The minutes and the hours slowly ticked by.

If the flight left on time, just after noon, it should be arriving in St. Louis just about now. I stared at the clock, another thirty minutes slowly swept by. I reached for another cup of coffee. I had consumed so many cups during the day that my head was buzzing and my body was wired. Even with the soft sound of the television in the background I could still hear the ticking clock. It was as though my mind was wiping out every other sound, other than that coming from that garish timepiece.

One more hour passed by. The tension was becoming too much to bear but if it felt bad for me, what was it like for Mo?

The piercing sound of the ringing phone made me jump up from my seat. I literally raced across the kitchen and grabbed the receiver off the wall. "Hello. Hello." There was a long pause. All I could hear was loud static. "Hello. Hello. John are you there?" Another pause.

"John it's ok. We got through."

My whole body went limp. I felt both physically and emotional drained.

"Tell me. What happened?"

"I really don't have time now to go into details. We are rushing to catch our connection. It was a nightmare. It was good I had Dominic with me. Can you believe I was actually heading towards the same man who stopped you two? What are the chances of that?" I smiled to myself and thought, why am I not surprised?

It was much later when the full story unfolded in detail. It turned out Mo's flight was full and with several planes landing at the same time the immigration hall was crowded with incoming passengers. Mo and the children joined one of the five long lines and shuffled slowly towards the passport cubicles.

There were just four people ahead of them in their line by the time they first got sight of the immigration officer. It was then that Mo felt Dominic squeezing her hand. At first she didn't think it was possible. She says she remembers looking down at his face and from his look of panic she knew it was true. She tried not to panic herself but she now faced the task of changing lines without anyone getting suspicious. She felt she didn't want to get on the end of a line and provide a better opportunity for the officer to question her in detail.

"What was the best thing to do?" she was asking herself. She only had seconds to make up my mind.

Time was just about running out. Only three people stood between them and passport control. There was no way she could cut into another line without risking someone complaining and drawing attention. There was just no other way. She had to join the back of another line and preferably as far away from this line as possible.

Juggling through her pockets as if looking for some document she backed up with the kids and waved the couple behind her to move forward. With the children following her like little ducklings, she eased back down her line and across to the next row and then to the one after that. Quietly she whispered to Dominic to pull his cap down over his face.

"I was trembling by the time I reached the cubicle. Fortunately the other lines still had people waiting so we didn't appear quite so obvious."

The officer in his dark blue uniform and seated behind his computer station gave a cheery smile. He also gave a long slow look at Mo and then dropped his gaze down to the three children. He made some remark about the joys of traveling with three youngsters, but Mo couldn't remember exactly what he said.

"I was having a controlled panic attack and desperately trying to concentrate on looking as natural as possible, although I know my smile must have appeared so false. I tried not to let him see my hand was shaking as I pushed our passports towards him. He asked why we were coming to America and I told him we were on our way to Florida. Before he could ask, I offered that we came via St. Louis because it was the cheapest way. *You know how expensive it gets traveling with three kids...* My voice trailed off. I didn't want to say too much."

'And where will you be staying?' he asked me.

"I told him, I have friends in south Florida and we will be staying with them. We want to travel around a bit...and visit Disneyworld of course."

"I was wondering if he could hear the pounding of my heart as I waited for the next question which I expected to be, 'May I see your return tickets?"

Trying to explain that she didn't have any tickets would have set off a big alarm signal. Who goes on vacation with one-way air tickets? Fortunately the question was never asked, nor was any reference made to the investor's visa stamped in her passport. Although she was prepared for both questions, she was delighted that neither one was asked. With the simple pointing of the finger, directing them to proceed towards customs, she realized they were through. "Enjoy your stay," she heard from behind her, but chose not to look back.

Mo said it was hard not to pick up the children and run. "I was literally shaking all over as we moved through the customs hall. I felt that at any second I would hear his voice calling us back."

Mo getting back into the U.S. was a huge relief all around. It did mean, however, she was facing a huge workload, dividing her time between running the business and running the home but there was no other option. Even knowing this was the only way, it did little to ease my feelings of guilt. But I still had my own set of problems to face. The first being, how was I going to raise three thousand pounds?

How times change in just a few short years. I contacted the bank I had used in London during my time in the publishing business. The same bank where I was made welcome and invited for a coffee and a chat with George Cole, the bank manager, any time I was in the area. George would even stop by our house on his way home on Friday evenings. Then the coffee cup would be replaced with a glass of gin and tonic.

I was left waiting in the reception area for nearly half an hour before being ushered in to see a loan officer. Everything had become so formal. There was a completely different feel about the place.

Poor George had suffered a massive heart attack while swimming and drowned in the Mediterranean Sea soon after we left for America. Now, years on, I was quickly realizing that this was proving to be a far different banking experience than I had enjoyed in the past.

The young female assistant asked my name twice before we reached her dark, uninviting office towards the back of the building. Again how different, I thought, to George's plush suite on the second floor where a request for a business or personal loan had always been quickly dispensed with a warm smile and a friendly handshake.

"How may I assist you?" asked the pretty young lady dressed in a dark business suit. I had already decided I was going to ask for a fifteen thousand pounds loan to cover the lawyer's fees, repay the loan to my parents and have a little buffer to help us back in America. I also required money to cover my living expenses during my unwanted exile.

I gave a quick introduction to who I was and reference to my long relationship with the bank. I explained where I was living now and just the briefest of reasons of why I needed the money. The loan officer listened to what I had to say and didn't change her expression when I asked for the money which I found encouraging. I explained I would use the monthly payment I was still receiving from my former partners to cover the repayment of the loan.

"And what can you offer as security?" she asked in a casual tone. Her question was unexpected and hit me like a hammer blow. "Do you have property here in England? Maybe even some stocks, bonds anything that we can use to secure the loan?"

Rather sheepishly I had to admit I had nothing like that. I didn't even have the household of expensive furniture we had left here with our friend.

John Kennedy had moved into a large manor house in the country with his new wife just before we left England. Our furniture was fairly new and expensive and we didn't want to sell it at that time, thinking one day we may have it shipped to Florida. John was happy to store it, delighted that he could fill many of his bare rooms.

John, who we had known for a number of years, owned the printing company where we had some of our magazines printed. We had always thought he ran a successful company but it turns out he had over extended himself and he filed personal bankruptcy about a year after we left. We later learned that the bailiffs, who came to his nine-bedroom mansion, wouldn't believe his story that he was just storing most of the furniture for his friends. Our three bedroom suites, living and dining room furniture, together with John's own stuff, was quickly loaded onto the three removal trucks waiting outside and hauled away.

"Are you hearing me Mr. Freshwater?

"We can certainly arrange a loan for you but we must have some security. Are your parents in a position to help?"

I couldn't help but smile as I thought of my mother showing up at the bank with an armful of cans filled to the brim with cash. "I'm really not sure," I said. "They do own their own home which is clear of any mortgage. Let me check on that."

That evening I was trying to explain to my parents, without giving them cause for alarm, the reason I needed a loan and why the bank required the deeds to their house.

"Well, the house is going to you and your brother when we die so I don't see a problem," said Mom in a usual matter-of-fact manner. "Just tell us what we have to do." Dad simply nodded his head in agreement as he sat back in his favorite chair with one ear, I suspected, half tuned to the television. Before leaving the house I made a quick call to my brother

Frank to explain what I was doing. As I expected, easy-going Frank saw no problem with the arrangement.

If I was beginning to think that everything was starting to fall nicely into shape then that belief was certainly going to be shaken with the phone call I received from Gudeon a few days later.

"I'm going over your application now and, to be honest, I'm not really happy. We have to show that your publishing company is a successful operation. The immigration people will see immediately that it hasn't made any real profits so we have to convince them of a brighter picture for the future. We must provide them with a positive business plan."

"No problem," I quickly countered. "I can begin working on that today."

"No," Gudeon said firmly. "You don't understand. It can't come from you. That won't carry any weight. It has to be presented by a highly-respected accountancy firm."

Immediately, warning bells started ringing in my ears. The alarm had gone off, sensing I was about to get involved in something that carried a high price tag. A business plan. Highly-respected accountancy firm. I figure these two together didn't come cheap. "How much is this going to cost?" I asked nervously.

"I'm not sure," was the guarded response. "We did get one done for another client some time back and the firm charged six thousand pounds. I know it's expensive but honestly I don't think we have a choice."

That evening I sat in Mo's sister's kitchen and began writing down on a pad a list of numbers. Under the right hand column with the heading 'Planned Cost of Trip' I wrote airline tickets and the figure $1,000 beside it. Underneath I wrote a second item: 'All Other Expenses' and beside that I wrote down $500.

In the right column under the heading 'Actual Costs' I first wrote down additional cost of airline tickets and the figures $950 and $750 beside it. Under 'Lawyer Fees' I wrote the currency exchange dollar amounts of $850 and $5,100. Alongside 'Business Plan' I wrote $10,200. I totaled up the figures and faced a whopping grand total of $17,850. Quite a difference from the original budgeted figure of just $1,500, and I wasn't home yet!

If I was beginning to get that familiar feeling that life couldn't possibly get worse before starting to get better, I was to be proven wrong once again.

Two weeks after Mo had returned to Naples, her mother passed away in her sleep. Everyone, including her father, accepted that Mo couldn't be there to attend the funeral. The important thing was that her mother would have understood. She was that type of woman.

Mo and I tried to limit our long distance phone calls. It came down to her calling only when she faced a major problem and wanted my input. In reality she had proven many times she could handle anything that was thrown her way, and I sensed on most occasions she already had a solution even before she called me. I guessed she was looking for an excuse to chat and give me an update on her and the kids.

A prime example of Mo's resourcefulness was when she was forced into finding a new form of transportation when her old car died on her one morning.

The mechanic at the local repair shop was honest enough to say it wasn't worth repairing because there were too many other defects that would soon need fixing. The car had been a loaner from Alan Boole, our investor in The Collier Advertiser. The old blue Cadillac had served us well, even though the air conditioner had packed up ages ago and its appearance had become a little embarrassing for Mo when she pulled up outside a client's business. The roof lining had fallen down and would blow like a curtain in the wind when she was driving along with the windows down. Recently, I had pulled out the lining, revealing an even more embarrassing sight of a rusty inside roof.

"There are ads in the paper advertising new cars with no money down. What do you think I should do?" Mo was asking over the phone.

Do we have a choice? I was asking myself. Clearly Mo needed transport to make her sales calls and for everything else in her hectic life and we certainly didn't have the funds to go out and buy a used vehicle which would have required some type of down payment.

"Go ahead and see what you can do," I said.

Again, a feeling of overpowering guilt swept over me as I put down the phone. I should be back in Naples and helping my wife resolve these sorts of problems.

Mo had never purchased a car in her life. She was very well aware when she went to the car showroom of what her needs were. It needed to be a small car, economical to run, inexpensive and with air. And one more thing, it had to come with absolutely no money down.

She quickly picked out the car she felt best suited her needs and haggled long enough over the price to think she had struck the best deal. "So how much can you put down?" asked the smiling salesman.

"Nothing! Just like you say in your ads," she said.

"We can do that....but you do realize there are some costs involved for delivery and plates and couple of other items."

"I'm not sure you heard me," Mo said with a determination in her voice. "I have absolutely no money to give you so if you want this deal to happen then you had better be creative." The tone of her voice convinced the salesman that this was one situation that required no further discussion. Poor guy. It may have been easier for him if he was dealing with someone with good credit but some recent late payments didn't help the cause.

It took the salesman twenty-four hours to eventually come up with a workable solution. He told us many years later that financing this sale was probably the hardest he had ever faced.

The following afternoon Mo drove out of the dealership in a white Chevrolet...equipped with air conditioning! It proved to be a wonderful tonic for her.

In the meantime, I was attending regular meetings with the accountant at Price Waterhouse who was responsible for writing my business plan. The young CPA just wouldn't be hurried. In his eyes I was just one of many clients and he actually got quite angry one time when I mentioned that speed was of the essence in my case. Even the hefty payment I was making didn't seem to matter much. It took him almost seven weeks to produce the thirty-two page detailed plan consisting of facts, figures and colorful diagrams. His conclusion was that he felt the paper had a bright future, largely based on the information I had provided. All true or not, at least we had our completed document and we were now finally ready to submit our application – almost three months after my return to London.

I suppose I should have seen the next problem on the horizon for it was to prove to be the biggest hurdle yet. I really thought I had it covered, but wrong again.

"How are you going to make the substantial investment in the company to satisfy the requirements in the application?" Gudeon casually mentioned as we were looking over the plan.

"Haven't I done that already?" I asked. "Surely the original $20,000 setup costs and not paying ourselves a salary in the summer months and no commission at all to Mo adds up..."

Gudeon looked at me with an air of disbelief on his face. It was clear he couldn't believe what I was telling him. Was he really wondering if I could be that stupid? "You are supposed to be operating a successful company here. Telling the immigration people that you can't afford to pay yourself a salary is like putting a gun to your head. Unless you can come up with something like one hundred thousand pounds, this application doesn't stand a chance."

A feeling of going back to square one had become an overly used expression in our lives. We had come this far and now we were facing a mountain as big as Everest.

This time our mountain seemed insurmountable.

Chapter Fourteen

Chris Simpson was an old business contact back in London who had become a close friend over the years. It was a relationship which really began the night our publishing company organized a boat trip for staff and clients on the River Thames. We were so fortunate that it turned out to be one of those all too rare, balmy summer evenings when jackets and raincoats could be put to one side and, seemingly, just about everyone aboard was up enjoying dancing to the reggae beat on the open deck under a canopy of twinkling stars. For one couple for sure, it was also a night that offered an air of romance.

Chris brought along a hot-looking Jeanette whom he had just employed as his secretary. Clearly the couple clicked on that first date and Jeanette went on to become Chris's wife, mother of his two children and full-time business partner.

At a young age, Chris had proven to be a successful businessman in many areas. He had not only built up the third largest chain of video stores in England, but he was also publishing a popular video magazine. He was regarded as a leader in the world of video rentals. Along the way, he had acquired investment properties and owned several apartments in London. Despite various business setbacks in recent years, Chris had always managed to regroup and forge ahead. His business skills were admired by all who knew him.

After staying with Mo's sister and her family for several weeks, I felt I was beginning to become an inconvenience. Their two children were sharing one bedroom in order to make room for me, and I was becoming the embodiment of "the fifth wheel." When I mentioned this situation to Chris, he immediately came to the rescue, offering me one of his vacant apartments. A big favor indeed, but now I was about to ask him for an even bigger one!

Chris and Jeannette had played a major role in our lives. When we first moved to Naples we probably still regarded them more as business acquaintances than true friends. During the last couple of years we lived in England we would run into them at various functions and parties, but rarely did we socialize on more than a token basis. To the best of my recollection they had visited our house only once for dinner, getting lost on the journey over, and arriving sometime after 10:00 p.m. In our eyes, they came across as a wealthy couple, enjoying the glitzy, London entertainment scene.

It was a little surprising to get a phone call from Jeanette during that first year we lived in Florida, explaining that she and Chris were planning a vacation in Naples and asking if we could find them a hotel. When we did the sociable thing, suggesting they could stay with us, we really didn't expect them to accept the offer. But they did, and we immediately regretted making the invite, concerned that a couple we hardly knew and used to London's swank nightlife, would find it boring to stay in a home with three young children.

We shouldn't have worried. Chris and Jeannette virtually adopted our children during the time they were with us. Chris, an ex-military man, spent hours on the beach with the boys, showing them how to build camps and catch fish. On the weekends we would barbecue at one of the beach parks and on one occasion I can recall, when Chris was left in charge of heating the can of beans on the hot coals, he revealed in his quiet, unassuming manner that a few weeks before he and Jeanette had spent more than five thousand pounds to stay for a few days in a posh Palm Springs hotel, "and I have to admit I didn't have half the fun I'm having now!"

On the last day of their stay with us, Chris and Jeanette were waiting around the house before driving off to the Miami Airport. Their London-bound flight had been delayed because of bad weather so they decided to kill a couple of hours by walking across the street to look at the model show home. When they returned an hour later we asked them if they liked the house.

They casually replied in their familiar, unpretentious manner, "Yes, we really did. We bought it!"

It was Chris, with his soon to be wife Jeanette, who asked our daughter Kirsty to be their flower girl at their forthcoming "high-society" style wedding in London. This invitation came at the height of our financial troubles and presented yet another embarrassing moment for us. We had to explain that, while we would love to be at the wedding, we just couldn't afford the expense of flying the family over. A week later, five round-trip airline tickets arrived in the mail.

It was Chris and Jeanette who, after staying with us on another occasion (shortly before we closed the spa), casually mentioned as they climbed into a cab that they had left a Christmas card on the bureau in the bedroom. After they left, we opened the card. Five thousand dollars in traveler checks fell out!

Before going to meet Chris, I had ascertained from Gudeon more details regarding the hundred thousand pounds necessary to fulfill the criteria of my new investment visa. He explained it had to be recorded by simply providing a photocopy of the appropriate bank statement. Technically, as it appeared to me, there was no demand for the money to stay there in the account, which left a door open that I was about to enter. I knew I was on sticky ground with what I was planning so I was careful not to say anything that could arouse Gideon's suspicion. The less he knew the better. I had absolutely no intention of getting him into trouble. My plan was to work within what I perceived to be a legal loophole. My conscience was clear, even if I was preparing to bend the rules to the breaking point. In my own mind I truly believed we had done more than enough to earn our legitimate stay in Naples.

I had not thought beforehand of what I was going to say to Chris so when I arrived at his office I simply blurted out, *"can you lend me a hundred thousand pounds for twenty-four hours?"* The request seemed to flow remarkably easy off the tongue, and before he could even start to answer, I quickly added what I was planning to do with the money. "I swear to you that the money will be back into your account in just a few hours," I was trying to assure him.

Chris took only a second before answering in almost an apologetic tone. "I would love to help, but you know I've extended myself opening these latest video stores." I knew that Chris had agreed to a master plan of opening 150 stores and then selling the whole operation to the country's largest video conglomerate. It was rumored that the deal would be worth eight million pounds to Chris, and he was only four stores away from reaching his target.

"I'll tell you what I can do," he offered, perhaps noting the disappointed look on my face. "I'm closing on a deal to sell my video magazine. When that goes through there will be fifty thousand pounds available for you to use if that will help." I didn't want to sound unappreciative, but this was only half the money I needed. I thanked him warmly and we left it that he would call me as soon as the money was available.

I had just received the offer of a loan for fifty thousand pounds and yet I was feeling a little dejected as I left Chris's building. I had to think positive and believe I was on track. There was one other possible source left to me...my two partners, Rob and Dennis, with whom I had worked closely with for more than ten years.

Dennis was always the serious one in our trio, and had naturally evolved into the conservative-minded partner controlling the finances. When Rob and I came up with ideas for various projects, Dennis would invariably act as the devil's advocate. It was a system that had worked extremely well and helped make several of our companies prosperous.

I had kept Dennis updated on my situation, except for this last little problem. I now needed his help in raising the other fifty thousand pounds.

As I took a seat in his office, I wasted no time in explaining my reason for being there that afternoon, "… and if the company can loan me the money I will have it back to you within twenty-four hours," I blurted out, remembering as I spoke, a similar situation I had with Chris just an hour earlier.

Dennis always answered in a slow and deliberate manner. It didn't matter what the question was. Even if you were to ask him about the weather, you would still have to wait while his mind worked overtime to give a carefully calculated answer. This occasion was no different.

"Well, we do have about that amount in what I call our rainy day account," he said. "Let me check with my new partners and see what they think. But we must be absolutely sure that this money is safe. Can you assure us of that?"

I had to be totally honest. There was no way I was one hundred percent sure, but at the same time I could see no reason why it wouldn't be safe. "The money won't even come out of the account," I offered. "It will just be sitting there for one day and then be wired back."

Just like the Dennis of old he spent the next thirty minutes analyzing the situation and trying to think of ways he could keep tabs on the path of the money flow. He was seriously thinking of tracking it himself as it made its way across the Atlantic and back again. Eventually, even he accepted that this idea was impractical.

"I'll get back to you tonight," he finally said.

I breathed a huge sigh of relief when, as promised, Dennis called. Calm as ever, he informed he that I had my temporary funding. The new group of shareholders at my old company agreed they wanted to do everything possible to help me, and with Dennis's assurance that he felt comfortable with the twenty-four hour loan, the money would be made available. I decided I would wait for Chris's money to come through and send the two loans in one lump sum. In truth, I did not trust the bureaucracy and incompetence of the immigration service, and wanted the records to clearly show a deposit of one hundred thousand pounds. As I went to bed that night I believed we were set to go, and that I was nearly on my way back to Naples.

My anxiety level rose over the next few weeks. The sale of Chris's magazine hit some last minute snags, and for a time it looked as if it may even fall through. I waited, and worried, and it was nearly a month later that he was able to give me a check. Finally the two loans were placed in my personal account and wired to The Collier Advertising account in Naples, Florida. Two days later, after being duly recorded, it was wired back to the UK. It was many years later when I revealed to Chris and Dennis that because of the change in the currency exchange rate in my favor, I ended up with two hundred extra dollars in the company account. They both thought that was amusing.

My biggest obstacle in returning to America had been breached. I was now ready to submit our application to the visa department at the American Embassy in London. Gudeon suggested it could take up to ten days for the application to be approved. "Give it one week and then call to find out the status," he said. "It shouldn't do any harm to make an inquiry."

Those seven days seemed an eternity. When they finally passed, I put a call through to the embassy. To my surprise, I was instantly put through to the office of the man in charge of Investor Visa applications. I was pleasantly surprised again when the officer himself picked up the phone. He seemed very friendly and didn't appear to mind in the least that I was calling him.

He told me to wait for a few moments while he pulled my file. With pulse racing and my mind recalling everything that had gone on in the past I immediately started to think the worst. I just couldn't help myself. It was like I was preparing myself to hear him say; "sorry, your visa has been turned down." As each second passed and I continued to hold, my hands became clammier. Now I was also becoming aware of the beads of sweat forming on my brow. I felt a mess.

The wait was interminable. A minute later and I had fully convinced myself that all of my efforts had been a waste of time. I had become a shaking wreck.

For a moment I was even tempted to put down the phone and call back when I regained control of myself but then his softly spoken voice broke the silence. He was explaining that my file was on his desk with three others he was planning to review at home over the weekend. "Call me Monday, after midday, and I should have an answer for you."

As I put the phone down I wondered if this man really knew the power he was wielding. With the swipe of a pen he could make or break a family's hearts.

Looking back I think it was the friendly tone in his voice above all else that gave me at least a hint of confidence. As the weekend passed I began to feel everything was going to be ok. That afternoon I began to think positive thoughts, I called the airline and booked a one-way flight back to Miami for the following Tuesday. Departure time was 2:30 p.m. and I was told to be at the airport at least two hours prior. In my mind I had formulated my own plan. I knew I would have to revisit the embassy one more time to pick up my visa. If it wasn't to be Monday, then it would certainly be Tuesday morning. I decided it would take an hour to travel from the embassy to Waterloo Station, before heading out to Gatwick Airport by the new fast, non-stop train service.

But, though I had convinced myself that all would be well, I still regarded that weekend as the longest of my life. My moods were on a roller coaster, high with confidence one minute and plunging to absolute despair the next. This yo-yo of emotions lasted for three days. I met with family and shared time with friends. I was trying to take my mind off the possibility of disaster and, in the same instant, was trying to believe this would be the last I would see of them for awhile.

It was excruciating, sitting alone in Chris's apartment Monday morning, waiting for midday to arrive. I tried reading. I tried watching TV. But most of the time I just sat in the chair looking into space. All this felt familiar. I missed my wife and children, and after four months away I desperately needed to be with them again.

Eventually, the old grandfather clock in the hallway struck twelve chimes. The noise vibrated through the hallway like a call to arms. I didn't want to appear too anxious by making my call so soon after midday so I fought off the urge to grab the phone and dial. I sat back in the large armchair for a few more minutes and closed my eyes.

At 12:20 I couldn't wait a minute longer. I placed my call to the embassy. I asked to be put through to the visa office, and when a woman's voice came on the line I asked if I could speak with Mr. Caulfield.

"Sorry," she said apologetically. "Mr. Caulfield has just stepped out for lunch. He should be back by 1:30." I could only smile into the mouthpiece as I thanked the lady and put down the phone. I watched the clock as its hands clicked past every minute. At 1:35 I tried my call again. The clammy hands and beads of sweat had reappeared in full force, and I suddenly realized that the Sword of Damocles was literally hanging over my head. I was only seconds away from getting an answer that would change the direction of my family's lives forever.

Mr. Caulfield, bless him, did not make me wait for long.

"Ah, Mr. Freshwater. I have good news for you. I have approved your application." The words washed over my head. I had difficulty focusing on what was being said. "You can stop by the embassy in the morning. We open at eight-thirty and you can get your passports stamped. Don't forget to bring in your wife's and children's passports as well." I sank back into the chair and let out a loud and massive sigh of relief. It had been a long struggle, but we had done it!

I had never told my lawyer that Mo and the children had returned to Florida. I reasoned that the less he knew on some matters the better. On one occasion he did indicate that he would need to see my wife, but that had been forgotten along the way. I had Mo send me all the passports a few weeks earlier, so I now had everything the embassy might ask for. I immediately phoned Mo with the wonderful news and spent the next hour calling family and friends.

As you can imagine, I was up well before dawn the following morning, packed and ready to go by 6 a.m. The apartment was only a short cab ride away from the embassy, and 7:30 found me sitting in a little coffee shop just fifty yards away where I could clearly see that big golden eagle sitting so majestically on the front of the building. Forty-five minutes later, with my body wired with three cups of coffee, I was standing third in line to enter the building.

I realized I may have cut it too fine by choosing to fly home that same day, but after four months I was beyond being anxious to board the plane. I figured I had already done more than my share of waiting, and could not imagine it would take but a few minutes to stamp a passport.

As I made my way to the embassy doors I couldn't help but recall how this nightmare had started back in St. Louis. I thought it was amazing I had heard nothing more about the 'necessary paperwork' ever showing up and I had to believe it had been long forgotten, residing deep in some office filing cabinet. But none of that mattered now. It was all behind me. I was going home!

Inside the embassy, a young corporal dressed in that familiar crisp white military uniform told me to take a number from a board which supported rows of hooks and hanging numbers. It reminded me of the type of thing you would see with valet parking. I was ushered to take a seat in an area marked "visa pick up."

The wall clock showed 8:40 a.m., just a minute slower than my own watch. I pulled out a book and tried to read, but the effects of the coffee were making it difficult to concentrate. The clock's hands moved slowly to 9:10 a.m. The room was filling up with people, but there was no action at the front of the room where embassy staff was moving around behind a large mahogany counter. At 9:20 a.m. I stood up from my chair and approached the counter. I coughed, and was suddenly aware that everyone else in the room was looking at me. The young corporal came over, wondering why I got up from my seat.

"You will just have to be patient and wait sir. They will start calling out the numbers when they are ready." The room was beginning to feel very warm. I was regretting the fact I chose to wear a suit and tie. Reluctantly I moved back to my seat.

At last a woman appeared, cleared her throat and called out the first number. A young black man got up from his chair beside me and made his way to the front. I couldn't hear what was being said, but I could see him hand over his passports before coming back to sit down. The woman behind the counter disappeared and then returned three to four minutes later and called out a second number. I was next. The same procedure was repeated and then it was my turn. "You have your passports?" queried the short, portly woman. I handed them over and sat back down.

Twenty minutes later the first person was still sitting and waiting. The only action had been with others who were each called by their number to the counter to hand in their passports.

At last the woman returned and called out a name. The black man rose from his seat and walked forward. He was handed back his passports which he quickly inspected. He handed over some money and appeared to sign a receipt before walking away smiling, with passports held firmly in his hand. The next woman was called, and then me. I knew we had to pay a fee so I reached in my back pocket for my wallet. "That will be two hundred and eighty dollars for each visa," said the woman. And almost as an afterthought, she added, "It has to be cash or a cashier's check."

I was completely unprepared for this. I had only about one hundred and fifty pounds in my wallet, which I had assumed would be more than enough to cover the visa costs. Gudeon had never warned me about this. "But you take credit cards?" I asked, knowing I had just enough left on a Visa card to cover the payment if they didn't take American Express.

"No, sorry, we don't. It has to be cash. There is a bank just down the street. They will cash a check for you," she said. This was long before ATM machines came upon the scene and I had already closed my bank account. All of my money had been transferred to Florida.

Panic began to set in. So near and yet so far. Who did I know nearby who could loan me four hundred and ten pounds right now? I ran from the building and found a phone box. Fortunately, unlike many of the public phones in London, this one was in working order. Desperately I called Dennis at his office, praying that he would be in.

I was relieved when he answered the phone, and I probably began to babble as I tried to get across, as quickly as I could, what was happening. "Dennis. I've got to come up with seven hundred pounds to pay for my passports and I only have one hundred and fifty and they won't take a check. I could really do with six hundred to cover the fees and the cab fare." Dennis knew I was planning to leave today and there was no doubting he could detect the panic in my voice.

"We don't have any cash in the office. I was going to the bank at lunchtime. I can give you a check to cash if you stop by."

It was now 9:50 a.m. and I realized there was a real danger I wouldn't make my flight. I had just over an hour and a half to sort out this mess before I was due to leave for the airport. Dennis's office was easily twenty minutes away and I knew the traffic was going to be bad. This was going to be tight.

Hailing a cab, I explained my situation to the driver as we headed across town. Probably sensing a good tip, he sped through the morning traffic like a maniac, giving me hope we could get there in time. I kept the cab waiting while I raced up the three flights of stairs to Dennis's office. I literally grabbed the check out of his hand, thanked him profusely and ran from the room. A few minutes later the cab was again left waiting as I raced into the nearby bank.

It was now 10:30 a.m.

Inside the bank my heart stopped. Before me were long lines of business customers snaking their way around the ropes. In their hands were the heavy bundles of deposits. Left with no other choice, and beyond the ability to be embarrassed, I ran to the head of the first line and pleaded my case for everyone to hear. I hoped that waving my plane ticket in the air would convince everyone this was almost a life and death situation.

I must have sounded either convincing or crazy. The elderly man at the head of the line waved me through with a cheery smile, and a couple of minutes later I was again back in the taxi and rushing to the embassy.

My watch showed 10:45a.m.

I felt I had stepped into a shower. The sun was shining and there was no air conditioning in the old London cab. My wet clothes were clinging to my body. Sweat was running into my eyes. My mouth was dry. I must have appeared frantic to everyone who saw me enter the embassy doors. It was like a parting of the waves as I ran towards the counter. Amazingly, no one tried to stop me. My portly, embassy woman appeared, as if on cue, from the back office just as I got there. I tried desperately to compose myself as I handed her the money. For one horrible minute I thought she was going to tell me to sit down and wait my turn. I jumped in before she could say anything.

"I'm really sorry, but I do have a plane to catch." She hesitated for a second, then turned and walked into the next room. She reappeared a minute later carrying a batch of passports. "Here," she said, placing the priceless documents in my hands. I handed her the money. "Sign here, here and here. Good luck."

The hands on the embassy had already passed 11:25 p.m., but it looked as though I was going to make it!

I was surprised to see that my cab was still waiting. I had already paid what had shown on the clock when I left to run into the embassy and wasn't sure the cab driver heard me when I yelled back over my shoulder to ask if he could stay around for fifteen minutes and wait for me. He was my knight in shining armor that morning, although in truth he was Ari in a turban who cut and weaved his cab through the London traffic. As we pulled into Waterloo Station, I pulled off a few pounds from my money clip to cover my train fare and airport needs, and dumped the rest in the hands of my new friend. I figured Ari had more than earned the tip.

I eventually arrived at check-in a few minutes before 1:45 p.m. I had to wonder if I was already too late. I was supposed to check in two hours before the flight – not forty-five minutes. I was the only passenger left standing in the check-in line for the 2:30 flight to Miami. The attractive, dark-haired lady behind the counter looked up and asked for my ticket. "I hope I'm not too late," I offered. "I've had some problems."

She had the bluest eyes I had ever seen. They seemed to sparkle and compliment her warm smile.

"I'm sorry," she said, "but economy class is now full. *Do you mind if we upgrade you to business class?*"

Chapter Fifteen

It was the pinnacle of happiness for me to be back in Naples with my family again. We had always been close, but my four months absence had served to strengthen the bonds between us. Just as Mo's Dad had promised his wife on the day he returned from serving overseas, I vowed openly I would never leave my family again.

Although our life was a financial mess, we still considered ourselves fortunate in so many ways. Above all else, we had our kids, who seemed to provide a ready escape from our day to day financial worries. We tried to find as much time as possible to be with them.

I guess one of the advantages of living in a place like Florida is that you don't miss the absence of vacations. If we couldn't afford to go on expensive trips, then it was easy to compensate by going off on the occasional weekend camping and canoe trips to places like the Peace River or Ginny Springs in Central Florida where we would all enjoy a lazy afternoon, tube rafting in the cool waters. Everyone seemed to enjoy these family trips and they cost us very little money.

I don't think climbing Everest was ever planned with any greater precision than our river expeditions. For these canoe adventures, we had acquired five gallon, plastic pickle buckets from our local McDonald's. We scrubbed them clean, using them to store our bedding and all the food we hauled along for our overnight trip.

Those weekends are mostly a non-stop slide show of happy memories. The three children would paddle their own canoe, while Mo and I paddled ours alongside. We got to see Florida's wildlife up close, including many different types of snakes, otters and yes, alligators too, as we floated downstream with the gentle current.

I did say 'mostly' happy memories. The kids thought it hilarious when, trying to navigate through a section of more turbulent waters, I once flipped our canoe. They hollered and screamed with delight, while their mother vented her disapproval by shooting me a somber look. Mo wasn't too happy to discover that the pickle buckets that had fallen into the water were not completely waterproof. Our bedding and food had become rather soggy. But, helped along by the raucous laughter from the children, she soon had a smile back on her face.

On another camping trip, we were awakened early one morning by what appeared to be the sound of stampeding cattle. The deafening noise seemed only a short distance away, and we half expected to be trampled underfoot as we scrambled out of our sleeping bags.

Fearfully we sprinted from the tents and looked for the cause of the commotion. As quickly as it had started, the noise quieted to a gentle mooing sound from somewhere yonder. It was a disappointed Dominic who pointed out that the 'stampeding herd' comprised of three or four docile looking cows now grazing contentedly on the other side of the river. We doubled over with laughter as we reconsidered our "close call" with death.

Perhaps the most memorable canoeing experience was the time Mo decided to experiment with her own method of overcoming the evening dampness problem which caused our clothes to get wet during the night. She had decided to bring along a huge commercial roll of plastic, which she planned to roll out to cover the entire campsite area on which we would be pitching the two tents.

Canoeing and swimming for most of the day left us tired and exhausted and by the time we finished our meal and washed the dishes we were all ready for bed. Even the children went to their tent without being told as Mo and I snuggled onto our air mattresses for the night. We recall later that we had both heard the rain in our sleep, but exhaustion stopped us from waking...that was until Dominic and Kieran poked their heads through our tent flap to angrily announce their tent was completely flooded.

Mo and I were now awake and fully conscious of the howling winds and driving rain pounding the canvass above our heads. Drops of water were dripping from the tent roof and falling onto our blankets. It was only when I climbed off the air mattress that I appreciated the seriousness of the situation. While a river was cascading through our own tent, over at the children's tent the situation was even worse. They had chosen to camp tough and not bring mattresses. Their entire bedding was submerged in a stream of water.

We now realized that Mo's plastic sheeting had acted as a catchment pond for every drop of water that hit our campsite. With our bodies soaked and cold, we were left with no other alternative than work together to try and rip up the plastic from under and around the tents. For the time being we were back to dry land, but our bedding and nightclothes were completely soaked.

We had no other choice than to pull the children into our tent and huddle together for warmth. Without checking the time, I figured it would soon be light and, hopefully, the return of the early morning sun would quickly dry us out. As I tried to control my shivering I looked down at my watch, and was both shocked and disappointed to learn we had been to sleep for a little over an hour. It was still only 11:00 p.m.

That had to be one of the dreariest nights in our lives. Although the rain eased up, water continued to drip from the canvas for much of the night. We managed to find some dry towels in one of the sealed buckets but they gave us only limited comfort and warmth. Soon they were as wet as the rest of the clothing. Each of us would doze off, only to be awoken a short time later by the cold. Sitting there in the cold gloom, body aching, I felt sure this would be our last camping trip.

But how soon we forget. It took only minutes for the rising dawn, with its warming sun under a clear blue sky, to make us all feel good again. Soon we had a campfire blazing and hot coffee brewing. With dry, warm clothes we all felt fine, and were soon laughing and joking as we dove into our bacon and eggs, a must breakfast on any of our camping trips.

Funny thing. Mo never suggested taking the plastic again.

Chapter Sixteen

In the summer of 1991 we were told by our printers that they had been approached by a new publishing company with very deep pockets. The firm's plan was to produce a newspaper that would not only kill off The Collier Advertiser, but would also compete with the Naples Daily News for advertising.

In the eyes of many companies, the wealthy residential base of Naples offered an attractive market. It seemed that each week, a new bank or brokerage firm would open its doors, seeking a slice of the lucrative local pie. It was certainly no different in the field of publishing.

During our time publishing The Collier Advertiser we had seen scores of new publications come and go. Some were better than others, but very few lasted more than one year. We rarely worried about the start-ups, but this time it appeared we were facing a far more determined kind of competition. Although we had never considered our publication a newspaper in the true sense of the word, we did compete for a respectable segment of the town's advertising dollars. Newcomers in the market were never welcome.

Over the next few weeks, we learned more about our new competition. To be honest, we were becoming very worried. Whichever way we looked at the situation, it didn't look good. The new publisher was a woman named Terri Hopkins, who came from a family with strong newspaper interests in New England. Her sights were firmly set on taking over the Naples market and she didn't care who knew about it.

The printers confided to us that Hopkins had moved in to purchase a large stake in their operation; her rationale being she wanted access and control of her own printing and pre-print facilities. She poached staff from other publications, ensuring she had quality, well-known personnel to help in her endeavors.

Neither our printers nor we knew what the future had in store regarding our own relationship. There were very few printers in southwest Florida with the capabilities of producing newsprint so we had to tread very carefully. I had become personal friends with the three printing partners, but I also understood the pressure that a new majority stockholder could wield upon them at anytime. It was easy to see that overall control of the printing plant would no longer be in their hands. On the contrary, the reins were held by our new competitor, who had made no bones about the fact that she wanted to see us out of business.

As it turned out, the new publication wasn't nearly the threat we expected. It wasn't a newspaper per se, but more like an up-scale entertainment magazine in newsprint format. In some ways, the arrogance of its publisher seemed to filter down into the editorial content. Most agreed that the publication was witty, but almost in a condescending way.

Our own opinion was that "The Express" was very attractive, and would likely pick up advertising from the more trendy stores in town. This was fine with us, as those businesses had never been our market anyway. After enjoying an initial gush of interest within the Naples business community - helped by some very expensive promotional parties - both Hopkins and her associates must have realized they weren't going to enjoy the impact they had envisaged. There was no way they would present any real threat to the Naples Daily News. They weren't even cutting into our business too badly.

Ron and I were surprised that we weren't told to find new printers, but we reasoned that our regular weekly print runs was still considered an attractive and lucrative contract. In fact, it was us who eventually decided we didn't feel comfortable being around the new regime. Ron and I once walked in when Hopkins was combing through our pre-press art boards, discussing our advertisers with members of her staff. The conversation might have been innocent, but judging by the abrupt silence when we entered the room, neither of us felt that it was. We had a nagging fear that the rug could be yanked from under our feet at anytime. The final straw came with a clash in printing schedules between The Express and The Collier Advertiser. We ended up with a terrible-looking paper, covered with ink smudges and unidentifiable photos. It turned out that The Collier Advertiser had been printed on an old, antiquated press, while Hopkins was printing her paper on the new equipment she'd purchased.

Although we received a refund for the job, it was time to move on. Our new printers were nearly 100 miles away in Port Charlotte, but the inconvenience of travel was balanced with a peace of mind.

Apparently, we weren't the only customers who had reservations about continuing to do business with Hopkins. More and more clients took their business elsewhere, and one day we received a phone call telling us that the doors to the plant had been padlocked. Like many who had come before her with big ideas, the Terri Hopkins "Naples Express" lasted just a little over a year. That was enough time to reduce the family fortune by $500,000. We later heard, unconfirmed, that her total loss on the entire printing and publishing operation was much, much greater.

We were beginning to think we must be doing a lot of things right, to stay in business for as long as we had.

The Naples Daily News had started out as a small weekly newspaper, owned by the Barron Collier family who were responsible for much of the early growth in the area. Because of their involvement in southwest Florida, and the vast tracts of land they owned, the Collier family name was chosen for the new county which bordered the Everglades to the east and the established county of Lee to the north.

It was Barron Collier's money which helped to complete the all-important section of the Tamiami Trail running between Miami and Naples. When construction ran into financial difficulties in the early 20s, Collier stepped in and saved the project, which ultimately proved to be one of the main influences spurring development of the area.

Until roads were built, Naples had been dependent on shipping traffic via the Gulf of Mexico. Steamers and even sailing ships brought in the early Kentucky settlers, and later, the wealthy northern vacationers in search of warm, winter weather. At the turn of the century, the busiest area in town was around the pier. Even today, the reconstructed pier, used by fishermen of all ages, remains the city's most famous landmark. The first hotel in Naples was built nearby, and from there the village expanded to the north and east.

Barron Collier came to the region and purchased many thousands of acres of land, much of it for around a dollar per acre. This land proved to be rich in minerals and ideal for farming. If that wasn't enough, as the years sped by, large tracts of the land later were rezoned commercial and swallowed up in the Naples urban sprawl. Today, that commercial zoned land is some of the most expensive ground in the United States. Although the Collier family is now split into two separate operations, the name continues to be synonymous with the continuing growth of Naples and southwest Florida.

In the late 1980's the Collier family sold the Naples Daily News to Scripps Howard for a staggering sum in the region of one hundred and fifty million dollars. It had changed from an afternoon paper to a morning one, now published seven days a week, three hundred and sixty five days a year. Its ongoing success can, in part, be attributed to enormous real estate advertising revenue. Every Sunday it will include up to five separate real estate sections.

For much of the time we published The Collier Advertiser we enjoyed a good, if distant, relationship with the Naples Daily News. I always considered that we were like a mosquito on their backs, maybe an irritation but never a dangerous threat. The relationship did become a little strained around the time our advertising revenue grew to more than $20,000 in some of our winter issues, and we heard from insiders that the Advertising Director down the street was holding weekly meetings to conceive plans that would thwart our growth. The paper even published special supplements, which included a near-exact copy of our advertorial style.

This brought a sharp rebuke from Ron in his popular page three editorial where, with tongue in cheek, we produced the front page of a new publication called "The Naples Daily Advertiser." Of course, we duplicated their typeface!

Corbin Wyatt was the man who moved up in the company to become the Publisher of the Naples Daily News. He was liked by everyone and respected for his generous contributions to the Naples community. On the couple of occasions we met, he was very friendly and gracious. It was during one of those meetings that he pulled me aside to tell me a story about our son Dominic.

Dominic had always been our little entrepreneur. From a young age he had an obsession for money-making schemes. Fishing golf balls out of the lakes at the nearby golf course, and selling them to golf equipment stores around town, was one of his more lucrative ventures. That business worked phenomenally well until the golf course owners called the police complaining that the diver they hired to collect the balls was having meager pickings and Dominic's little cash-cow was immediately halted!

Like his older brother, Dominic had decided to become a newspaper carrier for the Naples Daily News. For two consecutive years he picked up the top prize awarded to the carrier who brought in the most new subscribers. One year the prize was a shiny new bike, the other time it was cash which bought Dominic his own king-size waterbed.

"We have always been impressed with the numbers of new subscribers Dominic is able to sign up," Corbin told me. "The last time we were signing up subscribers, I had one of our staff go out and see how he does it."

"Maybe I shouldn't be telling you this," he went on, "but your son came up with his own sales pitch. We've now labeled it the Dominic Technique, and have adopted it into all our selling seminars we hold around the country!"

I was both dumbfounded and amused as Corbin gave me further details. "We've determined that Dominic is able to assess the situation at each house he calls on, and appears to have a story ready to meet every occasion. As an example, if an elderly person answered the door he would immediately come up with a story involving grandparents, something like if he could win the prize he would buy a special gift for his grandparents in England."

The publisher went on. "My staff person who never let on he was watching and listening, told me about another time when a man opened the door holding a fishing rod. In a flash, Dominic's opening line was that he loved fishing and wanted to win the cash prize so he could go out and buy his own fishing rod."

Laughing and feeling proud at the same time, I thanked Corbin for sharing the story. We've joked about it many times over the years.

Although The Collier Advertiser failed to bring us the riches we had hoped for, seeing so many other local publications failing made us believe we had still achieved a certain success. In making our decision to sell we had come to believe we had taken the publication as far as we could with our limited resources. We all felt we had sacrificed enough blood, sweat, and sometimes even tears to keep the publication going.

As planned, following one more successful season, we began making inquiries about finding a buyer. We spoke with several brokers and eventually settled on one out of Kansas City, Missouri, who had been selling publications for over half a century. The current owner was very positive about what we were doing, and came up with a value of between $350,000 and $400,000. I had no idea how he managed to arrive at these figures, considering that overall we were barely surviving financially. Still, his company had been in the business for a very long time and, with such an impressive long list of sales, we eagerly accepted the price tag they were suggesting.

In truth, we would have taken a much lower figure just to move on. We all agreed it would be nice to pay back Alan Boole the money he had put into the operation and to hand him a handsome profit. Ron, for his part, had grown tired of living the life of a poor bachelor in Naples, where he lamented he had probably dated every female gold-digger in town. From our perspective, after viewing quite a few of his dates, they always came in the same package; tall, long-legged and usually blonde. He was now eager to go to the mountains out west. Not ever overly fond of Naples, Ron hoped to recoup his investment, some of the back salary he was still owed and whatever else a sale may bring. Mo wanted to get back to the classroom, and I, apart from wanting my own share of the proceeds, was thinking about several fresh ideas for projects I wanted to pursue.

Several would-be buyers approached us during the summer of 1991, but for one reason or another none committed to making an offer. This had suddenly become a bad time for free-distribution publications. Only a few months earlier they had been a "hot" item commanding ridiculously high prices. Now the situation had changed. Because of a slower economy that had led to a decrease in print advertising revenue across the country, no one was in the buying mood.

Just when we were beginning to give up thoughts of finding a buyer, the owner of a New York advertising agency called to say he was interested in meeting with us. After the first meeting I was excited. The man said he was extremely interested. After a second meeting he announced that, providing we could prove our advertising revenue, he would certainly be making us an offer.

I wasted no time in providing him with copies of the accounts he requested. We spoke later on the phone and he seemed satisfied. "I will be faxing you my offer on Friday," he promised.

Perhaps it was a little too soon to be celebrating but that evening Ron, Mo and I cracked open a bottle of cheap champagne in anticipation. We were ready to accept any reasonable offer, and all of us were on cloud nine.

When Friday morning came, it was impossible for any of us to concentrate on work. We knew this was the day, and we all shared feelings of excitement as well as some anxiety. The staff was happy, knowing from our discussions that the prospective buyer planned on keeping everyone on board, as well as injecting more money to improve the paper.

By mid-afternoon we had still not received the fax. Our nerves were strung to the breaking point. Although no one was prepared to say it, we were now starting to have serious doubts that the offer would arrive. There had been several false alarms during the day, which found all three of us crowding excitedly over the fax machine.

Finally, at 4:00 p.m., the fax we were looking for started to come through. As it slowly pushed out of the machine we could recognize the name of the New York agency at the top of the sheet. I swear you could hear all three heartbeats pounding in that little room.

The single sheet dropped into the tray, and Mo quickly picked it up for all of us to read. As three sets of eyes raced over the words, our hearts sunk. There was to be no offer.

The fax explained that the agency's biggest client was threatening to pull out and place its huge amount of advertising dollars with another company. Our buyer said his priority was to stay and try and save the account. "I hope this proves to be just a short postponement," the message ended.

We were now well into summer. We were still current on paying all invoices but we knew the weeks ahead would be the slowest and we would be moving heavily into the red. We were all feeling deflated. As we all expected, we didn't hear back from our buyer the next week, or the next week after that. After three weeks I placed a call, only to hear that our would-be buyer was still fully immersed in trying to sort out problems at his agency. He really couldn't see himself coming back to us anytime soon.

I made one more phone call to the brokers. They offered similar depressing news. No one was buying free publications at this time, and the last few deals were at hugely discounted prices. I didn't have to think for too long before telling them to continue looking for a buyer.

That evening Ron came back to our home, not to crack open champagne, but to agree with our decision to give ourselves just a couple more weeks to see if the broker could come up with anything. As we sat at the kitchen table, we all accepted we had virtually come to the time to cut our losses and move on. We had given the paper our best shot but it just wasn't happening. None of us wanted to go through any more money-losing months.

For the first time since we started the publication our financial backer, Alan, had began putting pressure on us. He was sharing the disappointment of us not finding a lucrative offer at a time when his own pool construction business was going through difficult times. Alan had always been good about funding the project and there had been several occasions when we had been very grateful for his ongoing support. Often, in the early days, he would inject loans to help us get through difficult periods.

What he didn't know, and has never been explained to this day, was that Mo and I had also invested more funds ourselves from the bank loan we organized back in England, as well as loans from friends we have personally repaid many years later. I guess our reasoning for not telling him was that we didn't want him to know how much we were struggling at times, just in case he decided to abandon ship and pull the plug before we had a chance of finding a buyer. The three of us had always believed that these facts would emerge once we had sealed a successful sale. But, of course, that celebration never came. For some weeks Alan had been urging us to take any low-ball offer he believed was out there. Just about anything in fact so he could get back his original investment.

Feelings had been running high. Alan now wanted to take over full control and find a buyer himself. He still owned the majority of the shares and he was making it known that just about any offer would do to help him get out of his own troubles. Time had run out. After consulting with his lawyer, he had the business listed with a new local broker the very next day and within a few hours he was approached by someone from the Chicago area. Apparently the interest came from someone who was planning to relocate to Naples to be with his married daughter and grandchild.

Within ten days Alan had sold the paper for just enough money to repay himself back his investment money, while Mo, Ron and I walked away with empty pockets and some lingering debts. We never spoke to Alan and his wife Pat for eight years, until I ran into them by chance at the local airport quite recently and, after certain hesitancy, we all shook hands and decided to forget - 'it was all water under the bridge.'

As we had seen so many times before with other Naples businesses, the new owner of The Collier Advertiser rode into town full of new ideas on how he was going to transform our operation into a big money-making machine. He rode back out of town six months later. The Collier Advertiser was no more, and his saddlebags were more than $100,000 lighter.

Although we were relieved to be out of the paper there was hardly enough time to catch our breath. Our financial situation had become no easier. We both needed to work as much as possible. Although Mo didn't have a Florida Teaching Certificate, she was always in demand for substitute teaching. Better still, from time to time she was now being offered long-term sub positions which usually meant enjoying her own class for a whole term or more.

Apart from the higher rate of pay for long-term subbing, she also welcomed developing her own study plans, as well as the opportunity of really getting to know each of the students. She would step in for teachers on maternity leave and for those out of school on long-term sickness.

For my part, I had met a successful insurance broker when writing one of my last articles at The Collier Advertiser which gave me the idea of looking at insurance as my next career. The broker I interviewed was selling discount auto insurance, and during the previous six months he had opened four new offices in the Naples area. This rapid growth suggested he was making good profits for a much needed service. The coverage was mainly aimed at young people and low-income immigrant farm workers who stopped by the offices once a month to pay their premiums with cash.

We had talked about a franchise deal, but when I confessed I had absolutely no money, he suggested that I might like to work my way into owning my own office over a period of time. In the meantime, I could start working for him to learn the business.

This was the best, if not the only, business opportunity open to me at the time. I decided I had nothing to lose, and began studying to gain accreditation as a licensed agent. This new road meant taking and passing the state's insurance exam. As usual, Mo was there to offer support, encouraging me to use some of the money I had recently earned from a couple of painting jobs to enroll in an insurance school. The nearest school was located in a run-down building in a shabby part of nearby Ft. Myers. Walking out of the single story building after enrolling and taking note of the paint flaking off the walls, I suddenly realized I was going back to school for the first time in almost thirty years. I smiled to myself as I recalled my last classroom had paint chipping off the walls too.

I wish I could say that my return to the halls of knowledge proved to be an enjoyable experience, but it wasn't. The next five weeks proved to be among the most boring of my life. The instructor was old and crotchety, and his droning voice sent everyone in the class into a light coma. I could only wonder why the man didn't try to improve his teaching abilities; he must have known he was bad. Every time he looked up he would see half his class asleep, their heads resting on folded arms.

I learned absolutely nothing from these day-long classes, relying instead on reading the textbooks in preparation for the test. This strategy proved faulty, and I failed the exam the first time.

Before re-taking the test, Mo and I decided it would make sense if I used some more of our limited cash and enroll at a weekend preparation course. This time it worked. I walked out of the exam test building in Miami, three weeks later, with a license in General Lines insurance. This was actually the toughest license to pass and I was told that very few students are successful on the first attempt. It was pleasing to think that my failure to pass the first time didn't make me quite so unique. I was now licensed in most types of insurance sales.

I worked with my auto insurance friend for just one Saturday morning before realizing that, unless I was now prepared to learn Spanish to go along with my insurance license, there was absolutely no way I could perform the job. I estimated that thirty percent of the people who came into the office were unable to speak a word of English. I may have been able to pass the insurance exam, but there was no way I was going to be able to learn Spanish anytime soon. I could still so easily remember the difficulties I had learning French back in my high school days.

So now I had a license but nowhere to use it. Fortunately that situation changed two days later when I ran into Terry Harris, another British expatriate who ran his own insurance office selling senior health care.

Terry, with his tough looking appearance, came across as the very last person you would ever expect to deal successfully with older people. And yet, I quickly learned, he had built up a very successful and highly respected operation. His elderly clients adored him.

Back in the poorer area of London's East End where I had worked my first reporting job, Terry's father had successfully built a business selling confectionery out of stalls at various markets in the area, traveling from market to market seven days a week. Terry and his younger brother both left school as soon as they were able to work with their father. They both learned the art of thinking on their feet and acquired an advanced diploma in the 'gift of gab'. Although not a true Cockney in terms of being born within the sound of London's Bow Bells, Terry fitted the Cockney image to a tee. He spoke the Cockney rhyming slang, had a wicked sense of humor and was always looking for an opportunity to make some extra cash. I never questioned if all, or indeed any, of these moneymaking schemes from his past were regarded as being in any way legal.

He eventually got out of the markets and went on to own two pubs before selling out and moving to America. Unlike us, he chose the path of least resistance, and married an American woman. That union appeared to last just long enough for him to file his papers and become a permanent resident.

Terry Harris always had a story to tell, which proved to be a quality that helped him sell his Long Term Health Care and Medicare Supplementary policies with great success.

I became Terry's one and only employee, although he always referred to me as a partner. Our deal was that he retained his current sales area, which he had worked for nearly four years, and I was free to canvass and sell anywhere outside. In the first few weeks, as part of my training, I tagged along like a loyal puppy when he went out on appointments.

It was difficult to keep a straight face when I began to hear Terry relating the same stories over and over again, each time throwing in different twists, depending upon the customer. I was often reminded of how my younger son Dominic sold subscriptions to the newspaper. Terry would also change his story to fit the situation. "You have to paint the picture for the old people to understand," he would tell me. "When they can see the problem, and we show them the solution, then they will buy."

I never saw Terry do anything even remotely dishonest in his insurance business. In fact, knowing his background, I was quite amazed that he ran it in such a squeaky-clean fashion. But his story-telling was a different matter. Let's just say he embellished a little - or perhaps used a wide-ranging poetic license - that he utilized to grab the attention of his audience. Terry was always entertaining, and I often wished I had seen him in his market days.

If you believed Terry's sales pitch, his aging parents must have suffered from every illness under the sun, or certainly every sickness matching those suffered by the clients we met. His standard line was that he could relate to a client's pain, because his dear ol', sainted Mum or Dad were fighting the exact same malady. It really didn't matter what that illness might be. If a client had it, so did Terry's parents.

There were some scenarios he presented that were so obscure I never did understand their true meaning. I quickly concluded, usually while sitting silent in the background, that his clients were just as confused as I was. However, they never let on. They all loved Terry, and judging by the number of Christmas cards he received each year from clients, he clearly was offering a service that they greatly appreciated. I think it's fair to say that both of us would still be in senior health care insurance today, if the industry hadn't changed so much.

Terry acquired most of his clients when Supplementary Medicare policies were affordable and popular. These are the coverages that pick up costs the government program doesn't cover. When he first came into the industry, Terry was able to quickly build a strong client base from selling just these types of policies. Always one to look for a new angle, he was quick to see the potential of selling other forms of health care insurance as well.

He worked hard for four years to develop and strengthen his business. When I met up with him, he admitted his ongoing commission payments for the next five years was "enough to save me from having to get out of bed in the mornings if I don't want to." But that wouldn't be Terry's style. He needed new business to cover his extravagant lifestyle.

But the days of the good life in this area of the insurance business were destined to change. Rapidly increasing premiums in the senior health care field served to dramatically slow down sales. After enjoying a couple of good profitable years, I witnessed first-hand how those increasing premiums were cutting back on both sales and our commissions. While commissions took a spiral downwards, our costs for generating leads were spiraling in the opposite direction. After a year of watching this changing scenario, I began looking around for new work.

A year later, Terry also got out of the insurance business. Always one to land on his feet, and have an incredible time doing it, he opened his own Tikki Bar overlooking Naples Bay.

I had moved from selling health care insurance to selling hearing aids in 1997 with the father of the girl our son Dominic had been dating through college. Susan's father, Al, proposed the idea when he learned I had left the insurance business and was looking for a job that would still allow me the time off to pursue researching a plastics project that had landed on my lap, but more on that one later. Now I needed something where I had freedom to do both, and a sales job where I could set up my own schedule sounded like the ideal solution.

I soon learned there are strict laws governing the sales of hearing aids. I had to undergo intense training and, yet again, acquire appropriate licenses before being permitted to go out on appointments. Al had run his lucrative operation for several years, building a list of nursing home contacts throughout south Florida. He worked closely with a couple of major, independent physical therapy agencies that provided services in well over a hundred different nursing homes. The list had grown to the point where Al was unable to service all the outlets himself. He needed help.

After the initial training, I would go out to the nursing homes where the physical therapy staff had set up hearing tests for us to conduct, usually on a regular monthly basis. During the course of their own therapy work, they were able to detect patients with hearing problems. It proved to be a wonderful referral service.

This opportunity looked like a winner and would have been, had not the largest agency we worked with maneuvered itself into serious trouble with Medicare over questionable billing. This unfortunate incident came to light just a few weeks after I started my sales calls. The health authorities moved in, wasting no time in closing down all the rehabilitation company's Florida nursing home offices. My own list of sixty nursing home outlets was reduced overnight to just eight!

I thought it couldn't get worse, but I was wrong. Although Al's operation was completely independent of the rehabilitation company, most of the nursing home managers believed we were in some way connected. Restoring management confidence was a painfully slow process. Over the next six months I was able to win back about a dozen clients, but this was not enough to provide sufficient outlets and enough sales. I was barely able to cover my travel expenses, and as an independent contractor, I had no insurance benefits either. Again, it was time to move on.

Chapter Seventeen

We always tried to be close to our three children. They gave us enormous pleasure and very few problems. None of them could be classified as true academic students, preferring to be involved in many different school activities, both inside the classroom and out. We certainly encouraged, maybe you could even call it demanded, that they go to college.

Kieran was the first to leave high school. He never really did get into the books at that time of his life, always preferring a tennis racket in his hand, rather than a copy of Canterbury Tales.

He had become quite good at the game and had won several local tournaments as a teenager. I had given up playing with him when he was around fourteen because, quite simply, I had no more excuses left for losing. Along with his high school friend, Shelley Dee, he was planning to go to a two-year junior college in Jacksonville, located in the northern-most part of the state. It was about an eight-hour drive, but we sensed his desire to be away from home and to enjoy the opportunity of spreading his young wings.

It was early spring of 1993 when Kieran and I went to visit the college campus. With the six hour journey ahead of us, we climbed from our beds before 4:00 a.m., hoping to make it to Jacksonville and back on the same day and, therefore, bypassing the need for a costly overnight accommodation. This trip gave Kieran an opportunity to drive the family car and he sat happily behind the wheel for most of the journey. It was a little before noon on a baking hot day when we arrived at the sprawling campus.

On our walk from the car to the administration buildings we took our time to meander our way through the campus buildings. I could see that Kieran was impressed by what he saw. He was never one to show too much excitement, but it was obvious he was feeling good about the possibilities of coming to this college.

On this beautiful sunny day, all our visa problems were pushed from our minds. It just felt so good that our lives were back to being a little more normal. Here I was, just a regular dad, along with his son registering for college. I certainly never anticipated facing any problems.

Because of his recognized tennis skills, Kieran had hoped to get a partial scholarship to help cover the costs of books and tuition. He had written to the tennis coach at the school twice in the preceding weeks but his letters, with an accompanying videotape, hadn't yet brought a response. Kieran, true to form, merely shrugged his shoulders when we talked about it in the car. He showed no disappointment that he hadn't heard back and clearly accepted he would try as a "walk on" for the team if he had to.

It was because of our continuing financial problems that Kieran was restricted to attending a Florida college, where fees would be about a third of what he would have to pay at an out-of-state school. Fortunately, he shared our love for the Florida climate, and staying in state wasn't a problem for him at all.

He had worked hard at part-time jobs and had saved several hundred dollars towards his college expenses. We were still struggling, but we told him we would help as much as we could. He planned on sharing an apartment off campus with other students and continue working part-time. Although finances would be tight for all of us, we believed we could manage.

Kieran had completed the registration forms we had received in the mail by the time we located the college administration building. It stood at the far side of the campus, rising impressively at the end of a tree-lined avenue. I noticed that the surrounding buildings were a mixture of both newer and older styles. We climbed the steps and went inside the red brick structure, handing the paperwork to a friendly-faced woman in the enrollment office. She smiled warmly and invited us to take a seat and wait. We were there only a few minutes before being invited to follow her into an adjoining room.

After directing us to sit down, she took a moment to look through our yellow application forms she was shuffling in her hands. "I see from your paperwork that you are neither citizens nor resident aliens. What type of visas do you have?" The woman's eyes continued to scan the pages as she spoke.

"We have investment visas. They were renewed a few months back," I added casually, not anticipating that there could possibly be any problems.

"That's fine. We would love for Kieran to register at the school...but we will have to treat him as an out of state student!"

The impact of what she was saying resurrected an all too familiar feeling. "But we have lived in Florida for over twelve years," I retorted. "We have filed domicile here and pay our property and income taxes here."

The woman's raised eyebrows told me she had noticed the desperation in my voice.

"I'm very sorry, but there is nothing I can do. I'm very familiar with the situation. I had a German student in exactly the same situation here just last week. I can assure you, we simply have no choice but to treat Kieran as an out-of-state student."

There was an embarrassing silence for the longest time as we stood staring at each other. "And are the fees are three times more?" I eventually asked.

"Even a little more than that, I'm afraid," she responded. "There has just been an increase."

For a few more lingering seconds we sat there staring at each other again. No one seemed to know what to say next. I shifted my gaze to Kieran and saw the sad look of disappointment on his face. I placed my hand on his knee and suggested we go for a walk and discuss it between ourselves.

"There is just one more thing I need to ask before we go outside," I said. "Is there any chance we can meet with the Activities Director. Kieran is keen to play tennis in college, and he would like to know what his chances are of getting on the team?"

"Of course you can. I will get him on the phone right now," the lady replied, the friendly smile returning to her face. She turned to the phone sitting on the corner of the desk and began dialing. As she talked, Kieran and I strolled over to the window and looked out across the campus lawn. I put a hand on his shoulder and gave him a squeeze. "It's going to be ok," I whispered. Outside, in the blazing sun, a few summer students were laughing and talking as they walked between the buildings. It was a warm and happy sight. I knew how happy Kieran would be here.

"The Activities Director is busy right now, but if you would like to come back after lunch he would be pleased to meet with you," the woman said, replacing the phone on its cradle. "Shall we say, back here at 2:00 p.m."

There wasn't much to talk about over lunch. Kieran was feeling down, his face showing his disappointment at the news we had just received. I tried to be jovial, but struggling to come up with things to make him feel better. I wasn't having much success. "Whatever happens Kieran, we will definitely find the money," I finally said, trying to make it sound as though it wasn't going to present a big problem. He offered me a knowing smile. All three of our children knew exactly how tough things were for us financially.

At two minutes before two o'clock we found ourselves walking into the office of the Activities Director. Although I was feeling a little annoyed that the college's tennis coach hadn't responded to Kieran's two letters, I decided to stay silent, rather than say anything that could stir up trouble for Kieran.

Kieran has always been a reserved type and again he remained quiet in his chair as the Director and I exchanged small talk. I hoped Kieran was going to speak up, something we had talked about many times, but I quickly realized he was going to leave the talking to me.

"Before registering," I said to the Director, "Kieran wants to know a little about your tennis program. He's very keen to play on the team."

The Activities Director looked up with a puzzled expression on his face. "Why hasn't he contacted the tennis coach before?" he asked with a distinct surprised tone in his voice.

"But he has tried on two occasions. He sent two letters and a video."

I tried to make it sound as though the correspondence wasn't such a big deal and played the whole thing down. The last thing I wanted to do was to make the tennis coach look bad, figuring that could further jeopardize Kieran's chances of getting on the team. There are times when you just have to be politically correct, I reasoned.

"He didn't hear anything back but I'm sure the coach is real busy at this time of the year," I offered as an excuse.

The puzzled expression on the A.D.'s face turned into one of anger. "I'm sorry. Let me get this straight." Turning to Kieran he asked, "You wrote two letters and sent a video and you didn't get a reply. Is that correct?"

Kieran nodded his head slowly. "Yes sir, that's correct."

"Well, the first thing I must do is to apologize for the fact you didn't get a response. I will be honest and tell you we've been having a few problems with our tennis coach and there are going to be some changes made around here. I want you to give me thirty minutes. Please go and make yourself comfortable in the reception area. I'll be back shortly."

Kieran and I had no way of knowing where this was leading. I knew the tennis coach was going to get chewed out, and I felt uncomfortable knowing that this was not going to be in Kieran's best interest. But I also accepted the matter was now out of our hands. All we could do was wait and see what was going to transpire.

It was less than fifteen minutes later when the tall, lean figure of the Activities Director strode back into the room and walked directly up to Kieran and held out his hand. "Congratulations Kieran. We would like to offer you a full tennis scholarship to cover all your tuition, books and housing. How does that sound?"

I didn't know how Kieran was feeling on hearing this news but I could feel the tears welling up in my own eyes. A full scholarship! This was just unbelievable.

Before either of us had a chance to speak, the Director added. "And I know about the out-of-state situation. The scholarship covers these extra fees. Go back to the enrollment office. They know what to do."

We left the room wondering what had happened between the A.D. and the tennis coach. We will likely never know, but before leaving for college that fall, Kieran was notified that a new coach had been hired.

We were both on cloud nine as we left the campus. After making a quick phone call to his mother to tell her the wonderful news, Kieran jumped behind the wheel of the car. I had never seen him so happy. He was pumping the air with his fist and repeating over and over, "Is this really happening? Is this really happening?" He fired up the car and looked across at me. "Take a nap dad, you've had a busy day. I'll drive us home."

That long journey between Naples and Jacksonville, from one end of the state to the other, was one that Mo and I drove many times over the next two years. Kieran went ahead with his plans to live off campus with a small group of friends, including old school friend Shelley Dee, and within a couple of weeks he had found a job waiting tables at a small fish restaurant. For the first few weeks he was either cycling or borrowing Shelley Dee's vehicle to drive to and from work. This was an unacceptable ongoing situation. We later found out that there were many nights when Kieran finished up at the restaurant long after midnight and had to cycle the long journey home in darkness, often in pouring rain. He had never mentioned that situation to us, nor had he ever complained.

A friend of ours offered to sell him 'The Mustard Monster', the name we gave to the dirty yellow color car he bought for a few hundred dollars. Yes! Now our boy had his own wheels!

We are not sure how many miles 'The Mustard Monster' had covered because the odometer cable was just one of the many broken parts we needed to fix. The odometer registered 44,000 miles, but the condition of the vehicle suggested it was at least on its second go-around. But despite its unattractive appearance that commanded a parking spot well away from the other students' more sporty looking vehicles, the Mustard Monster served Kieran well for more than two years. It was still with him when he moved on to the University of New Orleans.

Kieran and Shelley Dee had always been part of a small close-knit group who stayed together through their entire four years at Lely High School. There were a few innocent romances within the group, but Kieran and Shelley Dee had always remained just friends.

During college, there were times when Kieran would go out on a date and Shelley Dee would be there to help him choose his shirt or pants. He was equally supportive of her and would never go to bed until she returned safely from her dates. It was a good and solid relationship.

At the end of two years, both Shelley Dee and Kieran applied to the University of New Orleans and both were awarded full tennis scholarships. It was still very much the same deal; just good friends and great traveling buddies.

Over the years, we had become close friends with Shelley Dee's parents, Sandra and Ted. It was when Kieran and Shelley Dee were in the final year at New Orleans that Sandra happened to mention during a family party. "Have you noticed Shelley Dee and Kieran these days?" Without waiting for a response, she quickly added: "I do believe there is something going on between them."

The comment sparked our curiosity and we started to observe a little more closely. Sandra was right. For the first time we picked up on the little touching that was going on between the two. We had never noticed it before, and we couldn't resist asking Kieran if there was anything going on with him and Shelley Dee. "Are you dating?" I asked one evening. There was no subtlety in my questioning technique.

Kieran dissolved into his shy mode and smiled "Maybe," he said, and left it at that.

He later told us that Shelley Dee had always been his best friend. She was there for him to climb mountains with, and as a skiing companion when they went with her family on trips back to their original home in Canada. It seems there was nothing Shelley Dee wasn't prepared to do.

Four years after they graduated college, their wedding invitation cards read. *"I'm marrying my best friend."* At the lavish wedding reception, paid for by Shelley Dee's parents, Best Man Dominic got up to toast the couple.

With more than one hundred and fifty guests ready to raise their glasses, Dominic looked across at Shelley Dee's father. Solemnly, he began to speak.

"Ted, you allowed Kieran to go on vacations with you and your family and you said, *'that's okay, they're just friends.'* You even allowed them to go off to Jacksonville together and share an apartment, and you said, *'that's okay, they're just friends.'* Then you allowed them to go to New Orleans and once again share an apartment, and you said, *'that's okay, they're just friends.'* Let me tell you Ted, those two being *just friends*, cost you twenty-five thousand dollars today!"

Chapter Eighteen

I enjoy playing soccer as much today as I did when I had aspirations of becoming a professional soccer player back when I was eighteen. Only this week I signed on to play another season in the over-35's local league. Needless to say I'm the oldest player in the area still playing league soccer.

When we arrived in Naples in 1981, soccer was just beginning to take a foothold. The local Optimist Club, a community group that ran various children programs, had started a recreational soccer league for boys and girls from ages five through thirteen. It was already in its fourth season, and each fall more and more kids signed up to play in Saturday matches at a local school field.

Word soon got out about my soccer experience and it wasn't long before I received a phone call from the president of the club, asking if I would like help out.

With the help of many dedicated volunteers, the program grew and grew. The second year after I became involved, we reached the magical number of one thousand children playing in the leagues. I was asked to help organize the training of officials, and to offer advice to the new coaches, many of which had never seen a soccer ball in their lives. These young moms and dads were called to duty only because their son or daughter's team was short of a volunteer coach.

No one at the Optimist Club was above using threats and pressure on both the dads and moms if it meant finding a much-needed coach. With more than sixty teams, it was hard to come up with enough coaches and assistant coaches. Still, we somehow managed to pull off the task season after season.

For officials we often used local high school students, selecting first the ones that played soccer at school. That was always our priority, but with so many school activities placing demands on kids, much of the officiating staff begged-off each week. Usually, by about the third week of season we were forced to add anyone to the roster who was capable of blowing a whistle.

But it was such a successful program that the shortfalls were taken in good spirit and we rarely faced any serious problems.

I am often reminded by my wife of the one time we received a phone call from one frantic female coach. It was the evening before her son's team's first practice and the head coach had to go out of town unexpectedly on business. He wouldn't be around to take charge of practice. What was she to do? The first practice was planned for the following evening and it was already 9:00 p.m.

I tried to explain a few concepts on the phone, but the woman was having difficulty comprehending. After about twenty minutes she moved from worried to desperate. "Would you mind if I stopped by your house so you can show me what you are talking about," she pleaded.

By the time she arrived we had pushed most of the furniture back against the wall and removed the more delicate glass objects. She stayed over for an hour, receiving a crash course in soccer coaching. The lessons fell into three basic areas: stopping the ball, kicking the ball and trying to avoid bumping into the sofa. The woman left happy, feeling capable she could run her first practice. We waved good-bye from the front door, relieved that no family heirlooms had been destroyed by the soccer ball.

Our newly recruited coach stayed with the program for more than five years, proving to be a big favorite with the kids.

It wasn't long before Naples soccer became so successful that we ran out of practice fields. The sport was developing at every age level. After several years with the Optimist Club program, I was asked to help setup The Naples Traveling Soccer Club, which recruited over 200 of the better players to play in competitive games and tournaments around the state. That was the group I was supposed to chaperone to Colorado during that dark period when I was stopped at St. Louis Airport and ordered to return to England.

In the three local high schools, girl's soccer was added to the agenda. Adult men's leagues also began to flourish, and we estimated we had more than two thousand Naples residents playing soccer on a regular basis.

While the high schools had fine facilities for their players, the other teams faced a serious field shortage. Our appeals to the Collier County Recreational Department met with little success. Their argument seemed to be that soccer was no different than any other sport. Everyone was facing the same problem of no practice space available. Baseball didn't have enough fields, nor did the youth football leagues. This was clearly a sad situation. Here we were, in an affluent community and in a position of getting all these young people involved in sports, and yet we were seriously lacking the facilities. We decided something needed to be done.

Along with two other members from the Optimist Club we decided it would be our mission to go and find the much needed fields. At that time the school board held land-banks for future school development, and we tracked down one site that would be ideal for a soccer complex. Unfortunately the land was targeted for a new middle school and school board administration building at a yet to be determined future date. Although the school board turned down our request, they did offer some land adjoining another middle school in the area. This parcel adjoined a small park that the Collier County Parks and Recreation Department had been given by a local developer.

Getting the two authorities to agree to a joint deal involving the two parcels of land was only the first stage. Now we had to get the county to come up with the money to build a soccer complex.

I always maintained that if you stood at the Saturday soccer games long enough you would meet the majority of Naples parents. It seemed that just about every young kid gave Optimist soccer a try for at least one season. Among those parents included government officials, school board members, judges, doctors and so on. Thus, when it was time to make our presentation to Collier County Board of Commissioners, we knew there would be some sympathetic ears. We recognized one parent and one grandfather on the dais as being regular spectators at our games.

But even with this type of support, we weren't going to take any chances. The County Commissioners meeting just happened to fall on a teacher's planning day, and all the children had a day off from school. With the local newspaper, radio and television stations alerted, we arrived at the courthouse steps with more than fifty parents and one hundred children, all dressed smartly in their soccer uniforms.

Although we had to wait our turn on the agenda, which meant the parents and children sat and patiently waited for nearly four hours, it proved an easy battle to win. The only real concern of the commissioners was whether the proposed fields would be used enough to justify the costs. We had brought along graphs and a slide presentation to indicate just how heavily they would be utilized, and the eventual final vote gave approval five to zero.

As one commissioner quietly told me later. "You have to pick your battles carefully. I have learned not to fight issues involving kids and pets!"

When the fall soccer season rolled around, we had a beautiful, $300,000, six-field soccer complex with changing rooms and concession stand. Floodlighting was added two years later to help accommodate the growing number of teams that wanted to practice.

Continuing on the sport's theme, Disney world was always an exciting place for us to visit when our finances permitted. It was during an early trip to the theme park that planted the seed in my mind for a new business venture.

Even way back in the early 1980's it wasn't difficult to envision Naples developing into a prime vacation spot. With its rich blue skies and beautiful golden sandy beaches it was attracting more and more visitors and year-round residents. The flood gates had been opened.

Part of the Naples attraction has always been its laid-back atmosphere. Still, I wondered, what might become of the area if an appealing and exciting attraction was added to the pot. If Naples lacked anything, it was activities geared towards the younger families visiting the area. There seemed to be an opening for something classy that would fit into the Naples lifestyle, something that people of all ages could enjoy. To me, a sporting complex of Disney-size proportions seemed the perfect answer.

With our involvement with the spa at the time, we felt we were in touch with the growing trend among adults to keep fit. Women were buying up the Jane Fonda workout tapes, new health magazines were appearing on the newsstands every day, and health food stores were springing up all over the place.

I could see a demand for a sports complex. The first stage could be a water theme park of the type that had already become popular in Florida. The next stage would add a hotel offering a wide range of sporting facilities and coaching for teams and individuals. There would be meeting rooms for sporting groups, maybe even facilities in which Olympic teams could train. The complex would be suitable for people of all ages. Apartments and villas could be added later as the complex continued to grow.

It took me a little over six months to write my own business plan, researching both the vacation and sports industries. By the time I finished, the plan was more than sixty pages thick. Over the next year I mailed a copy to almost 100 different companies. Sadly, a package sent to Disney came back unopened, with a letter from the legal department explaining that they simply didn't look at unsolicited ideas. On a brighter note, a phone call back from the promotions department at McDonalds said they were extremely interested in the project and would be considering it further at a future meeting.

The developer of the newly constructed The Ritz Carlton hotel in Naples (who used to buy his shrimp for fishing from Dominic when he was working at the marina) was handed a copy of the business plan. He responded by saying that while he liked the project, he believed it could become competition for his hotel.

Over a period of nearly two years I met with local developers, the Collier County Economic Development Council and various tourist associations. Each new contact led me to two or three others. I had Realtors checking with investors, stockbrokers running it by clients and for a time there appeared to be a lot of genuine interest. It had become a jigsaw puzzle that just needed to be pieced together.

Unfortunately each piece was dependent on another piece and it just never worked out. The business plan still sits in my bottom desk drawer, the corners of the file now a little dog-eared. Each summer I go with my soccer team to play in a national tournament at Disney's Wide World of Sports complex, consisting of a baseball stadium, soccer and football fields, indoor basketball and volleyball courts, cafes and restaurants. I come away thinking to myself, that's what I had in mind twenty years ago!

Chapter Nineteen

Apart from the cardiologist telling Mo she needed to reduce the stress level in her life, he also warned her there was a strong possibility she could require a second angioplasty sometime down the road. One way or another, we had to get her full healthcare coverage, and quickly. But it wouldn't be easy. Due to her now pre-existing condition, this situation presented us with an extremely difficult challenge.

We had been putting off the inevitable all the time I was working on a plastics project that I will tell you about later. At the time I believed this was the business venture that would provide the solution to many of our needs. But it had lost its way and we had reached a stage of believing it probably wasn't going to happen. While we may have been undecided over what to do regarding certain aspects of our lives, the area of health care coverage was definitely not one of them. Health problems staring you in the face have a way of sharpening one's perspective to crystal clarity.

I had moved out of insurance business and into hearing-aid sales, but the move there certainly hadn't provided a solution either. The job offered no benefits and no where near enough in commission payments to cover expensive insurance once we had lost many of the testing outlets. The time had arrived for me to find a new employer, one that could provide that all important health coverage for me and my family. An important decision was made. I was off to join The Ritz Carlton hotel.

I had hoped that my soccer buddy, Paul, who ran the hotel's transportation, could pull some strings on my behalf but he said quite simply that he couldn't. I would have to stop by the employment offices in Human Resources and fill out an application in person. Apparently, the hotel follows very strict hiring guidelines over employing and training its staff. No problem, I thought, making sure I was at the hotel bright and early the next morning.

After going through the process of filling out and submitting my application, I began making my way towards the door, figuring that was it for now and I would be contacted sometime later about setting up a proper interview. But before reaching the exit, the attractive young lady seated at the reception desk, called over and asked if I could spare a few minutes for a short interview now.

I smiled back with 'of course', thinking to myself this was great. Get it over and done with as soon as possible. I certainly felt no pressure and was fully relaxed as we moved into the small conference room to sit in chairs facing each other, on either side of a small desk. The young lady, offering a warm smile, introduced herself as Kendal. We got straight down to business. Confidently I answered a dozen or so of the questions she was reading from a printed sheet. I could see her scribbling down my responses in the blank space next to each question. There was nothing on her face to indicate what she was thinking. After I answered what I could see was the last question on the back page, she placed the cap back on her pen, stood up and reached across to shake my hand, indicating the short interview was over. I was feeling very positive as I stepped outside, totally convinced I would soon be hearing I had been offered a chauffeur position.

But a week passed and I received no contact from the hotel. I waited a few more days before phoning Paul. "I'm a little surprised I didn't hear anything about the job yet," I confided.

"It usually takes a couple of weeks," Paul replied, giving no hint I should be concerned. "Let me call down to the employment office and see what I can find out. Maybe you didn't fit the profile!" I could sense the chuckle in his voice.

"No need to do that," I said. "I'll call them myself."

When I got back with Kendal I immediately detected a definite detached coolness in her voice as I identified myself. Quickly, she explained that there was a letter in the mail to me. "You should receive it by tomorrow," she offered.

"Can you tell me now what it says?" I asked, never imagining I could possibly be turned down for a driving position.

There was an embarrassing silence.

"It thanks you for coming for the interview, but we don't feel we have a position available which is commensurate with your experience and interest..." I got the impression she was reading from a script.

I don't know if I was hurt or offended, or both. This was my first real job interview since my days applying for journalist work, a lifetime ago, and I was being turned down. I couldn't recall a time when my pride was so badly shaken.

That evening, as I casually mentioned the situation to Mo, I tried to shake it off as an unimportant issue. But Mo knew better. She tried to make a joke of it by suggesting I was too old, which really didn't make me feel any better at all. Yes, my pride was wounded, but I also knew I was a good candidate for the job. That evening I drafted a letter, which was in the mailbox first thing the next morning.

The letter was addressed to Melanie Smith in the Human Resources Department of The Ritz Carlton. It read:

Dear Ms. Smith,

I can't recall now the exact words your office used when it rejected my request for driving employment. It said something to the effect that you didn't have a position available which matched my experience and interest. At another time I would accept this as a polite brush-off and continue on my merry way. After all, you should be permitted to employ whomever you like.

But, over the past couple of days, since receiving the rejection letter, I have felt increasingly uncomfortable about the matter, Firstly, because of some inconsistencies in the stated reason for the decision. More important though, is this. If I was rejected because I didn't fit the company hiring profile, which I suspect to be the real reason, then I would certainly like to be told what that criteria entails. With that knowledge, I may be able to remedy the situation for my next job interview.

Now, all this may sound a little silly coming from a 54 year-old man who has enjoyed some success in the business field, currently holds several professional licenses and has successfully steered three children through college. Perhaps my wife says it right when she suggests I'm hurt because my ego has been bruised and I should move on. But you know how stubborn we men can be!

It was by sheer coincidence that I called your office the same day your rejection letter was being mailed. I was told on the phone, by one of your staff, that you were pursuing more suitable candidates for the position. I mention this only because this statement confirms that a driving position was available, but it just wasn't going to be given to me. Those working in your transportation department also confirmed there still is a driving job vacancy.

So do I qualify as an experienced driver? Well, I've driven for 36 years. I have never had points on my record and I have "safe driver" stamped on my CDL Class C Florida license.

So now the confusing part. Why didn't my profile fit? I truly am aware of my weaknesses as well as my strengths, and personally knowing some of the drivers your company has employed, I really can't see why I wouldn't be considered appropriate for the position. I am intelligent, clean, articulate, honest, professional, respectful and well-mannered. I could even provide you with character references from more than twenty local dignitaries - including one mayor, two judges, two county board commissioners, two school board members, three school principals, a former County Manager and the Sheriff's Department. I have been asked to serve on a variety of local community and school committees.

I can't think of anything I may have said or not said at my brief interview to damage my application. I have an English accent, which I can't imagine to be a bad thing in the hospitality business. I also have an awareness of what guests require when they visit a hotel like the The Ritz Carlton. Maybe, just maybe, you view me as being over-qualified. But really, I'm not.

I come to you today harboring no malice towards your department or the hotel - just seeking a little information. Maybe you've read enough here to feel I'm worthy of another interview. If I was head of a department like you, I would certainly want to know that my staff was doing a good job, especially if someone had gone to this much trouble to point out there may have been some type of oversight. Next time, I promise not to show up wearing the clown's outfit with the big floppy shoes and red ball on my nose.

There, I feel better already,
Respectfully,
John Freshwater

I can only assume that I received the phone call within minutes of my letter arriving on Ms. Smith's desk. Without explanation she simply asked me when I could come for my second interview. There was no mention of my letter, nor any reference to my earlier interview.

That same afternoon I was back at the hotel, sitting down in front of a different woman who was asking new questions from a different printed folder. In between questions, I noticed she was looking over my letter placed on the top of my thin file. I sensed this was the first time she had read it, and it was amusing to see her various facial expressions as she glanced over my words. A couple of times she raised her eyebrows. Once or twice her mouth even broke into a wide smile. At the very end she burst out laughing and her entire body rocked forward on the chair.

The interview lasted about forty-five minutes.

"How did I do?" I asked.

"Oh, you did just fine," she said, "But I do have one final question. *Did you really show up in a clown's uniform for your first interview?*"

Two weeks later I was employed as a chauffeur, not as a clown, and three months later Mo and I had full medical benefits. It proved to be a smart move. Less than a year later Mo took me up on that offer, my joking about being able to have as many angioplasties as she liked once we had medical coverage. She was back in the hospital having her second.

Mo was happiest when teaching but to be able to pursue it full time she knew she would have to go back to college and obtain a degree. It was an essential part of qualifying for a Florida Teaching Certification.

Although she had taught in England for six years, Mo didn't need to take a degree course in college, opting instead to attend a teacher's training college. Now she was left with no alternative but to complete the more stringent criteria for Florida. If she wanted to become a full-time teacher she had to have a bachelor's degree.

She visited with the local colleges and received conflicting and confusing advice. No one fully understood exactly what path she was required to follow.

Whatever way Mo ultimately chose, it was going to be both lengthy and expensive. Firstly, she was told, she would be required to round up all her prior qualifications and mail them to the World Education Center in New York. There, her education background would be evaluated - for a $400 fee – and she would learn what further credits were necessary.

She sent off the material and we waited three months for the assessment to come back. With that information in her hand, she went to meet with the admissions staff at the newly opened Gulf Coast University.

"From the way I see it, all you need is a degree in something, maybe even basket-weaving," the young Admissions Director advised her with a smile. "If I was you I would find out which degree you could finish in the shortest time, with the credits they have already given you."

Having no interest in basket weaving, Mo chose Business Administration. She learned she could take the course at nearby International College over three semesters, which would mean she could graduate in little over a year. The one big downside was the cost of tuition and books. Although costing less than any other college we contacted, it would still be setting us back almost $10,000.

We didn't hesitate in making our decision. We would apply for student loans to cover the expenses. This was something Mo wanted to do and now it was my turn to offer full support.

But getting into college wasn't going to be that straightforward. She would first have to provide more paperwork. Bureaucracy being what it is, this paperwork included going back in history to prove she had graduated high school, more than thirty-five years ago! And then she would have to take her college entry SAT exams. I could see she was thinking that at fifty-two years of age, was it really worth it.

But with the family's encouragement she pushed ahead, even though proving she had graduated high school in England proved to be a major challenge. The education system in the Greater London area had been revamped over the years, and the old records had been moved out of the city and filed in different parts of the country. Our search took us to an obscure little town in the north of England. The warehouse there supposedly held all school records for the area we were searching, dating back to who knows when. But it still took many expensive phone calls and several letters to track down the required proof. Finally, she had the evidence in her hands and she could prove without a shadow of doubt that she, Maureen Vanessa Braddle, had in fact, graduated Roseberry Grammar School For Girls in Epsom, Surrey in 1964.

But this was only part of the solution. Mo still had to successfully complete her SAT exam. She quickly discovered that much of the material was completely new to her. "I feel like I'm reading a foreign language," she confessed one evening as she ploughed laboriously through the study books.

Long ago I learned not to underestimate Mo's abilities. Not unexpectedly to me, her exam results came out higher than those of our three children, which elicited a lot of light-hearted ribbing at the next family get-together.

With Mo working and studying and me now in full-time employment, our lives embarked on a new phase. With one son already graduated from college, the other in his junior year and Kirsty in her senior year of high school, life took on a quality more pleasant than we had experienced for many years. Yes, the nagging credit card debts remained - we still found them impossible to pay down - but the reduced stress factor the doctor ordered was slowly becoming evident in our day-to-day lives.

Again it seemed a safety rope had hauled us back up our mountain. It was time to lift our heads again and appreciate the view.

Mo's graduation ceremony was held at the luxurious Naples Philharmonic where, dressed in her black graduation cap and gown, she glided happily across the stage to accept her diploma. And why shouldn't she have a bunch of celebration balloons thrust in her hands for the pictures afterwards? What does age, and the fact she was the oldest one graduating that day, have anything to do with it!

The principal at the school where she was subbing had made Mo a standing full-time job offer, one she was eager to accept as soon as she received her Florida Teaching Certificate. She wasted no time mailing off her application package to the state educational offices in Tallahassee. Everything now seemed set. She had the long-term subbing job until the end of the school year. After that, there was no doubt in her mind she would take over her own fourth-grade classroom.

There was no way we could have predicted the contents of the letter she was to receive a few weeks later. We had both arrived at the house together and Mo collected the mail from the mailbox. She was so excited as she grabbed the envelope displaying the return address of the Florida Department of Education. Here was the certificate she had worked so hard to get. She tore open the letter as I was sifting through a familiar stack of bills and junk mail. The first time I realized something was wrong was when I heard her muttering, "Oh no!"

I looked across to see her eyes welling up with tears. I noticed both hands were grasping the letter so tightly that her knuckles had become white. Her moist eyes were racing over the contents of the letter again. Finally, her arms dropped to her side and a gasping noise broke the silence.

"They say I still don't qualify. I still have zillions of courses to take before they will give me my teaching certification." She was speaking in a voice that was flat and without emotion. She was shaking her head in disbelief. I could see her whole body becoming limp as she collapsed into the chair beside her.

In silence, I walked over and pried the letter from her grasp. I read it through once, and then again to be sure I was reading it correctly. Sure enough, the state was saying it required Mo to take more educational classes. Our climb to the top of the mountain had quickly been halted!

It was obvious the anger and frustration Mo was feeling as she tried to get answers during the next few days. She called the university that had given her the original information that all she needed was a degree to satisfy the education requirements. They were puzzled and sympathetic, but couldn't offer any advice. All they could provide were condolences. "We are just as surprised as you," was their feeble response.

While her school principal showed considerable sympathy, as well as disappointment at the fact that he was not going to get the full time teacher he wanted, he admitted there was nothing he could do. The matter was out of his control. He did offer to write a letter on Mo's behalf but regretfully explained that the offer of a full-time teaching position would have to be shelved.

From the highs of just a few weeks ago, we had suddenly crashed to the lowest of the lows. For the next couple of days Mo walked around the house like a zombie, not knowing the next step to take. I desperately wanted to help, but other than writing a letter to the Department of Education myself, there was nothing I could do. This was surely bureaucracy gone mad.

We were back in our swirling sea, being pulled down, it seemed, into the troughs.

It took Mo a couple of weeks before she felt like discussing the situation. Come the end of the school year she would again be out of a job. It would always be like this, unless she acquired her teaching certification. She couldn't give in now. She had put in too much time and energy to get this far. We agreed we would somehow find a way.

That evening she was back on the computer trying to gather more information on the required courses she still had to take, as set out in the letter. At first glance, it looked like those requirements would take at least another year, and whole lot more money.

The 2000 school year was coming to an end and on this particular day Mo was taking her class out on a field trip. Back at the school, the principal was meeting with a member of Governor Jeb Bush's educational task force, which was traveling around the state gathering up data. The head of the task force was visiting various schools in the Naples area, hoping to hear ideas from local educators on how to improve the state's educational program.

"If you could have five minutes with Jeb Bush, what would you be asking him?" the woman posed to Mo's principal. After a long pause the principal replied.

"Why can't we sort out this mess with one of our teachers? She's one of the best you will find and she's being given the run-around by the Department of Education."

Clearly not expecting this type of response – more likely waiting to hear a request for new equipment or a change in teaching policies - the smartly dressed lady took a step back in surprise.

"Tell me what this is all about," she said. "You obviously feel very strongly about this matter."

No one mentioned this meeting to Mo when she returned to school that afternoon. Thus, she was surprised to hear the message on our answering machine when she arrived home around five.

The voice on the machine was the woman from the task force. Her message explained in detail what had been discussed with her principal that afternoon. "...obviously your principal thinks you are a great asset. If you can get all your paperwork to my hotel before I leave at 6:30 this evening I will take up the matter in Tallahassee," she said. "I'll see what I can do for you."

Thinking that these were probably no more than sympathetic words from a politician, Mo decided she had nothing to lose by gathering up all the material and dropping it off at the hotel. It was only a few minutes before the deadline but the woman was still in a meeting when Mo inquired at the reception desk. She never got the opportunity to meet with the educator but left the thick manila envelope, containing transcripts and a copy of her degree, for her collection.

We had both forgotten about the matter, until Mo was called into the principal's office just a few days later. "I have some wonderful news for you Mo," he blurted out. "I have just received a phone call from Tallahassee to say you are exempt from having to take any more classes. You are a certified teacher as of July 1st. I would now like to formally offer you the position of fourth grade teacher for the next school year!"

In just a few days Mo had gone from the lowest of the lows to the highest of the highs. It was just the tonic she needed in her life.

We learned later that the state was planning to introduce legislation aimed at helping teachers just like Mo. If they could prove they had sufficient previous experience, coupled with the necessary college degree, they would be exempt from having to acquire all the educational qualifications. This new legislation would be effective as from July 1st, and Mo would be one of the very first teachers to take advantage of the new ruling.

Chapter Twenty

Not many people get an opportunity to hug the world's best-known soccer player, but I got that rather unique opportunity after chauffeuring the great Pele around Naples for four days.

Just about everyone in The Ritz Carlton transportation department where I had been working for the past three years had become aware of my passion of soccer, especially the office manager and his chief dispatcher, two younger guys who I had played soccer with over the years. One of them, Paul, was the one who suggested I applied to the hotel for a job.

I guess the 'days wanted off' calendar hanging on the wall of the dispatcher's office also provided ample evidence of my love for the game. My weekly initials alongside 'soccer training' or regular requests for a weekend off to play in a soccer tournament told the story. Paul, and his dispatcher, Ray Fowler, must have decided as soon as the reservation came through that the Pele pick-up from Miami Airport was an assignment right up my street.

The arrangement was that I would leave Naples around 2:00 am and drive the brand new, luxurious, dark-blue limo over to a hotel in Miami to pick up one of Pele's business agents, along with his assigned bodyguard who just happened to be English. We would then continue down to Miami Airport to meet the 'red eye' from Rio with Pele and his small entourage on board. The legendary Pele was coming to Naples to do some promotional work on behalf of Pfizer Pharmaceuticals and their product Viagra!

Although it was still very early when we arrived at a deserted Miami Airport, I assumed there would still be the usual police traffic squad hanging around waiting to pounce and to hand out tickets for unlawful parking. Even though I was about to pick up a celebrity, it really didn't change anything. Experience had taught me that unless you are actually loading passengers, celebrities or not, the airport vultures have no hesitation in pulling out their booking pads and immediately start writing a ticket, no explanation accepted. I had witnessed it happening a score of times. And for us drivers, most times settling a ticket was down to us, so I wasn't planning on taking any chances.

I explained this situation to my two passengers on the way down to the airport and we agreed I would drop them at the entrance to the custom hall and go off and wait in the limo holding area the thirty minutes or so before the scheduled arrival time. One of them would call me when they had made contact with the group and I would drive up to meet them.

It was a clear but humid and muggy morning outside as I sat parked on the empty lot. I knew from being there before that later in the day, this same area would be overflowing with gleaming black and white stretch limos. The big temperature clock across the way was already showing seventy-five degrees even at this early hour so I felt fortunate I was sitting in the comfort of the air-conditioned car. The sky to the east was just beginning to waken as the heavy nighttime blackness began turning to pale yellow, heralding the beginning of another sunny south Florida day. The radio was softly playing a familiar golden oldie. I turned up the volume and smiled to myself as I realized I knew just about all the words. I looked over at the paperback lying on the soft leather, front passenger seat and I thought for a second about easing back in my own seat to read the last few remaining unread pages. As I stretched across, my eye caught sight of the small luminous clock on the front panel and I quickly decided there wasn't enough time to get into the book just now. I could enjoy that later. Instead, I loosened my tie, relaxed and watched the sunrise as I caste my mind back to some of the exciting Pele action I had seen on television over the years. It gave me quite a buzz to think that in a few minutes I was going to meet the man who had become nothing less than a soccer icon.

As the minutes slipped by I began to feel a tiredness sweeping over me. My eyelids were beginning to feel very heavy. I had time for just four hours sleep before the alarm woke me in the middle of the night. For a moment I was tempted to push the seat all the way back, stretch out and close my eyes but I knew this could prove to be a costly mistake. It would be a disaster if I slept and didn't hear my cell phone ring. I tried the old tired driving trick of licking my fingers and wetting my eyelids as I pushed the button to ease down the car window, hoping to enjoy some refreshing cool air. I stuck my head outside, only to be met by a warm wave of high humidity. I quickly decided it would be more beneficial to crank up the air to keep the car cool and me awake.

Even with our pre-set plan, I was becoming increasingly nervous as each minute ticked by. What happens if the agent can't get a cell phone signal inside the terminal? I begin to toss around different possibilities in my mind. Here I am, sitting almost half a mile from the terminal building and out of sight while the agent with her VIP is standing at curbside desperately trying to get hold of me. I check again to see if my cell phone is charged.   My nervousness builds to anxiety as the bright green digital numbers on the limo clock change again, and again. It is now almost twenty minutes since the plane was supposed to touch down. I call the airline to check if there has been any change to the ETA. The recorded information is still the same as it had been the last two or three times I called. I also check my phone to see if there had been any missed calls while I was getting the flight information. I accept I'm getting a little paranoid. A minute later I decide I've had enough of waiting here in the darkness, it's time to move out.

Hey, I'm driving a stretch limo here and I'm picking up one of the greatest sporting legends of all time, I say to myself. There has to be a different set of airport rules to cover this scenario, but really, who am I kidding. I know otherwise.

I edge up to the curb outside the custom hall. It is still relatively dark here amidst this mass of concrete support pillars and low ceiling but the airport lighting is reflecting brightly on the highly-waxed vehicle making it stand out like a showroom model. I figure I will have no problem seeing my group when they come through the doors even though I'm still about twenty yards away, the closest I can get to the automatic glass doors. A few airport workers are milling around aimlessly. I feel lucky. There is no sign of any cops to make me move along at best, or hand me a ticket at worst. This unusual quietness at such a large airport creates an almost unreal and eerie feeling. Any other time I've been here the place is sheer pandemonium.

Nervously I start tapping the central armrest and begin to wonder how long will it be before I am spotted and reprimanded like some school kid for doing something he knows to be wrong? I will the phone to ring. But instead of the call coming I become aware of something else coming my way. In the side mirror I can see the clear outline of a cop in a dark, it looks like brown, uniform moving out of the shadows and heading in my direction. With his hand already reaching into his back pocket, he walks with a slow but deliberate gait towards the back of the vehicle. No time to panic. Instead, I decide to take the initiative. Instinctively I open my door and jump out and before the cop can say his piece, I blurt out what I hope comes across as a friendly and courteous greeting......'*You play soccer, sir*?"

The Hispanic-looking cop stops in his stride. He stands motionless, except for squinting his eyes as if trying to fully comprehend what I am saying. After a long pause he answers my question with his own question. "Soccer! What do you mean, do I play soccer?" he growls in a heavy accent.

"Just wondering...cus' I'm picking up Pele.... and he will be coming out of those doors in just a couple of minutes." I mouth the word P.E.L.E very deliberately as though I'm speaking to a deaf person. I want to make sure he picks up on the name.

"*Pele*" he screams. I could see his whole body puff up. "*You mean the one and only Pele is coming here?*" I'm excited. I realize immediately that I have hit the jackpot, or more precisely, the weak spot of this Miami cop.

"*You, you wait there,*" he stammers. "*Get back in your limo and don't you move...Let me go and get some help.*"

I also realize this stroke of good fortune is never ever going to be repeated in this location again. No one gets an opportunity to wait curbside at Miami Airport, not even someone driving a limo.

Two more cops have now joined my new friend. One is positioned at the front of the vehicle and the other at the back. I'm not quite sure why they are feeling it necessary to guard my limo but that is not for me to worry about. Brazenly I bring my feet up onto the dashboard, clasp my hands behind my head and think mischievously to myself, let me savor the moment.

I wish it had been longer but after less than ten minutes the sound of an incoming call breaks the silence. The agent's voice is breaking up but I pick up enough words to comprehend that the group is moving through the terminal. I jump up and move around to the curbside to be in a position to greet my guests and to open the door. A little nervously I run my hands over the lapels on my jacket, straighten my tie and brush back the hair over my ears to ensure I look the part.

"They're here," I say to my three buddies who have now straightened their stance and appear almost comical as they try standing to attention, waiting for the moment for the double glass terminal doors to open.

Despite his larger than life image on the TV screen where he appears to have always out-jumped and out-run anyone on the soccer field, Pele is only about five feet, eight inches tall, so at first I couldn't see him. The group jostling around him has swelled to about twenty people and he is completely hidden from view. The first time I notice him is when he is only a few feet from the limo and becomes separated from the main group. Three or four people jump into the vehicle and, as Pele turns to wave farewell to his excited followers, I grab the opportunity to ask the favor I had been considering for the past few minutes.

As quickly as I am able to, I ask Pele if he would mind signing autographs for my three special friends, explaining that they had been a great help in taking care of me. That warm Pele smile, the one I had seen a hundred times in interviews, spreads across his face......."*Of course I will......where are they?*"

Enjoying this temporary power that has suddenly been bestowed upon me I summon the three cops. I gesture with a scribble motion in the palm of my hand and beckon them with my finger to step forward. They immediately get my message, moving in close and pulling note pads from their jacket pockets. Eagerly they begin patting Pele on the back and shoulders like some long-time buddies as he cheerfully signs his name and message in their pocket books. He doesn't seem to mind. I guess he is used to this sort of adulation from his fans around the world. Moments later we are pulling away from the curb and I can't help but smile as I think about all the other times I had been confronted by the airport cops. I have to wonder if these three will remember me the next time I come to the airport.

Later that afternoon, after catching up on a couple of hours sleep, I receive a call from the office saying that Pele's agent has asked if I would be their chauffeur during their four day stay at the hotel. I felt quite honored, even if the work only means just driving them to local restaurants. The first evening, as I'm standing to one side of the large lobby doors waiting for my guests, I'm thinking it a little strange to see Pele appear with a soccer ball tucked under his arm. He doesn't say a word. He just flashes one of his brilliant smiles and throws me the ball. I quickly read the black handwriting. *"Good Luck John. Pele"*

It didn't take long for the word to get around in the Naples soccer circles that I was driving Pele around town. Everyone was hoping that I would bring him out to our Wednesday evening practice. Actually I did invite him but he said he couldn't as he had a promotional dinner at the hotel. *"You go...and score a couple of goals for me"* he joked. I was amazed the next day when he asked me if I had scored those couple of goals. I felt a little guilty when I lied that I had. Although he appeared to enjoy going out for lengthy lunches and late night dinners he was still the fittest looking 63 year old I had ever met.

On the third evening I was waiting for his group to take them to yet another restaurant in the downtown area. The agent had called to apologize for running late, but they were now on their way down to the hotel lobby. It was already past 10 pm and I knew the restaurant would soon be closing. I realized this could become an embarrassing situation if we arrived at the restaurant to find the kitchen closed. After all, this is small town Naples and certainly not a sophisticated city where restaurants stay open very late. I decided to phone the restaurant to explain the situation before my guests came out.

The female voice on the phone listened to my concerns and asked me to wait a moment while she tried to find her boss. A moment later I was explaining to a charming owner that we were on our way, but wouldn't be at the restaurant for another thirty minutes.

"Not to worry" said the friendly voice. "For the great Pele my restaurant stays open all night!"

My two soccer-playing colleagues back at the office couldn't hide their envy when I proudly showed them my autographed soccer ball. I should have guessed the requests that were going to follow. Could I get them autographed balls too? Then Mo asked if I could get some signed pictures of Pele that she could use as rewards at school. I wasn't sure how many nine year-olds would know the Pele name, but that didn't seem to matter.

When the time came to take Pele to the airport for his departure, I still didn't quite know how I was going to get the autographs. For the journey to Ft. Myers Airport there was only going to be Pele, his agent and the bodyguard in the limo. This time the trio was flying over to Miami where Pele alone would be catching a connecting flight back to Brazil.

We had become quite chatty over the four days but I still felt awkward about asking him to do my autograph session. To ask a guest of The Ritz Carlton hotel for their autograph was a big no-no. I had heard that staff had been fired for breaking this hotel policy. Hey, I wasn't going to let that little obstacle stop me, I decided. This was an occasion to throw caution to the wind. I figured Pele could only say no. And how was the hotel going to find out anyway.

Inside the limo I had already placed two soccer balls on the back seat. Close at hand I had half a dozen small sheets of paper we would use if he agreed to sign some autographs for Mo's school kids.

I knew I had to make my request before the soccer star climbed into the vehicle and came face to face with the two balls. Trying to explain why they were there as I was driving wouldn't be easy. It's like being a full-size soccer field away when you are driving a stretch limo and your guests are seated in the back. I was very conscious of the possibility of Pele thinking I was being presumptuous and taking advantage of his friendly manner.

I need not have worried. As we walked away from the main hotel doors towards the limo I quickly made my request. The seemingly always cordial and friendly Pele gave another of those warm smiles and said simply "Of course I will...no problem." Better still, instead of signing his name on plain pieces of paper he asked his agent for some of his promotional pictures she was carrying in her briefcase. On the journey to the airport I could see him in my rearview mirror sitting back smiling and writing personal greetings on both the soccer balls and a dozen or so photographs.

When we arrived at Ft. Myers Airport there was security staff to greet the limo as arranged by the hotel. In the few seconds it took for the car door to open and Pele to climb out, a group of inquisitive travelers had quickly gathered to see who was the celebrity being greeted by a couple of uniformed cops. It soon became obvious that even here in southwest Florida people instantly recognize Pele, even though I would bet, few of the excited onlookers had ever watched a game of soccer. As I stood there holding the door and without warning, Pele threw his arms around me and held me in a bear hug for several seconds..."Thanks," he said warmly. "Hope we will meet again."

Being the new 'hot shot' soccer player when I first arrived in town - well, maybe I'm exaggerating a little here and more likely the buzz was simply based on the fact that someone had arrived who appeared to know ALL the rules - I was quickly invited to referee an adult soccer match.

Now despite playing the game most of my life, I had never actually refereed a proper match and, to be honest, I had never wanted to. It always seemed such a thankless task. You know, twenty-two players kicking the hell out of one another and you are the one singular, all-uniting enemy on the field. You step in to help and get yelled at by both camps. Nah, that's not my idea of fun; I'd rather kick the ball and the opposing players for 90 minutes - and let off some steam by shouting at an incompetent idiot of an official. But, our new life brought a new attitude. Why not be a ref? It might be a good way to make new friends and stay fit. Never know, I might even be good at it. Also, the man who asked me to referee the match said that two experienced linesmen would be there to help, so how difficult could it be?

Buoyed up with my newly-formed positive attitude over officiating a game, I turned up early this Sunday afternoon to find an expansive, open-playing area with a neatly marked out pitch. I was keenly dressed in my recently purchased all-black referee's outfit. Yes, I was taking it *that* seriously. If I was to referee my first match, I thought, then I would give it my best; with integrity, impartiality, authority, and certainly looking the part. I was the first one there and, as I waited, I began to feel a strange feeling stirring in my gut, which I immediately recognized as an attack of very bad nerves. This is stupid, John, I said to myself, you'll be fine. If anything is disputed, the two linesmen will be there for back-up, just relax. But I didn't feel any better. Not only did I feel uncomfortable, but I started sweating profusely. Was it being caused by just the temperature which I guessed was soaring way up into the mid-90s. Alone, and standing in the middle of the field, I felt like a lone ant caught under a sadistic schoolboy's magnifying glass.

For no other reason than wishful thinking, I was expecting two teams of middle-aged American guys in patchwork uniforms to arrive who were out for a happy-go-lucky kick-about and maybe a few pointers from me on the etiquette of the game my old country had brought to the world. Instead, I got two teams of snarling, mutually loathing Mexicans in their teens and twenties who had spent the week probably working for a disgusting pittance in the orange groves and tomato fields of south Florida. I greeted the first few guys cheerily, but there was clearly little time for pleasantries. Well, their English was limited in the extreme and my Mexican didn't go beyond a drunken *Ariba* after a shot or two of Tequila. Besides, they weren't exactly friendly or up for chitchat. I began to fear the worst when both teams began changing separately at the furthest two points of the touchlines, without so much as a wave of 'Hola' to one another. They slipped into immaculate kits; one was radioactive green, the other was chemical yellow and I discovered later that the words emblazoned on the shirts were the names of their fiercely opposing native areas of Mexico. Polished boots came out, shin pads were strapped on and oil was rubbed into rock solid legs.

I stood in the center circle watching all this unfold, my stomach turning over, slowly melting, and looking anxiously around for my two linesmen. I was hoping that either one of them was bi-lingual in today's second language, or at least had some experience in cross-Mexican diplomacy training. My heart sank and I sucked in some hair-dryer air through gritted teeth when I saw two men skipping merrily towards me across an otherwise empty sports area. Either they were my co-officials, or they were two lovers hopelessly lost after an all-night session at the local gay bar. The older looking of the two was wearing the skimpiest black running shorts imaginable, yanked up painfully high – dressing to the left if I remember correctly - and a black skin-tight running vest; pristine knee length white socks finished off the outfit. At least he was in black. The other was about 19, funeral-parlor white, and had decided to express himself today. He was wearing a neatly-ironed, red polo shirt, flawlessly tucked into gray and white striped shorts and barely visible ankle socks.

Maybe he was the more feminine side of this odd couple. We said our hellos and I decided to quickly get the game going before either these two have a row, or I pass out. With one big, brave blast of my whistle I called the captains in for the coin toss to decide who kicks off. There was plenty of chest crossing, a cursory half smile from the captains to me, and then we were off.

It was obvious from the start that this was a grudge match and no place for the meek. Tackles flew in high and hard and the players slid in with abandon despite the ground being baked rock hard and barely covered with a thin topping of grass as tough as an old garden brush. I was quick to the whistle; got to get a grip of this game by the scruff of the neck right away, I thought. Show who's boss. My first few decisions brought chaos. Shouting, swearing, sneering, finger pointing, I got it all. I would probably have been offended if I could understand a word of what they were saying. Then they got on with the free-kick and the frantic, bone-crunching pace continued. The first real problem arose when I suddenly heard the blast of a whistle; the game stopped, the players looked at me menacingly, but my whistle was no-where near my mouth. I heard the noise again and then I saw the older linesman waving a flag and blowing for all he was worth on a shiny whistle. I stared at him in disbelief, then trotted over. I expected to have confrontations with anyone of the twenty-two emotional Mexicans but I never thought for a second that the first would come from my co-official. He was adamant that he had studied the offside rule and that multi-whistling was essential to controlling the game from the side lines, just like in basketball and American football. Of course he was completely wrong. Anyone who has played the game knows that only the center referee carries a whistle. A "yes, yes", "but, but" conversation ensued until he finally agreed, with a bit of a sulk, to put the whistle back in his pocket.

Virtually every decision I made in that first half was contested fiercely but it was remarkable how I coped and the protestations bounced off me harmlessly. In fact, with my arm raised and a whistle in my mouth, I was suddenly decisive, resolute and fair minded... the epitome of an English referee. To my amazement I had magically become one of those officious bastards in black that I had always shouted at as a younger player. And it felt great. I was even amused when amidst all the hollowing and shouting that greeted every call I asked one player who I had determined could speak English, what his goalie was shouting at me. "Not good", he said. "Something bad about your mother!"

"And what are the others saying?" I asked. "They are all agreeing with him!"

I fought off chronic dehydration and ran around like a demon to keep up with play. I admit that I looked on nervously when things got messy in the penalty area, but thankfully I did not have to make any game-changing decisions. By the second half, both teams had calmed down and followed my decisions like lambs. Either that was down to my impressive control skills, or the sheer exhaustion in that heat. The game ended in an agreeable 2-2 tie and there was much backslapping, hugging and genuine camaraderie between the opposing players.

They were particularly appreciative towards me and that was the first of many games I refereed for both teams. In fact, the only people rowing at the end were the two linesmen, who stormed off about fifty yards apart. Quite what their argument was about, I do not know. I wasn't that interested. I just wanted to get home and take something for my pounding headache and soothe lotion on a face that had become as red as a plate of Mexican chilies.

The only time I ever encountered personal physical abuse during almost twenty years of referring soccer games was during a Sunday afternoon men's match involving a Mexican team from the agricultural town of Immokalee, thirty miles east of Naples, and a local team made up of mainly British expatriates.

Naturally, one would expect that such a match up would create a difficult situation for me. Accusations of making bias decisions to the benefit of my fellow countrymen would be expected, but strangely that never occurred. I think it's fair to say that over the years I had gained the reputation of being a fair and impartial referee – most definitely I didn't always make the right calls but I was never accused of showing any favoritism. Any referee will tell you whatever call you make during a game will be wrong in the eyes of fifty percent of the players and the fans.

This particular game, as I expected, turned into a physical but fair one. There were no more than the usual number of fouls and certainly not anything to be considered too serious. By the time we approached halftime and with the game still scoreless, I felt I had everything under control. Wrong!

It all began with an innocuous incident when the Immokalee full back shoved the opposing winger off the ball. Whistling for the foul, I ran up to the ball to ensure the defending players were going to take the required position of standing at least ten yards back.

"Fuck you ref."

Did I hear that right? I looked all around to try and locate the source of the abuse. This really didn't make any sense. No one could possibly argue the call and it appeared everyone was cool and moving on with the game.

"*Fuck you ref.*" I looked at the line of players making up a wall defending the goal and caught the eye of the player who had committed the foul. His mumble had now turned into a strong voice, almost like a chant. "*Fuck you ref...fuck you ref!*"

What the heck was he so upset about? I'm thinking as I tried ignoring him. If he had stopped there I would have feigned a certain deafness which is sometimes required in refereeing and continued with the game, but he didn't. His voice was becoming louder and angrier. I decided I had no choice but to take some action before this incident escalated into a team problem.

I stepped in front of the ball and paced a couple of steps closer to the offending player while, at the same time, gesturing for him to come and meet me halfway for a little chat. At that time I still hadn't planned on giving him an official yellow card warning...just a few words to defuse his action that I really had difficulty comprehending.

Although we were now standing face to face I didn't see this as any real confrontation. Giving a friendly verbal warning often happens in a game. But before I could say anything he started up again in that heavily accented monotone voice repeating the expletive..."*Fuck you ref*"

I had no choice. I reached in my back pocket for my wallet containing the notebook and yellow card. In a casual voice I told him there was no need for him to cuss and spoil a good game, at the same time writing down his shirt number in my notebook before holding the plastic yellow card aloft. I figured an official caution would be the end of the incident. Wrong.

As I turned to walk back to my spot close to the ball the cussing started up again.

"*Fuck you ref...fuck you ref*" I couldn't believe my ears. This was a situation that wasn't going away. I reasoned with myself that I had given this player every opportunity to get over whatever frustration he was harboring and to get on with playing the game.

"The next card will be a red card and you will out of the game," I called out in a stern voice.

"*Fuck you...gimme a red card.*"

I was aware that all eyes were on me, wondering what I was going to do next. This was a scene from the Wild West, gunfight at the OK Coral.

No backing down. Once again I traced the familiar steps, moving towards the player while reaching into my pocket for my wallet. I opened the book and for the second time started to write down details of the booking offence.

Without any warning the fist came flying up through my notepad and the cold-cut undercut landed squarely on my chin. Wham!

There was no immediate pain…just numbness in my head before a murky haze drifted through my brain. I was still conscious, aware that I was lying on the floor and aware of the commotion going on around me. I knew I needed to get back up on my feet, not only to protect myself from further attack, but to try and control the ugly situation that I sensed was about to develop. There was no time to be frightened. I stood up and looked around. My attacker was just standing there motionless. It was as though he was in a dream. Perhaps on drugs. His face expressionless. No anger. Nothing.

Fortunately the incident hadn't sparked a battle between the two teams as I feared, just a lot of pushing and shoving between opposing players. There has to be some valid reason for teams wanting to fight each other and apparently, watching the ref being hit wasn't one of them. I doubt whether any player on the field had ever seen a referee knocked to the ground before. Certainly I hadn't. My attacker's action was so bizarre that even his own players were looking confused by the whole incident. Several of them had joined the group from the home team who were crowding around me asking if I was ok?

I'm not sure why but I think I felt embarrassed more than anything else. I just wanted to get on with the game. I looked around the field and saw that everything appeared to be under control. Even my attacker had moved away, making his way to the sideline and the shade of a tree. After quickly jerking my head from side to side to ensure there was no jaw damage and brushing off the dust and grass cuttings from my uniform I blew my whistle to restart the game.

Unknown to me, one of the fathers watching his son play on the Naples team had already called the police. As the game continued I became aware of the distant sounds of sirens becoming louder and louder. A moment later, two police cars with emergency lights flashing came to a screeching halt in the nearby parking lot.

I guess it must have appeared strange to the cops to see a nice, friendly game in progress. More so when it was explained to them that the person who had been attacked was still out there in the middle of the field. I got the impression, when giving them the information at halftime, that they thought this incident was more amusing than serious. They did, however, handcuff my attacker and haul him off. As they lowered his head and sat him in the car I could hear the faint cry......*"fuck you cops...fuck you cops!"*

I felt better, knowing this wasn't anything personal.

Chapter Twenty-One

Many times during our worst financial days we were asked if we were planning to file for bankruptcy. This was not such an unusual course of action in Naples, where the slow summers caused hardships for so many business owners. It appeared that no operation was exempt from the financial pressures that came about when the hot summer months arrived and up to half the population migrated north.

Even the more popular restaurants, where it was not uncommon to wait ninety minutes for a table in season, were half empty by June. A well-used local saying was that during the summer you could fire a cannon down Route 41, the main drag, and not hit anybody!

In the less hectic years of Naples it was not unusual for stores and restaurants to close their doors during the summer months, but that changed when higher rents and overheads forced the owners to operate year round. Whatever money was taken in summer helped to bankroll the operation and keep hard to find, trained staff. Still, for some it just wasn't enough. By September, a familiar sight in the downtown area were the large *"going out of business"* signs pasted inside the storefront windows. The "businesses for sale" listings in the newspaper grew from half a column to three or four.

Mo and I talked over the personal bankruptcy situation many times, but we always talked ourselves out of taking what we considered was the sign of failure. We felt it would be a label which would hang over our heads for life, even though we tried to rationalize that our huge credit card debt wasn't really our fault, but more a predicament that had been caused by the fraudulent deal at the spa, the ongoing lawyer's fees and all the costs we incurred with our immigration woes.

We listened to both sides of the bankruptcy argument. We knew of one friend who had filed bankruptcy when his real estate venture failed. He was left owing nearly one hundred thousand dollars to the credit card companies who had financed, unknowingly, the expansion to his business. He looked at his situation in the following unemotional manner.

"Just suppose I can find a job which pays enough for me to be able to pay back twenty thousand dollars in interest charges a year. That will take me ten years, and that's without paying off any of the principal.

"If I go ahead and file bankruptcy now, I get the credit card companies immediately off my back and in two years I can start rebuilding my credit."

Mo and I watched as he did exactly that. In fact, after less then one year he acquired a secured credit card with a card limit equal to the cash amount he deposited into the account. Within two years he was offered non-secured credit cards and it was as though there was hardly a blemish on his financial file. Long before ten years was up he had bought a new home and was back in business. He vows he will not make the same mistakes he made before, learning a valuable lesson about the dangers of using credit cards to finance a business operation.

But for us we chose a different path. We contacted the credit card companies and arranged an extended repayment plan. In a couple of instances the companies even agreed to stop adding interest charges. Although it has been many years since the worst of financial times, we are still paying off small monthly amounts including a monthly payment to our attorney, Nelson Faerber. For us our total debt has been reduced drastically and there is clearly a bright light at the end of the tunnel.

Like so many other families who are stretched financially, it seemed for the longest time that just as we were getting close to clearing our debts a new incident occurred which pushed everything back.

Even though we can recall many long negotiations carried out over both the phone and in letters, the only credit incident that still really irks us today is the one involving the finance company that handled the lease for our desktop computers at The Collier Advertriser. Ron and I both had to sign personal guarantees.

Although we had paid the company nearly $20,000 of the $22,000 in the three year lease agreement, the company chose not to work with us when the paper was sold, insisting that we send back the equipment even though I told them I had someone prepared to either take over the lease payments or, if they wished, purchase the equipment at a fair price which was a lot more than what was still owed.

The leasing company remained adamant. They would sell off the equipment themselves to settle the debt. Of course we didn't expect to see any money back on the deal, and neither did we expect to see what was going to appear on our credit files. It was several months later when we were reminded of this incident.

Although we were paying off the credit card companies with monthly payments, we suddenly found ourselves being turned down when we applied for any new credit to purchase a much needed item.

When we investigated the reasons we discovered our credit report was showing that we had "items seized" by the computer finance company. The credit reports showed we still owed two thousand dollars. It took a lot of pressure from us to learn the leasing company was claiming they were unable to sell the equipment and refused to discuss the matter further. As a result, we were left unable to get any credit for the next *seven years*!

Chapter Twenty-Two

We have introduced several British friends to Naples who have enjoyed the place so much that they ended up buying a vacation home here. Chris and Jeanette were the first, and others have followed. Mo's younger sister Melanie and her family went one stage further, moving here permanently about ten years ago.

Their move began when they were visiting one summer. I was busy finishing up another application form for the green card lottery when Melanie casually looked across at me working on the word processor and asked what I was doing. I told her that I was completing these forms and explained what the lottery was all about. After a few seconds silence, Melanie casually asked if I would send in an application for her.

This lottery process was introduced, we were told, as a result of a Congressman with Irish roots complaining that the Irish were not getting a fair deal with their quota of green cards. After debating the issue, Congress agreed to increase the numbers of visas that would be handed out to the Irish applicants, but decided, to be fair, they would also have to increase the numbers issued to applicants from other European countries. Twice since living here they have held this lottery. Anyone wanting a green card simply sends in their name and address and waits. We have known several families get lucky. As it turned out one of those, wouldn't you have guessed, was Melanie's family.

I clearly remember that day in October, 1992. A few weeks after the family had returned to England, a jubilant Melanie called and began screaming into the phone. "Guess what?" and before giving us anytime to respond she answered her own question. "We've won the lottery. They are going to give us a green card!"

Mo and I were delighted for Melanie and her family, but a little disappointed that we hadn't been given similar opportunity. I'm not sure we actually thought it was unfair, but we had come to believe we had earned our right to stay on a permanent basis without any fear of further hassle. We had already talked about the situation, and had decided that if we were unsuccessful this time we would take whatever steps were necessary to get our own green cards.

With The Collier Advertiser behind us, we had become technically illegal again. We still had our second investor's visa, but if we tried to leave the country and return, we would be in the same horrible mess as before. Apart from not wanting to face that nightmare twice in one lifetime, the children were now growing toward adulthood. They regarded themselves as true Americans in every sense and it was obvious to us that they would want to continue their lives in the U.S.

For Melanie, it took about six months to process the paperwork for her green card. She and her husband - Spanish born Pepe - sold their home and the small construction business they had started in England. They moved to Naples, along with their two teenage daughters and, after seven years of being here, Melanie became an American citizen. This permitted her to eventually bring over her twenty-four year old son, Jason.

The first time the lottery system was introduced, there was no restriction on the number of entries each person could submit. Like so many others, we figured the more entries we sent the more chances we had of winning. The overall effect of all those entries arriving in Washington DC at roughly the same time was absolute chaos, completely clogging up the local postal system. There were literally millions and millions of applications. For several days it became a nightmare for postal staff.

For the second lottery, a few years later, the immigration department, learning from the mistakes of the past, decided they would have to change the policy, accepting only one entry from each applicant. Anyone attempting to send more than one would supposedly be automatically disqualified. Exactly how they were going to work that out we were left to wonder.

Apart from Melanie, we knew of about ten other couples who won their green cards through the two lotteries. In addition to the lotteries, the immigration services have also offered amnesty to illegal aliens a couple of times while we have been living here. This program was aimed mainly at the thousands of Mexican farm workers who cross the southern borders each year to find work in the agricultural areas of California, Arizona, Texas and Florida.

While many of these illegal aliens return to Mexico once the annual harvesting is finished, many thousands choose to stay. Someone in Washington, even back then, apparently decided it was too difficult to track down all these people, and so they adopted an "if you can't beat'em, tax 'em" approach and so the amnesty was offered.

While keeping in touch with the lottery, we also began making inquiries about qualifying under these amnesty programs. We had to believe that because we had always supported ourselves financially, in what we could claim to be trying circumstances, and had never been in any trouble with the law, that we would qualify. Wrong!

Our early inquiries took us to the offices of our local Congressman, whose staff promised to research the matter on our behalf. They sent letters to officials in Washington and several weeks later we were passed a copy of the government's written response. Listen to this, you are not going to believe it. The letter stated we didn't qualify under the amnesty program because we entered the country LEGALLY! This program was only for those families who entered the country ILLEGALLY! In other words, because we followed the rules and tried to stay honest, we were the ones being punished.

One of the British families who came to Naples on vacation, and later bought a holiday home here, was Fil and Wendy. They had been introduced to Naples by Chris and Jeanette, and shared a business interest in the video magazine which Chris had sold that enabled him to give me that loan for our investor's visa. The couple lived in Bolton in northern England where Fil had been named "Video Store Owner of the Year" a couple of years before. Like Chris, he had built up a very profitable video store operation over a number of years before selling out and moving into several other business ventures, including the publishing operation with Chris.

Mo and I had become friendly with Fil, Wendy and their young daughter Sammie. We would often visit with them at the huge community pool in the nearby Winterpark development. It was during one of these visits that we were introduced to another English northerner, named Roy Wallwork.

Roy was a big man who waddled like a penguin when he walked. He had red wavy hair and a constant warm smile on a ruddy face that almost matched the color of his hair. He spoke with one of those strong, north of England accents that almost everyone subconsciously impersonates within a couple of minutes of engaging in conversation. Roy was a talker, and it wasn't long before anyone who cared to listen knew everything about him, his family and his business.

Roy had a true rags-to-riches story to tell. Admitting to having no formal education, he dallied in various jobs before starting out from the very bottom in the plastics industry. "Starting from the bottom" simply meant Roy was calling on small retail stores in the industrial town where he lived and loading up his bike with any recyclable plastic the storeowners were planning to throw out. With his bike laden down with the plastic, and him waddling beside it, he would make his way to the local plastic recycling plant where he would be paid for anything considered recyclable. He was paid only pennies per pound, but over the months he was able to save up enough to purchase a beat up, old rusty truck with the sides hanging off.

"Ehhhh by gum! It was a scary sight seeing me and the truck cum driving down the road," Roy announced with a huge grin.

"I would pile the plastic as high as it would go. I had to be careful going under bridges," he joked.

Despite his rusty old truck proving unreliable, Roy decided his next investment wouldn't be another truck, but a bailer. With this piece of equipment, held together with a "wish and a prayer" (he admitted a full service on the machine was changing the string holding it together) he was now able to compress the plastic into bales and load down his truck even more. The operation grew to a size where he was eventually able to open his own small and very basic recycling plant. Using old equipment no one wanted, Roy and a partner soon built up a flourishing business.

"We had to be sure to buy a fresh ball of string every Monday to keep most of the machinery up and running," he said, laughing.

As he sat around the pool enjoying a beer, he cheerfully admitted, without too much prompting, that his business was worth over eight million pounds! He was now regarded as one of the biggest independent plastic recycling operators in the United Kingdom.

"Got anything like that 'ere?" he asked in his thick Lancashire accent.

"I have absolutely no idea," I replied. "Never ever thought about it until you mentioned eight million pounds. I think it's time to find out."

I quickly learned that Roy was a workaholic, even when on vacation. It was amazing that he was so large, seeing as he never sat still for a minute.

"Let's go and take a *looksee.* We can soon find out by looking for recycle bins at the mall and at the back of businesses around town. Eeeh," he said. "This reminds me of when I first started."

I couldn't help but wonder, even at this early stage, if he was already expecting me to go out and buy a bike and a ball of string!

This day, the sun was shining out of a cloudless blue sky, and the temperature was in the low eighties. It was hard to imagine it was only two days before Christmas. Before day's end, Roy, Fil, Roy's son Daryl and myself had covered most of the town, searching for dumpsters loaded with plastic.

We must have looked suspicious, driving up and down alleyways in Roy's big, black rented sedan because a police cruiser soon started following us. The cop inside must have been mystified, watching as we checked inside each bin before driving off to find another. I'm not sure if the young cop understood Roy at all when the big fella tried to explain what we were doing. From my seat in the back of the sedan, all I could see was a puzzled cop scratching his head and nodding. In the end I think he just gave up trying to understand the explanation of this weird Englishman as he waved us off.

Roy seemed delighted with what we were finding. "There's plastic out there so it must be going somewhere," he said excitedly. Looking directly at me, he added. "There's a business for you here, son!"

The day after Christmas, and with me taking an extra day off from Terry's insurance business, Roy and I went down to the county complex to see what we could learn. The staff was very friendly and helpful and explained that all the plastic picked up at curbside went through Waste Management, the huge national firm, contracted to handle all the waste in Collier County. It was generally assumed by the county staff that, apart from any private arrangement (which was indeed a possibility with the enormous amount of plastic waste picked up from the big town mall and strip malls each week) all the domestic plastic waste went to the county landfill.

This was both good and bad news to Roy. "Someone is missing out on making a fortune here," he said in an excited tone that made my ears perk up. I began to think seriously that here was a business idea that had already been shown to be extremely profitable by the very man standing beside me. It was beginning to show signs of exciting possibilities!

"We are leaving here to go home the day after tomorrow," Roy informed me as we left the county complex. "But let's stay on this. Let me contact the Italian manufacturing company that provides me with my new equipment. I know they have an agent working in the U.S. We'll call him and see what he knows about plastic recycling in Florida. He should have a handle on things."

A few days later I received an e-mail from Roy, with the name and phone number of the agent. He said he had spoken with his equipment suppliers in Italy and they confirmed that this one agent in the US was responsible for supplying much of the plastic recycling equipment currently in use throughout the country.

Determined not to waste another minute I went immediately to the phone. I wanted to try and setup a meeting as soon as possible. It was only when I began dialing the number that I became aware what keys I was punching. 1-941-775.... This was the very same telephone exchange as our own!

The agent I was calling not only lived in Naples, he lived less than half a mile away from our home! And it also turned out his wife taught in the same school as Mo. Another incredible coincidence in our lives that was almost too much to believe. This was surely one of those occasions when fate was bringing us together for a purpose, I thought at the time.

Not knowing exactly what information I was looking for, I arranged to have lunch with Jim Scott the following week. It turned out to be a memorable meeting and one that was going to lead me into a two-year project with mind-boggling prospects. There were going to be times when I really believed we were about to crack it big time in America. Was the top of the mountain finally coming into view? I was to be asking myself.

Over lunch, Jim quickly assessed from our conversation that I was eager to get into a new business venture. He smiled across the table and explained that his deceased boss, who had also lived in Naples, had put together a business plan that involved setting up a local plastic recycling operation. The idea was to recycle huge amounts of agricultural plastic pulled annually from the fields in Collier County. Having no ongoing use, this dirty plastic had been dumped over a number of years at one of two Collier County dumping sites. The tomato growers and other users not only had to haul the plastic to these centers, but also had to pay a dumping feet.

The growers, I learned later, were left with no choice but to pay the fee. By law they couldn't bury the plastic, nor would the environmental agencies allow them to burn it. That past year, Jim told me, the county had paid out more than $300,000 to bury more than 50,000 tons of plastic themselves, and the county was now left in the position of having to stockpile another load. It had become a major headache, and one they desperately wanted to remedy. It was incredible. Here we had an endless supply of free plastic waste that could be recycled into valuable plastic pellets and sold back to the plastic industry.

As we talked, Jim pulled out a dog-eared folder from a briefcase and laid it on the table. "I think you will find this interesting," he smiled. "It's the business plan my boss and three others put together. They had raised just over three million dollars to build a plant."

"So why didn't the project take off?" I asked.

"A few weeks before it was due to start, my boss died suddenly of a heart attack. A few weeks later one of the other partners also died."

Jim went on to explain that the two remaining partners decided not to go ahead with the project, and handed Jim the business plan with a suggestion that he could use it anyway he wished if it would help him sell some new equipment. The plan had been sitting in Jim's briefcase for nearly two years.

"You are welcome to it," said Jim in his warm and friendly voice. "I'm not looking for anything out of it, other than an opportunity of selling you the equipment if you decide to go ahead."

The business plan was comprehensive in the way it set out the project. But the data was three years old and needed updating. After that, all I needed was several million dollars!

As I read the plan over and over, I couldn't help but again think that fate had brought me to Jim Scott. There had to be a reason for us getting together like we did. I really believed that this project was going to happen.

I had been working on the plan in my spare time for several weeks when Jim called me. "I think I may have some good news for you," he said excitedly, something of a rarity for Jim. "I ran into one of the financial backers involved in the original partnership in a restaurant last evening. He asked me how it was doing and if I had found someone yet to get it going."

"I told him about you and he sounded real interested. He mentioned he had a good tomato harvest this past fall and was looking to invest some money. You had better give him a call. Do it right away. He had been drinking heavily and may soon forget what he told me!"

I didn't waste a second. As soon as I put down the phone I was dialing the offices of Kent Manning. I was on such a high that it was a big disappointment when the woman who answered the phone told me Mr. Manning was out of the office for the next couple of days. I explained briefly who I was and left a message for him to call me.

I learned a long time ago never to expect callbacks. I didn't get a call from Kent Manning that week, or the next. I tried calling his office several times but was repeatedly told he was out of the office. I decided as my last resort to drop off a copy of the updated business plan together with a friendly cover letter.

Another week went by and still no call. Three more unsuccessful attempts to contact Mr. Manning were sufficient proof that he really wasn't interested. I accepted it must have been the drink talking the evening he met with Jim Scott. I have to wonder why these things happen this way. Is it just to tease?

But despite my disappointment I was determined not to give up and I continued to work on updating the business plan, as well as starting a campaign to find the financial backing the project required. Going on Roy's advice, we were now looking at introducing more equipment as backup and to secure twenty-four hour production. The project had grown considerably since the original plan, and the funding we were looking for had also increased. I assessed we now required over four million dollars!

This was happening at a time when many new things were happening in our lives, including the time Mo was back in college getting her degree so she could get back into full time teaching.

As part of her college business course studies, Mo had to produce a business plan. We both thought it was most fortunate that her professor agreed she could take my plastic project and use it as the subject of her plan. At the end of the semester, using much of my data, I was handed a professional looking, updated plan that had secured an "A" grade for Mo.

Now, armed with the plan, it was time to go and find the funding. I realized that with no money of my own it would be impossible to locate funds from regular banking institutions. My only real chance, I thought, was to talk with private investors and venture capitalists. I won't even try and recall the number of companies I met during the next year or so. I do know that I combed the venture capital lists and sent out nearly two hundred, professional looking information packages. Each relatively expensive mailing was skimmed from our meager savings.

I followed up on every response, but soon learned my timing couldn't have been worse. This was around the period when nearly all the venture capital companies were tying up funds in the dot com start-ups. "Any other time and we would take a serious look at your project, but not just now," seemed to be the standard reply.

But even with so many negative responses I still believed the idea was good enough to succeed. My search had taken me deep into the Naples business community. It seemed that everyone who read the plan thought it was a sound idea. Just when I thought I had met with everyone I was suddenly introduced or given the name of a new contact. From there I was able to draw up a new list. As long as there were still people to see, I was prepared to go out and make my presentation. From one contact source I was led to another. There was a period when I convinced myself I was meeting with an unbroken chain, believing each new link was getting me closer to finding my backer. I wasn't prepared to leave any stone unturned. I tried to be relentless in my search.

The business plan, with Mo's fresh input, was indeed solid. It brought lots of compliments. But all these, while helpful and inspiring, would be useless if the plan didn't bring the money I needed.

After working on the project almost full time for nearly two years, we became desperate for me to once again earn an income. The project was taking much longer than we had anticipated in getting off the ground and still there were no firm assurances. We couldn't allow ourselves to fall back into the financial quicksand. I needed to earn money and that's when I made my application to work at the The Ritz Carlton.

It didn't escape me that, working in a five-star hotel, I would be in contact with some of the wealthiest people around. Without ever trying to be pushy I never missed an opportunity to mention the plastic project. I don't know how many of my hotel guests were genuinely interested or were just being polite, but I handed out many personal business cards that went along with my comment: "If you know of anyone who could be interested."

On one occasion I picked up a guest from the hotel to drive him thirty-five miles to the airport. As he settled down in the back seat in the plush Lincoln Town car I could sense an air of excitement in the vehicle. It was like a powerful electric charge. I couldn't prevent myself from mentioning that I sensed he was really excited.

"You bet," he said. "I've just had some good meetings and I'm just about to put a deal together that will make my company one of the biggest venture capital operations in the world!"

Was this a call from heaven? My heart was pounding as I began thinking about the possibilities. Clearly my passenger wanted to talk about his good fortune, and I was anxious to turn the conversation around to my project. Somewhere between the hotel and the airport I was given an opening, an opportunity to mention my plastics idea. I didn't pause for breath, realizing that here was my golden opportunity. I took the silence in the back seat as an indication that my passenger was listening to my story. I looked into the mirror and could see that he was leaning back against the headrest, seemingly listening intently.

As we climbed out of the car, less than fifteen minutes later, he handed me his own business card and, in what seemed to be a genuine manner, suggested I send him my plan. As I stood on the edge of the curb and watched him disappear into the airport terminal I believed I had found the last part of my jigsaw puzzle. I couldn't remember a time when I had felt so positive as when I drove away from the airport and back towards the Ritz.

The business plan was in the mail the next day, and a follow up phone call was placed a few days later. I never did get to speak to my hotel guest again. He did write, saying that my plan had been received and passed on to one of his VPs. He further explained that the word had come back to him that I had a sound idea but "this really wasn't the best time for this type of investment."

Despite the crushing disappointment I was able to bounce back immediately. Even I was amazed at how resilient I had become to rejection. I was able to brush this one aside and look for the next move.

Someone suggested I speak with Ray Holland, president of the Florida Community Bank in Immokalee, hub of the country's agricultural business. It made sense to me that if any bank was going to listen to my proposal then it would be the one that served the tomato growers, an establishment that had a real interest in seeing new businesses and new jobs come to this poor, rural community.

Ray Holland was as "country" as you can get. From his cowboy hat hanging on the hat rack standing in the corner, down to his leather cowboy boots, he was a born and bred Florida boy. I half expected him to be chewing tobacco and to be spitting into a spittoon as we talked, but fortunately we just drank coffee as we discussed the plan.

I quickly decided that Ray Holland had a type of personality that didn't allow him to get too excited. Or, at least, he wasn't the sort to show it.

For almost an hour I was treated to nothing more than "hmmmmm" and "I see" as I went through the plan step by step. For a moment, after I finished talking, I wondered if Ray really understood the project. He sat back in his chair and didn't say a word. His head was bent forward and his eyes seemed focused on his twiddling thumbs. Suddenly he looked up and I could see from his expression that he was excited.

My heart started pounding when I realized he was hooked. I was suddenly aware he was telling me the level of funding his bank was prepared to offer. "We could certainly fund sixty percent, maybe go as high as eighty percent in certain areas, but this is not the way you want to go. I can see you don't have any money of your own to put into the venture. I have a better idea."

The bank manager went on to explain how he could put me in touch with someone who handles applications for rural development grants, via a federal agency handling new businesses in agricultural areas. "I know they can guarantee you getting practically all the funding you need," he said as he rocked back in his chair, placing his shiny leather boots on the table. I smiled back. This wasn't the type of bank president I was used to meeting.

An appointment with Bob Knox - the grant applications man - a couple of days later continued to charge my enthusiasm. After reading through the plan he said he felt confident I could get up to ninety percent of the funding via the agency. "I've handled several of these applications and they've all been successful," he smiled confidently.

Bob explained that the federal agency guaranteed the loan made through a local bank. "I know Ray Holland has a couple of these going on right now, so that's why he sent you to me," he said. "As you can expect when dealing with the government, there's a lot of paperwork to do on the application. My fee is $1,500 to handle the whole process."

When we discussed my meeting that evening, it wasn't easy to tell Mo about the fees. We were slowly getting back on our financial feet and slowly paying down the credit cards. We both accepted that for us to come up with $1,500 would set us back financially. And yet, we both had a lot of confidence the project could work. It may have appeared that we were rushing into this without too much checking, but alleviating that concern was the fact that it was the respected bank manager himself who was recommending this course of action.

We had already discussed the possibility of getting both Dominic and Kieran involved in the recycling operation. "Why not see if either of them would be interested in coming up with some of the money?" Mo suggested. "They are both working and doing ok."

We only had to suggest the idea to Dominic for him to jump in. After graduating college he had been working in a bar, deciding what career he wished to pursue. Since he was a child he had wanted his own business, and he had been closely following the developments of the plastics idea. "Treat it as a loan to the company," he joked as he wrote out a check to cover his share of the fees.

Although we realized the government funding wouldn't cover the entire amount of the project, we reasoned it would be much easier to reapproach private investors if we could show we had secured up to ninety percent of the money. Once again, I was starting to believe we were getting close to making our plastic project a reality.

The plan now required some fine tuning. Our application required that we had everything in place, including the location of the site, staffing, equipment we would install, even down to the trucks we would be using. Our business plan had grown to over one hundred pages, as every facet of the operation was covered in detail.

Although Bob Knox was ready to submit our application to the rural development committee, I decided we should hold off until I felt confident we could secure the remaining ten percent of funding. If questions were asked of us I wanted to be able to show that we were well-capitalized. In truth, I think I was beginning to feel the first ripples of concern. I could sense a changing attitude within the financial world. Stock prices were beginning to drop and there was a general uneasiness in the air as investors held on to their money.

Those senses proved accurate. The general economic slow down was also being felt in the plastic industry. Almost overnight, scrap-plastic prices plunged, resulting in a glut of recycled plastic in the world market. Prices, which had stayed around .27 cents per pound for a couple of years, had fallen to below .14 cents.

A plastics agent in Miami who had told us he would buy all the recycled plastic pellets we could produce, was having second thoughts. His price had dipped to eleven cents. The general feeling I was getting from the industry was "it would be better to wait and see." While our costings showed that our break-even figure was only nine cents a pound, I could understand the hesitancy of people to invest. It appeared I had lost my window of opportunity. The project would have to wait until the situation improved.

Our hearts sank. For almost two years I had worked continually on getting this plan ready. Now, in the space of a few weeks, I had come to the "realization that it wasn't going to happen."

Today, almost five years later, the business plan sits with several others in that special drawer of my desk.

Chapter Twenty-Three

I have enjoyed playing all types of sports for most of my life, but I will admit that running was never one of my favorites. I can easily run for the ninety minutes required in a soccer game, but as for running on a track or on the streets, forget it.

As much as I dislike running, I dislike my own birthdays even more. Actually, it isn't the actual birthday so much as the fact I'm reminded I'm getting older. New Year's Eve works pretty much the same way.

So as I approached my fiftieth birthday, you can easily imagine the concerns in the family household. Both Mo and the children were fully aware of an approaching crisis. A time when dad goes into his sulk.

While the rest of the family gathered to come up with a plan to humor me, I had already decided things were going to be a little bit different this year. I wasn't going to be immature and selfish and mope around the house with a sullen expression and make everyone else feel miserable this birthday, I would do something memorable. Something that would lift my spirits and make me forget the occasion.

But what to do? It needed to be something that wouldn't cost a lot of money, yet present a big enough challenge to give me a sense of excitement and satisfaction. It needed to be something that I could look upon as some type of accomplishment years down the road.

It wasn't easy coming up with a suitable project, and I pondered the situation for several days. Perhaps, I thought, I should try and overcome my fear of heights and do something like bungy jumping, or even skydiving? Tackling either of those and the fear I would feel would certainly take my mind off having another birthday.

But a hero I am not. Why be stupid about picking a challenge that would make me feel so uncomfortable? My feet needed to stay firmly on the ground. How about running a marathon?

My birthday was only two weeks away but it didn't matter. As I didn't enjoy running, I had no intention of doing any training. I was fit from playing soccer and exercising with weights in the garage, so why did I need to do anything more just to run twenty-six miles!

A couple of days later, and my plan firmly fixed in my mind, I drove down towards Marco Island and marked a spot just over thirteen miles from home. It was a mile or so short of the Marco Island Bridge. My turnaround point would be just before the new road construction area.

Mo gave me one of her confused looks and an exasperated "whatever!" when I told her the plan. Although my birthday was the following Sunday, I planned to run my personal marathon on Saturday, the day before. I figured if I got out of the bed and really didn't feel like taking my early morning jaunt, then I had another day to try it. My wife's job was to get out of bed at 4:00 a.m. and accompany me, just in case I needed to be transported to the hospital's emergency room. She would also be carrying the water supplies.

The night before the run I must admit I started to have second thoughts. At soccer practices I usually got bored after running just a couple of warm up laps around the field and here I was, proposing to run for twenty-six miles. I went to bed around 9:00 p.m., thinking to myself that this may not be the best idea I had come up with.

After a restless night's sleep I woke before the alarm at around 3:45 a.m. I felt good, really good. I was psyched, and ready to give it a try. I looked outside and the clear starlit sky made me feel this was definitely the day to go for it. The air was cool and fresh. I couldn't ask for better conditions.

I slipped into my dirty trainers, Budweiser tee-shirt and black soccer shorts. I felt no need to dress up for the occasion. I woke up a not-too-happy wife, loaded water jugs into the car, and took off down the street.

For the first few hundred yards I felt nervous. I remember asking myself what was I going to feel like after running roughly the equivalent of 450 laps of the soccer field. Will my legs seize up, or my body close down?

The early morning air felt good. There was no need to race. I had no time to beat. I had to strike a pace that I felt comfortable with for the next few hours. The first mile was easy and so was the second. I felt comfortable as I ran along the dark, unlit Tamiami Trail heading towards Miami and the Marco Island turn off. Around five miles I still felt good, just a little pain in the calf of my right leg. Nothing serious I thought.

Another mile and the calf pain became more intense. Although I never experienced cramps in all the years I played sports, I sensed I was just about to discover what they feel like.

With every stride the pain seemed to grow more intense. I knew I was facing an important decision: to take a car ride home, or try to run through my minor crisis. I needed to cross the highway and, as there weren't many vehicles around at that time in the morning, I chose to walk across. I grabbed some water from Mo and enjoyed the luxury of catching my breath and allowing the pain to subside. But I knew I had to get back into a stride. Too much walking and my legs would think they had finished their workout and would start to relax. Then the aches would start to set in.

I got back into running stride and picked up the pace. I was getting close to the Marco Island road. I had run six miles. Only another twenty miles or so to go I remember thinking. This was by far the furthest I had ever run in my life, or at least since my school days when I was forced to run cross country. I could still feel the pain of the cramps but it was beginning to feel a little better. The intake of water seemed to be helping.

I was on a stretch of road with no sidewalk and no street lighting. I chose to run towards oncoming traffic and it soon was obvious no driver expected to come across a runner on this road at this time in the morning. High beams blinded me time and again until the oncoming driver saw my silhouette and dimmed the headlights.

With the cramp pain now almost gone, I felt surprisingly good. My breathing was easy and my legs felt strong. I can't recall any of the thoughts rattling through my brain at that time. It's likely I didn't have any. I think I may have picked up on Mo mentioning the word 'braindead' as we were leaving the house, but I couldn't be sure. I've heard marathon runners talk about experiencing walls in their runs. My mind must have started functioning again as I began to wonder when I would hit mine.

Choosing not to wear a watch, I had no idea of the time, but the dawn-yellow sunrise was breaking over the mangroves to my right. Everything started to get bright in a hurry, and suddenly I felt I was in a new environment. Up ahead I thought I could make out the outline of the Marco Island Bridge. If it was the bridge, then in another mile or so I would be at the turn... halfway through my birthday run.

The halfway stage came without emotion, except for the desire to stop, sit down and drink lots of water. I knew that to stop running now would spell disaster. I had to keep moving.

I grabbed more water from Mo's outstretched arm. My legs still felt good but, surprisingly, it was my arms and my shoulders that were beginning to ache. For the first time a tiredness swept through my body. The tough part of the run was beginning to hit me; I sensed I was about to come face to face with my first wall.

I became conscious that I was losing the spring in my stride. My soles were coming down flat on the pavement and my pace was dropping.

I needed to recover my style if I was ever going to make it back to the house. The time it took was unimportant.

A gentle breeze was coming off the avenue of mangroves. At first it was pleasant and refreshing as it cooled my body, but it was also taking on a negative effect, working like a barrier as it pushed me gently sideways and almost backwards. I had no previous experience to draw from. I just knew it was time to lower my head and bite my lip. I had made the turn long ago and I was approaching the main highway. I had run two thirds of the distance. I only had another eight miles to go. I was not going to be beaten, at least not just yet!

This was a stage of the run I can hardly remember. Perhaps I ran it in a semi-conscious state. I can only recall making the left turn back onto the Tamiami Trail and some time later thinking, "only five more miles, I am nearly home."

This good feeling was to be short-lived; the strength was draining from my body with each new stride. Everything until now had been a physical challenge; now it was definitely mental.

The voices in my brain were telling me I had done enough. They teased me I had run over twenty miles, why run any further? There was no conscious effort about making the legs move; they had been mechanical for a long time now. It was now all about winning the battle of the mind.

The backlash from the rush of wind as trucks sped by was now presenting another challenge to overcome. It was like being beaten down every time one went by. I looked up and saw the familiar sign of Lely High School, where the kids had gone to school. I lowered my head and ploughed forward but when I looked up again I got the feeling I hadn't moved any closer to the sign. I tried holding my gaze down longer this time, but again I experienced the same effect. It seemed like an eternity before I eventually reached and passed the school sign.

I was now back in my own neighborhood. I could easily walk home from here I thought. What a tempting offer. Slow down, take a drink, walk the last mile or so...even climb into the car.

It would have been so easy to give in, but I knew I was so close to finishing. Why give up now? My pace had slowed to almost a fast walk. Out of the corner of my eye I could see Mo leaning out of the car. She was smiling and thumping her hand on the side of the door. I sensed she was encouraging me to go on, but I could hear no sound.

Finally I was on my street. And finally I was in my house. My legs felt like jello as I walked through the door, hoping to hear the yells of congratulations from my daughter, the only one in the house at that time.

Behind me stood my wife. "Hey Kirsty" she called out to our daughter, who was still asleep in bed. "Dad has just ran a marathon." There was a brief silence.

"Is he dead?" was Kirsty's only comment as she rolled over and went back to sleep. But then it was, after all, Saturday morning. Nothing in the world interrupts a teenager on Saturday morning.

The few real marathon runners I've told about my run look at me in two ways. The first is with complete disbelief, and the second is with a look that tells me they think I'm completely stupid. In the week that followed the run I was of a mind to agree with the latter assessment. I'd never known such aches and pains as I experienced during those days. I hobbled around the house, barely able to stand straight, having to rely on the furniture to keep me from crashing to the ground.

It was two years later when the second part of this chapter unfolded. It was Kirsty's eighteenth birthday, and Mo and I was asking her what she wanted as a gift. It didn't take her long to come up with her perfect gift idea. "I would like to go skydiving…but dad has to come with me!"

Anyone reading this who is into skydiving (and isn't scared of it) will think of me as a wimp. But as I've already admitted, I'm not into heights and really not a great lover of small planes either. There was absolutely no way I wanted to go up 12,000 feet and jump out into the big blue yonder. It didn't matter that I would be attached to an instructor with hundreds of jumps to his credit. I just didn't want to do it, and no daughter of mine was going to make me.

So here I was sitting on the floor of the plane with the vibration of the single engine shaking my entire body. My throat was dry and I felt that any moment I would pass out from the fear.

This was a midweek afternoon. Our family had already driven out to the airport on the two previous Saturdays, only to see the clouds roll in and our planned jumps postponed on both days. The first time we were slated to be on the sixth airlift, but the thunderheads appeared when we were just one planeload from going up. The second time, with Dominic signed up to come along too, the weather was so bad, no planes were allowed to take off.

Sensing how disappointed Kirsty was after the second postponement, I suggested she take a day off school the first time we saw a clear morning. She had already finished all her senior class exams, so taking a day out of school posed no problem.

This had seemed like a perfect day for killing myself! It was warm and clear and the weather forecast was perfect. It would remain like that for the next few days. I called the airport and booked our jumps, along with a photographer who would record Kirsty's jump on video as part of her birthday gift.

Unlike the two previous Saturdays, the skydiving lounge was quiet and almost empty. We were told that we were the only first-time jumpers around today. Everyone else was an experienced skydiver, who would be jumping out at different heights as part of their training program. We were introduced to Mike, a powerful looking, handsome guy, who was going to be our instructor. His reassuring smile made me feel a little better. Kirsty was smitten.

Because Mike was the only instructor at the airfield that day, Kirsty and I had to go up separately. I quickly jumped in and offered to be first; I wanted to get this madness over as quickly as possible. A smiling and confident looking Kirsty had no problem with that. "It will be fun to watch you come down," she said.

The instruction class lasted about four minutes. Basically it consisted of helping to get me into my jump gear. Mike said there were just two hand signals for me to look out for. The first was "thumbs up" to show that we had cleared the aircraft and the other was a "pulling" sign to indicate it was time to yank the cord and open the chute. He explained how I should lift my legs - by bending my knees - as we approached the ground. His legs would be taking care of the impact.

Did I want to pull the cord, or would I prefer to leave that job to him? I chose to be in control of the situation and pull the cord myself. Already I was feeling there was too much for me to remember. What would happen if I went into unconscious shock as we jumped from the aircraft? A feeling of mild panic was beginning to set in.

We left the hanger with about eight other jumpers and turned the corner of the building. That's when I first saw the aircraft. The beat-up, yellow plane with its single engine did nothing to build my confidence. This was possibly another one of those 'worst moments' of my life.

For everyone else climbing into the plane it was a different scenario. There was an air of excitement and eagerness as they each took up their allotted positions on the floor. Mike indicated for me to take a seat in front of him on the closed side of the fuselage. I was very pleased not to be seated too close to the open door.

Suddenly the quietness was shattered with the roar of the aircraft engine. A few minutes later the vibrating shell eased away from the side of the hanger towards the single runway. The plane appeared, at least to my mind, to be vibrating uncontrollably. I wondered if everyone could see my body shaking in a kind of unison with the engine. I doubted if they cared. It was good that I wasn't expected to speak. My mouth was completely dry.

The plane roared down the runway and I realized with each passing second I was getting closer and closer to the scariest thing I had ever faced in my entire life. The noise was almost unbearable. I was convinced the aircraft was having difficulty in gaining enough speed to get airborne. From the open window I could see the trees at the end of the runway getting dangerously close.

Just when I thought we were about to run out of room, I felt the aircraft lift off the ground. The engine shrieked as the plane gained height, almost clipping the trees underneath.

We were now in a spiral pattern. The vibration and engine noise reminded me of an old motor you would find deep in the hull of an ancient tugboat. Around us, the other jumpers were making preparations. For two who had moved to the open door space, there was a quick final pull of their shoulder straps before taking one pace forward and hurling themselves out into space. I could barely watch. Fortunately there was something for me to do to take my mind off my fears. Mike was gesturing for me to shuffle up closer to him. With my back facing him he began to adjust the straps and I could feel myself being locked to his huge frame. There was something about his size that gave me some much needed confidence. One by one the others jumped from the aircraft. Now there was just Mike and I...as well as the pilot I hoped. The engine was whining and wispy white clouds floated by the open doorway.

"Start to move over to the door and sit on the edge," Mike spoke calmly in my ear. "I'll count three, two, one and then we'll go. Don't you do a thing."

I had thought about offering Mike a financial incentive to get us down safely but quickly discounted that as a ridiculous suggestion. After all, we were strapped together!

There was no time to feel fear. I took one look at the earth below and I was suddenly aware I wasn't sitting on the edge of the door anymore. Instead, we were drifting through the sky and I was very conscious of what was happening. It wasn't an unpleasant feeling and there was none of the churning sensation in my stomach I'd anticipated. We rolled over a couple of times before straightening out onto a level plane.

Mike's arm stretched in front of my face and he gave the thumbs up sign. I suddenly felt relaxed. I began to believe I wasn't about to die!

Everything moved quickly. Although we were falling in space for a full minute, it seemed only but a few seconds before Mike was indicating I should pull the cord. My right hand moved across my chest, and I was quickly reminded that my body was still in a nervous, almost numb mode. I felt for the cord and it wasn't where I thought it should be. The panic lasted just a split second as I looked down and saw the red handle. I grasped it tightly and yanked it with probably more force than I needed. There was a loud whoosh and we were dragged upwards as the chute opened.

Then...all became strangely silent! No sound and seemingly no movement. It was as though we were suspended in space. The airport and open fields lay before our feet. There was calmness like I had never experienced before. Mike's voice, asking me if everything was ok, broke the silence. I nodded my response. "Want to have a little fun?" he asked with a mischievous grin.

"Like what?" I asked gingerly, thinking to myself that being suspended several thousand feet above the ground was all the fun I needed just now.

"How about this?" he laughed, pulling the chute straps so we began to swing wildly. I had the horrible feeling the erratic movement was causing me to slip through my straps. I also had this vision of watching myself crashing to the ground. My whole body stiffened and I called back over my shoulder for Mike to stop. I figured I had nothing more to prove. I had been brave enough for one day.

Our landing was soft and uneventful. We landed just a few feet away from Kirsty and the cameraman, who had recorded the last part of the jump. I should have realized then that my stiff, unnatural grin would be chosen to grace the opening credits of Kirsty's video.

Now it was her turn. I lay on the warm grass watching her board the plane without showing the slightest hint of fear. I was now totally relaxed, relishing the satisfying feeling of what I had overcome that April afternoon. I knew that I would be able to draw from the jump anytime I faced a danger in the future.

It had been a wonderful experience...one that I had absolutely no intention of ever repeating.

Chapter Twenty-Four

Once we were out of the newspaper business in the summer of 1991 we were again on borrowed time where our E2 Investment Visa was concerned. Although we could legally remain when the visa expired in less than two years time, we would be in that same precarious position of having to apply for temporary yearly extensions. A familiar black cloud was beginning to loom above our heads. After all our efforts, we would be back in exactly the same position as we were in at the time of the spa closing; me unable to be employed and our family unable to re-enter the country if we ever traveled overseas. If we chose to stay, we would become virtual prisoners.

And what about our children? All three were getting closer to graduating college and would soon be looking to embark on their own careers. It was apparent none of them had ever considered living anywhere other than the USA. But how could they possibly stay if they were unable to work! The time had arrived for us to do whatever was necessary to obtain our green cards.

Our assortment of British friends living in Naples provided a variety of visa scenarios. Several had acquired green cards through the lottery system, some qualified because they had family ties to US citizens, while others had obtained them through employment. A few, quite simply, were living here illegally.

Brian and Vivian Stuart, our friends from The English Pub, shared with us their own concerns about being able to stay in Naples. They were also here under the E2 investment visa, and were facing the possibility of ending up in a similar precarious position as our own. They had a grown son, James, and after running the pub for nearly twenty years the couple was considering selling what had become a very successful operation. If they proceeded on that route, under their current visa, they would be giving up the right to stay. What then? James had no plans to leave the country. He had moved north trying to enter the New York music industry, and like us, Brian and Viv had long regarded Naples as their permanent home.

Fortunately for them, Brian, while operating the pub, had picked up a sound knowledge of wines and was able to solicit the help from one of his large wine distributors who agreed to offer him a consulting job that would fulfill the green card qualifications. The couple had already contacted an immigration lawyer in Miami who told them he saw few, if any, problems if they decided to make an application. They immediately set the green card ball rolling by committing to a $6,000 lawyer fee.

Unfortunately I didn't share Brian's enviable position of having a work sponsor. Time was ticking by and the renewal date for our current visa was getting closer. At that time I was working with Terry Harris as an independent insurance agent. Terry's own position of also being an independent contractor didn't qualify him as someone who could sponsor me. For me to find a qualified sponsor I had no choice but to look elsewhere!

Terry always had a generous nature, and after hearing my plans, he offered to help as best he could. Being the jovial fellow that he is, with a quick wit and a ready story that had helped him in his various careers, he possessed the kind of personality which attracted a long list of bar buddies. He was known all over town, especially at after-work drinking holes. At Harold's Chickee Bar, his favorite haunt for almost twenty years, Terry appeared to know just about everyone who came in. Because of his never missed daily appearance, I'm convinced there were some customers who accepted he must be one of the owners.

Among his acquaintances was a man who operated what was generally considered a very successful brokerage firm in town. After a few drinks one evening, and with Terry carefully explaining my predicament, the friend offered to help me. I was amazed. This was a complete stranger to me, and yet he was generously agreeing to take on the responsibility of becoming my sponsor. He said he was prepared to go through the complicated process by offering me a job as an office manager with his company.

I had heard from others that the road that lay ahead for sponsors could be far from smooth, and looking back at our own complicated track record, why should we expect anything different? We acknowledged that there were going to be many requirements demanded by the immigration authority. Firstly, and most importantly, I had to prove I was the best candidate to fill the position being offered. It wasn't just a simple case of me being offered employment. I had to compete for the advertised position.

But I didn't see this as being a major problem. I felt confident I could prove I had plenty of experience in running a business and my knowledge of insurance had to be a big plus, I thought

Brian's lawyers in Miami explained the full picture when I went to see them for an initial thirty-minute free consultation. They told me that the position we came up with would be advertised in the local newspaper and all the candidates who responded and appeared qualified would have to be interviewed. They also explained that careful records would have to be kept of each initial telephone interview. After that, my sponsor would have to provide full documentation of the personal interviews with the final two or three selected applicants, one of those obviously being me. In the end it came down to a situation where, in the eyes of the Labor Department, I was selected because I was the best candidate.

When I told the lawyers about my stockbroker angel, they agreed I had found a good match. That anticipated fee of $6,000 was a figure that seemed to roll easily off the tongue of the young, red-haired lawyer sitting in front of the huge panoramic window. "A third today, a third when you get approved by the Department of Labor and the balance when you receive the green card," he said without missing a beat.

I tried to appear nonchalant as if the fee wasn't going to present a problem. Mo and I had already discussed the matter and agreed we had no other choice than to refinance our house once again to raise the money. Over the years we had seen the equity build in the property and again it was going to be put to good use. As I sat across the desk, it occurred to me that it was a little strange that the red-haired lawyer should have an Arabic name. He picked up on my smile as I looked down on the business card he had handed to me at the beginning of the meeting.

"My father is from the Middle East but my mother is from Ohio," he said smiling. "They met while he was in college there." From his matter of fact style of explanation I guessed he was used to offering up this same story every time he handed out his business card.

I smiled back. From fourteen stories up the view of the Miami skyline looked magnificent. Out in the distance I could see the Miami beaches and the monster cruise ships slipping past the cranes lining the causeway. Closer were the majestic buildings of a new Miami. There was an exciting vibrancy about the city that was attracting more and more visitors and residents. It was easy to experience a feeling that Miami was clearly a town on the move.

My thoughts were interrupted when the lawyer handed me several forms which he said would have to be signed by my would-be employer. "The sooner we get these back, the sooner we can get started," he said.

I wasted no time in getting the documents to Terry who made arrangements the same day for his drinking buddy to pick them up, read them over and to sign them. Everything was looking good...but then I should have known better.

For two weeks neither the friend, nor the forms, showed up at the bar. Terry thought it strange that such a loyal regular daily customer hadn't been seen around the place. Stranger still, no one knew where he was. Without my urging, Terry offered to find out what was going on by calling his friend at home.

Apparently there was no response to Terry's phone call that day, nor in the days that followed. He left message after message, but after nearly two weeks he still hadn't received a response. It turned out to be a chance meeting when Terry ran into his friend at the local shopping mall. It was immediately obvious to Terry that my sponsor was embarrassed and it wasn't surprising to hear he had been trying to avoid him.

Apparently after reading the small print on the bottom of the immigration forms which referred to penalties, including hefty fines and imprisonment for making false statements, our friend had gotten cold feet. It could be argued that while in no way were we attempting to break the law, we were planning to bend the rules as much as possible to best suit our application. But on this occasion it wasn't going to work. The printed warning was sufficient to scare off our sponsor who clearly valued his brokerage license too much to go out on a limb for someone he didn't know. We were left with no other choice but to look for another angel.

Finding a new sponsor proved to be extremely difficult. For one reason or another, every name we came up with presented a problem that eliminated them. Some operated a business that was either too new or couldn't show adequate history. Others owned a business that in no way related to the skills I possessed. And then there were those business owners who simply didn't have an operation with a strong enough balance sheet to meet our requirements. It certainly wasn't easy asking people to reveal to the authorities how much profit their company was making. But ask we did. This was one of many requirements set down by the immigration department.

As the weeks went by and a desperation mode began to set in, it was Terry again who seemed to come up with a solution. Yet another drinking buddy who had become very critical of immigration policies over the years became very sympathetic over my situation. He coolly said he would be delighted to help out in any way he could. Without any hesitation he said he would be willing to offer me the job I needed. So once again we collected a new set of forms and had them delivered to my new sponsor's office for signature.

I should have sensed immediately a repeat of the same problem when the signed forms didn't come back after the second week. This time I called the sponsor myself, but got no response. I tried for three days until I eventually got the recorded message announcing that the number was no longer in service. Can you believe the company was out of business. My willing angel had flown the coot!

Terry had now exhausted all his contacts and I had, long ago, considered and rejected virtually every person I knew. For several weeks we seemed to be in limbo as Mo and I desperately racked our brains for the name of one special person who would fit the demanding criteria set by the immigration service.

The solution finally came to me one evening as I sat watching soccer on television. I had become friendly with Tom O'Reilly many years ago when I first started refereeing high school soccer games. I had even coached his two sons when they played on my travel team.

Tom was part owner of a large chain of fast food restaurants. My mind was quickly racing with ideas. Tom was perfect. His company organized sporting events all the time. Their soccer tournament in Tampa was regarded as one of the very best in the nation. How about convincing him to offer me a job as special events coordinator for his franchise? I didn't sleep a wink that night as I kept going over and over in my mind just how perfect a choice was Tom. The next morning I first ran the idea by the lawyers, who immediately gave their approval. All I had to do now was to convince my friend.

Luckily for me, Tom is one of the nicest people in the world. And I say that not just because he readily agreed to answer my cry for help as we sat in his office the next day. I carefully explained everything that would be required, and apologized up front for any inconvenience the situation was going to cause him should he agree to help. He pondered the matter for just a few seconds before flashing a smile and agreeing to my request. Within a few days Tom signed the first batch of papers and for the first time I allowed myself to believe that our application for the green card was for real.

Our application to refinance the house mortgage was approved, and suddenly Mo and I realized we were in the best financial shape since the early days of arriving in Naples. It wasn't so much that our debts had reduced; in fact they had grown with the new attorney's fees. But with two regular salaries now coming in and a little extra money from refinancing the house, we were able to comfortably cover our weekly household expenses. There was definitely a feeling of less pressure on us. Without question, we had joined what had become an all too familiar way of life for many American families. That being debt consolidation!

Although the lawyers warned us that our application was going to take time and that we needed to be patient (they were estimating a two-year wait) we started to feel our lives were coming together at last. Mo and I joked that our footing on our mountain had become firm.

Tom proved wonderful about doing everything that was asked of him. He would return all phone calls, and fax back any information that was requested the same day. It was immediately obvious I couldn't have come up with a better choice.

It was about three months later that the lawyers called to say they were ready to place the required job ad in the local paper. It's no secret that the game plan in these types of situations is to word the ad in such a way that I would ultimately be defined as the most suitable candidate. In an ideal world, I would be the only one responding to the advertisement. But of course, that would never be the case. The lawyers said that from their years of experience in these matters, they would be expecting at least half a dozen or so suitable applicants.

As skillfully as our ad was worded, the response still brought an unprecedented 35 replies! Thirty-five people living in Naples and nearby Ft. Myers wanted the job as Events Coordinator for Tom's fast food chain. From my telephone conversation with the lawyers a week or so later, it was obvious they were clearly surprised by the number of replies to the ad. "This will make it a little more difficult, but it doesn't change the situation," they said with an air of confidence.

All the replies had to be recorded with the offices of the Department of Labor, who closely monitor the entire interview process. My lawyer advised me that half of the applicants could be disregarded immediately as being either unqualified or unsuitable. Of those remaining, Tom would be required to give a ten-minute phone interview, keeping a detailed log of each conversation.

I felt guilty in asking Tom to do so much when I knew he had such a hectic schedule, but I shouldn't have worried. He merely gave me one of his warm smiles and said it really wasn't a problem. I got the impression he was actually enjoying the whole thing and feeling good, I guessed, about being in a position to help me.

With his set list of questions provided by the lawyers sitting in front of him on his desk, Tom began the interviewing process. Everything went well at the beginning, with Tom performing his task in the professional manner I had come to expect and appreciate. Each response from the person being interviewed was carefully handwritten beside each question. The interview process took up big chunks of Tom's time over the next three days. It wasn't possible to contact all of the applicants during the day, so the phone calling sometimes went on late into the evenings.

Eventually the phone interviews were all completed and the large envelope containing the detailed logs was mailed to the Department of Labor, with a copy going to the Miami offices of my lawyers. There was nothing for us to do now but wait.

The first hint of a problem was when the lawyer phoned me a couple of weeks later and asked me to contact Tom to see if he had any paperwork on a certain named applicant. I learned from the phone conversation that the Department of Labor had received a complaint from this person claiming he had been unfairly treated in the application process. He argued he was very qualified for the job but hadn't been called back for an interview.

Tom's detailed records showed he had attempted to call this applicant no less than fourteen times over a three-day period, both during the day and during the evening. When we investigated further we learned that the man protesting had sent in his application two days after the published deadline and didn't even qualify to be on the interview list. We were spared further investigation by the Department of Labor who accepted our explanation without any more discussion.

The process now required that Tom should invite four of the applicants, myself included, for a personal interview in his office. Of course there was no need for me to go along. As Tom was setting up the appointments, I took the opportunity to look over the other resumes. Wow, I was truly amazed at the high quality of each applicant. If anything, all three were over-qualified for a job that was advertised as paying just $25,000.

Once again Tom rose to the occasion, and judging by his comprehensive notes that were mailed to the Department of Labor, he clearly did a thorough and professional job of interviewing each applicant. The interview process was now successfully complete, or so we thought!

While the interviewing was taking place in Naples, the lawyers in Miami were getting together the rest of my application package. Among other things, I was required to show proof of education, my planning and business skills and evidence that I was able to perform all the requirements for the events coordinator position. My file was already an inch thick. By the time we were finished there would be enough material to fill two large binders.

Proof that I could organize events was covered with my involvement in planning and setting up various soccer events, as well as my role in helping to organize the Optimist Club Soccer program which was now signing up over twelve hundred youngsters each fall.

I was also President of Lely High School's Sports Booster Club where one of our pet projects was to produce a discount golf card. This card was sold to local golfers and allowed them to play various Naples courses at huge discounts during the quiet summer months. During my two years as booster club president, this one project alone had raised more than $50,000. Although much of the legwork was carried out by a small core of hard working parents, rather unfairly, it was I as committee president who received much of the glory.

We also came up with the idea of the first "one million dollar hole-in-one competition" in south Florida which helped to put more dollars into the booster coffers. My thick application file was now beginning to look quite impressive.

When I was asked to come up with character references I was able to meet the request with little difficulty. I was in a very fortunate position of being able to pull from the files I had kept from making an earlier visa application, back when we were still operating the spa and we had many local dignitaries as members. Of the twenty one letters I sent out at the time requesting a personal reference, I received no fewer than twenty back, as well as one telephone call from a prominent judge. He said he was not permitted to write a reference on paper, but would happily give a verbal one if the authorities contacted him by phone. All this stuff in my file was making my application look strong. That was until that black Friday afternoon, at a time I was finishing up on another part-time wallpaper-hanging job I had worked into my schedule.

I broke off to call Mo who wasn't subbing in school that day and had just come back into the house after collecting the mail. We were expecting a letter from the Department of Labor to confirm everything was ok.

"It's here," she said excitedly. "Hold on and I'll read it to you." As I waited for her to tear open the envelope and pull out the letter I felt relieved that we were about to close the final chapter on our immigration worries. I reminded myself what the lawyers had told us earlier. Once the Department of Labor have given their approval, the rest is a mere formality. My thoughts were suddenly interrupted.

"Oh no," Mo sighed over the phone. "We've been turned down!"

I swear my heart stopped. This just couldn't be happening.

"What did they say? What did they say?" I was repeating loudly into the mouthpiece. Slowly, Mo started to read the letter. It was short and to the point. Just a single, five-line paragraph. The letter stated that the department had found irregularities in our interview process, and they were refusing to accept my employment. At the bottom of the page, almost as an after thought, the letter said I had thirty days in which to appeal.

My entire body was shaking as I left the paper hanging to phone my lawyer. I was told he was out of the office and was advised call back in an hour.

This was yet another one of those longest hours of my life. I was unable to work. I just sat down on my neighbor's kitchen chair and focused on the wall clock. Here it was again. That familiar clock watching routine and one I could certainly do without. Alone in the house I tried to focus on positive thoughts, but all I could think about was that we had finally been beaten. The authorities appeared to have won. There was no way we could expect to get our green cards now.

I watched the hands on the clock move slowly forward. Precisely one hour later I was back on the phone. This time I enjoyed better luck. My lawyer was there to take my call.

"Have you seen a copy of the letter?" I asked in a panic tone. "Yes, we received a copy this morning," he answered in an unexpected reassuring manner. "Don't worry; this often happens. I feel sure we can sort out the problem once we know what it's all about."

With this unexpected assurance I felt a wave of relief flow over my body. I should have called Mo immediately with the news but I wasn't thinking. I jumped in my car feeling much better than when I had first heard the contents of the letter.

As soon as I walked in the house I realized my mistake of not calling. I could see Mo had been crying. She was slumped in the chair on the patio with the crumpled letter still held tightly in her hand. She was just staring into space. I'm not sure she even noticed me standing by her chair.

I gently touched her shoulder and her body stiffened as if noticing my presence for the first time. "Hey, don't be down. I've already spoken with our lawyer and he really feels there is no major problem. It happens all the time!" I'm not sure she completely believed me.

In the days ahead, we learned from the lawyer's inquiries that when the Department of Labor followed up and contacted the three people who had come in for personal interviews with Tom, one lady had mentioned that there had been a brief discussion about soccer. It turned out that during the latter part of the interview she asked Tom what type of events she would be expected to organize if she was offered the job. Tom had rattled off a list, which included the possibility of arranging a local soccer tournament like the one the company sponsored in Tampa. He explained that it had become a national event, attracting young soccer players from all over the country.

According to Tom, the woman had smiled across the table and said she felt it best she was excluded from further consideration. She had absolutely no knowledge or interest in soccer.

This lady could have been viewed as a very strong candidate for the job. Her resume revealed she had vast experience in organizing various fundraising events. She was also an ex Naples councilwoman and well-known in the area.

The Department of Labor informed our lawyer that because our ad in the paper made no reference that knowledge of soccer was a requirement, it therefore failed to give a fair and accurate description of the job being offered. We had supposedly violated their guidelines.

After speaking extensively with Tom about what had actually been said during the interview, the lawyers felt we needed to contact the woman and try and get a letter from her stating that she didn't feel she had been misled in any way. I was beginning to feel uneasy with what was becoming a difficult and complicated situation.

I felt concerned that I was involving Tom with more than he had bargained for when he first agreed to help. I also wondered what the woman's reaction would be to our request. But I also knew we were left with no choice. I had to put my concerns to one side. If this was our only course of action then I had to do my part in meeting the lawyer's request.

I shouldn't have worried. After explaining everything to Tom, he said he didn't see a problem in contacting the lady again and would have it done by day's end. Thank god for Tom, I was thinking as I put down the phone.

True to his word, Tom called me at the house later that evening with some wonderful and amusing news. I could sense the excitement in his voice.

"I contacted our friend and guess what? When I explained the situation she got real angry...not with us but with the authorities! She said she would be firing off her own letter to the Department of Labor and would be sending me a copy of the letter."

It turned out that the woman was angry with the department for assuming she wasn't intelligent enough to be able to assess for herself whether or not she wanted the job.

A copy of the letter which we received a few days later blasted the officials for what she called unprofessional conduct on their part.

"The topic of soccer was just one of many things discussed during the very professionally conducted interview," she stated. "I didn't feel anything was hidden from me. I chose to excuse myself from further consideration only because the more I was told about the job, the more I realized it wasn't for me."

Ten days later we received the news that the Department of Labor had reconsidered the matter and had given approval for our application to go forward to the Immigration Service.

With that wonderful news, Mo and I believed nothing else could go wrong. After all, the lawyers had told us it was now just a rubber-stamp job. All we had to do was be patient and wait.

We felt so confident that everything was going to be ok that we stopped thinking about the green card. For as long as we could remember this was the first time there wasn't any major upheaval in our lives. We joked again that we may actually be getting closer to the top of our mountain.

It was several months before we heard from our lawyers again. The Immigration Department was working its way through a backlog of applications, and ours was now only a month or so away from final review stage. That "month or so" turned out to be closer to six, and it was almost two years to the day since first filing the application. We were told that once our application was approved, we could expect to receive the all important green card registration numbers within a few days, and then the actual card in our hands within ninety days after that. What a relief!

I can't remember too much about the phone conversation I had a few days later with our lawyer. All I can recall him saying was something about there being another hitch. "A problem has arisen, but I think we can easily sort it out before I go and meet with the immigration official in the morning."

The lawyer explained that the immigration official conducting a final overview had noticed a time discrepancy regarding the dates of when we had owned The Collier Advertiser. Apparently the dates didn't exactly coincide with the dates we had stated on our application. This wrong data, it turned out, had been a genuine mistake on the part of our lawyer. We weren't trying to hide anything. But we now had to prove that we were the actual owners of the publication during this particular time frame in question. Copies of the publication with the relevant dates on the cover, and our names on the inside masthead, would supposedly solve the problem.

"It covers a three month period, involving about twelve issues," explained our lawyer. "I need those copies with me tomorrow when I meet with the lady in charge of the department. I can't put it off. She's doing me a great favor by seeing me personally to try and sort this out."

"Look," he continued. "I don't want you to panic but I think it would be a good idea if you were over here as well, just in case we need for you to go in and meet with this lady yourself. We only have one shot at this, and if I feel the meeting isn't going well I want to bring you in. You may have to fall to the ground and grovel."

At first I thought he was joking but hearing the sincerity of his voice I began thinking, perhaps he wasn't.

"Bring all the copies with you," said the lawyer. "They are insisting we have full copies of each publication."

We had kept a number of issues of the paper as mementos, but a couple of hours spent scouring through filing cabinets in the garage and boxes in the attic could only produce publications from a different time period. Covered in sweat and grime, Mo and I started racking our brains trying to think of somewhere we may have stored them. We hunted through every drawer of every room in the house as a feeling of panic and frustration began sweeping over us. The lawyer said there wouldn't be a problem if we found them, but what would happen if we couldn't? And the meeting was set for tomorrow morning!

It was still early evening when we began phoning around. We were able to track down several of the salespeople who we employed at The Collier Advertiser during the period in question, but with no luck! No one had kept copies, even an odd copy for nostalgic reasons.

Where could we go, who could we call?

"Ron!" We both shouted together. If anyone kept copies it would be Ron, now tucked away in the backwoods of Montana.

No one will easily believe what I am about to say, but I swear it happened just as Ron told me over the phone.

The first part of the good news was that Ron was at home to take my call, relaxing in front of an open fire with his three giant dogs sprawled at his feet. The first storm of the winter was passing through the Tobacco Root Mountains northwest of Yellowstone Park, and already more than a foot of snow had settled on the gravel road in front of his house. Ron had been living in Montana for a number of years and had recently sold the weekly newspaper he founded. A few months prior he had moved to the tiny and remote ghost town of Pony, partially for its beauty and partially to escape the near-stalking behavior of his ex-wife. Ron had been briefly married to the younger sister of the actress Glenn Close, and had explained to us that the brevity of the union stemmed from his wife's failure to inform him of her severe bi-polar affliction until a few months after they had tied the knot. He was happy that the madness was behind him and was taking it easy, writing for various local and national magazines from the deep woods of Big Sky Country.

After we had taken care of the formalities and quick updates on our lives, I quickly explained to my former partner what we were looking for.

Now for the second part of the good news. "You won't believe this," he laughed, "but I cleaned out my garage today and the copies you're looking for are sitting on the porch. I planned to take them to the dump in the morning. Hold on and I'll go and bring them in."

This couldn't be so. If the copies were there, then it meant Ron had been holding them for more than five years and was getting ready to throw them out the very next day!

The delay was nerve-racking. My palms were sweating as I held the receiver to my ear.   Mo's head was resting on my shoulder as she listened in on the conversation. I noticed that her breathing was uneven and heavy. I swear it was the longest two minutes of our lives.

"Yep, looks as though they are all here." came Ron's heartwarming news. "Tell me the dates you're looking for and I'll get the copies in the mail."

"Sorry Ron. That's not going to work," I said. "Our lawyers, and maybe me as well, are meeting with the immigration people in the morning at ten o'clock. They must have the copies with them."

There was a long silence on the phone.

"Then you have one huge problem. I can't even overnight them to your lawyer's office. It's a two-hour drive to Ennis in this weather, that's the closest pick up point, and I won't get there in time. What now?"

There was only one possibility left. "Still got your old fax machine Ron?" I inquired

"Yeah, it's still here in my office. Use it from time to time."

"Sorry to do this to you, Ron, but you'll have to fax over the copies...all twelve of them," I said, finding it difficult to get the words out. "And they have to be the complete issues!"

I just realized what I was asking Ron to do. I was asking him to fax over twelve issues, each one having no fewer than twenty-four pages and some as many as thirty-six pages. Each side of the page would have to be manually fed into the machine.

Then I'd better get started," he said without hesitation. "Make sure you have plenty of paper in the machine at your end."

"Don't worry," I replied. "I will be standing by the machine all night!"

As I put down the phone I began to wonder just how long it was going to take to fax over more than 400 pages of newsprint that had to be carefully cut, folded and hand fed into this antiquated machine. Poor Ron was up for most of the night. He told me years later his old, faithful fax machine never recovered from that night's work, and has never worked successfully again.

I slept very little that night myself, sitting on the chair next to the machine as it very slowly spat out page after page. Every so often there was a malfunction and Ron would have to redial to reconnect. It was after 3:00 a.m. when the last page and Ron's sign off message appeared in the tray. He had done a wonderful job. I just hoped his efforts would be enough to save the day.

As I turned my back on the machine, and the stack of faxed pages, I realized I would have time for just a couple hours sleep before getting up for the one hundred mile ride to Miami. I figured that to have enough time to get through the Miami rush hour traffic, I needed to be on the road by 6:00 a.m. Sleep came quickly as I sunk into a world of immigration monsters making more and more demands.

At the attorney's offices the next morning, the simple strategy was explained to me. The two lawyers who had been handling different aspects of our application would go to the immigration offices together. They would meet with the woman in charge to try and sort out the problem. If they felt they weren't winning the argument, I would be called over. The offices were only two blocks away and I could be there in minutes. Again, I was reminded that the lawyers had called in a lot of favors to set up this meeting with this top lady official. This would be our one and only chance to get final approval. I didn't like their serious tone when they mentioned again that I may have to go down on my hands and knees and grovel if all else failed.

What a situation. Here I was, paying a huge (for me) sum of money in lawyer's fees, and the decision could well come down to me groveling on my knees and kissing the immigration officer's feet. What a scene. I couldn't help but smile as I thought about it while consuming my fifth cup of coffee of the morning.

As I waited in the reception area of the lawyer's office, the clock on the wall reminded me of all the nail-biting situations I had been in before. This bloody clock scenario again! This was not unlike the time I was waiting at the American Embassy in London, or the time in Chris's apartment. The sound of my heart pumping played a familiar cadence in my ears.

Thirty-minutes. Forty-five minutes. An hour went by. I stood up, paced the floor in the windowless reception area and sat down again. I opened up a magazine, turning the pages but not reading the words. I was becoming very nervous, having convinced myself to expect the inevitable wasn't going to be good. At any moment now, I figured the frosty glass window will be pushed aside and the receptionist will pop her head out and tell me to take a phone call. I will be summoned to the immigration offices in a last ditch effort to win approval for our green cards.

The wait was agonizing. For the umpteenth time I asked to borrow the key to the men's bathroom. I wasn't sure I wanted to go, but the walk down the corridor gave me something to do. Each short trek burned up a few more nerve-racking minutes.

It was now 10:57. The two lawyers had been gone for well over an hour. I was about to ask for another cup of coffee when the door to the reception room opened. One of the lawyers moved slowly into the room with his head bowed low.

"What happened?" I asked frantically. The figure came closer with its chin pressed down into his chest. All I could see was a mop of red hair. Slowly the head was raised and the mouth softly voiced the words..."I'm sorry."

Before I could react, the second lawyer burst into the room and leaped across the rug. "He's only kidding! Everything is ok. They've approved your application."

I can't remember if Mo and I went out to celebrate that evening. I'm sure we did, but in the release from so many years of stress and struggle I can't remember where.

Chapter Twenty-Five

I wish I could say that the 'approval' for our green cards was the end of our immigration nightmares, but it wasn't. We were soon to discover our fight was far from over and the worst scare, if you can believe it, was still to come.

In the weeks leading up to Thanksgiving and Christmas, and with the preparation that goes into planning family festivities, we had pushed the subject of green cards into the back of our minds. We had been approved, so there was nothing more we could do but wait.

It was Mo who first waved the caution flag one evening over dinner. The two of us were relaxing outside on the patio one comfortable December evening, enjoying the tranquil setting around us that always served to remind us of what we enjoyed most about Florida. Noisy crickets out in the shadowy darkness were breaking the silence in the moments before a gentle breeze came up to trigger other softer tones from the three or four wind chimes that hung between our flowering pots. The sky was clear and alive with twinkling stars. A full moon was casting a soft glow that illuminated the surrounding trees and shrubs. We turned down the lights on the patio, lit two candles and bathed in the simple and magical charm.

"It may not mean anything," Mo announced with certain hesitancy in her voice. "But do you realize Kieran will be twenty-one March,1st? That's only twelve weeks away. What happens if our green cards haven't come through by then? Think it will be a problem?"

Her statement jolted me back to my senses. I took a large gulp of wine and tried to comprehend the significance of the question. I had no idea of what to say, but I knew the issue was important enough for me to run it by the lawyers first thing in the morning. We had both assumed the cards would be arriving long before the month of March. But maybe Mo had a point. What happens if they don't? We had faced unexpected delays time after time. I just hoped this wasn't going to prove to be an uncomfortable twist of fate I thought, as I quickly changed the conversation.

I didn't sleep well that night and didn't waste any time the following morning in placing a call to the lawyer's office.

"Yeah this could present a problem," came back the response from what had quickly become an anxious sounding tone at the other end of the line. "We must have those cards through by March 1st."

"And if we don't?" was my rather obvious next question.

"If we don't then your son simply doesn't qualify. That's the way it stands. It will be left to you, as his parents, to sponsor him…and that can take up to eight years the way the process is currently running. And it's likely to get even worse!"

"Eight years!" I was stunned. "This doesn't make any sense. All this effort and money and our son won't be able to stay here?" I felt anger building up inside as I gripped the phone.

"You sure have had your run of problems," noted the lawyer, perhaps trying to ease the situation. "I would have to say your family has encountered just about every nightmare they could have come up with." If he was somehow trying to make me feel better he really wasn't succeeding. Instead, he was reminding me about the time he first explained those nightmares several months ago. He told us then that there are about twenty potential obstacles facing green card applicants. "Most of our clients get to face one, possible two. You hit the jackpot, hitting just about every one!"

Perhaps sensing my building frustration, he quickly added. "Let me get on to this right away. It won't be easy, but let me see if I can get them to speed up issuing the cards." With the phone hanging loosely from my hand, and the earpiece resting against my chin, I could hear the click of the phone being replaced at the other end. I must have stood there for several minutes pondering what I should do next.

Firstly I had to explain to Mo what was going on. I knew this was going to be a crushing blow and once again I was worried about the effects all these problems were going have on her health. Again it seemed just when we felt everything was going to be ok, yet another obstacle was thrown at us. As I drove home from the office to tell her about the morning's conversation, a picture of a mountain flashed through my mind. I couldn't help but wonder how far we had slipped this day.

Not unexpectedly, Mo didn't take my news well. "Why? Why? Why?" she repeated over and over as she paced the room. "This all seems so unfair!"

There was nothing I could say to comfort her. The news that the lawyers would try and get the process speeded up sounded hollow. We both realized we were being immersed in another "wait and see" scenario.

By the following week we came to realize that our daily phone calls to the lawyer's office were achieving nothing. They had nothing new to report. We had to accept they would contact us just as soon as they heard something from immigration. We were left with a situation that did nothing to alleviate our growing sense of panic. Each day brought us closer to Kieran's birthday. January came to an end and we moved into February. Still we had heard nothing new.

"All we can tell you is that all your paperwork is in, and has been approved, and it's just a question of issuing your family with your green card numbers. Believe me, they can be issued any day." This was the standard answer we were given each time we called.

The worrying consumed our lives. Neither Mo nor I could sleep and much of the workday was interrupted with thoughts of what was going to happen to our son if he didn't get his green card.

It was now the third week of February. Too quickly the time was draining away, and there were now only a few days left. With our pushing, the lawyers agreed there was nothing to lose by them contacting immigration one more time. But the response was the same as it had been each time before. Our numbers were there ready to be issued.

Three more days passed without any news. We had reached a stage where we were barely able to function. February 26th, my birthday - no news. February 27th - no news. Mo went out and bought cards and gifts for Kieran. They would have to be mailed that day if they were to reach him in New Orleans in time for his birthday.

February 28th. I called the lawyer. I wasn't surprised to hear he had no different news. "I have a gut feeling they will be through today," he said. "We have been promised."

By 7:00 p.m. that evening, having received no phone call from the lawyer, both Mo and I crashed into bed. We were both so exhausted that we couldn't think straight. The worry had ground us down so far that we both passed out the moment our heads hit the pillows.

Early the next morning we dressed and drank our coffee in silence. I knew Mo was feeling just as sick as me as we left the house to drive off to work. We were like two zombies. Although I didn't feel one bit like working, I had insurance appointments to keep and would be out of the office for much of the morning. Around 11am I placed a call to Terry to see if I had any messages. "Just one," he said in a casual tone... *"Your lawyer called with your green card registration numbers. You want to jot them down?"*

I was in a daze as I interrupted Mo in class with a phone call to give her the good news. You can't imagine the excitement in our voices as we whooped and hollered over the phone. Strangers in the street must have been wondering what all the celebration was about when they saw me jumping up and down and screaming into the pay phone. I had no idea what the kids in Mo's class were thinking.

As we both calmed down enough to speak, I explained to Mo the little I knew after my conversation with the lawyer. "There is only one more thing that has to happen." Immediately I could sense the tenseness in my wife's voice when she asked, "and what is that?"

"The numbers have to be logged on the immigration computer in Washington before the end of business today. It won't be a problem. They will be doing it straight away."

We never found out what went on between the time of being told "they will be doing it straight away" until the actual time they were logged in at 3.45 p.m. All we know is that the numbers were logged just fifteen minutes before close of business on **February 29**. If it hadn't been a leap year Kieran would not have received his green card, and he would have been unable to stay with us in America!

....

On May 8th, 1996 we all met up in Miami to pick up what had become known in our family as the "elusive green cards." Kieran drove down from New Orleans with Shelley Dee, while Dominic and his wife to be, Susan, drove from the University Of Florida in Gainesville. Kirsty was still in her final year at the local high school, so she drove over in the car with us.

Our lawyer had set up an appointment for 8:00 a.m., and we had arranged with the kids to meet up the night before and enjoy a celebration meal together. We also wanted to avoid the possibility of any last minute travel catastrophes that would prevent us making the appointment. We were all in a festive, holiday spirit as we booked into a nearby hotel and enjoyed a family evening. In that atmosphere it was easy to forget all the trials and tribulations which had brought us to this point.

After all that had happened along the way, the final act could only be described as anticlimactic and frankly, no one was too disappointed about that.

It was fun sitting around the table in the restaurant and reminding ourselves of events that had happened over the past fifteen years. Kieran and Dominic were doing a sort of double-act comedy routine as they recalled the only time I lost my temper with them both.

I was reminded it was in the early days of us being in America, at a time when Mo had taken advantage of a low-price air deal to go over to visit her parents. The boys were laughing as they relived the incident which proved rather embarrassing for me.

Our friends Chris and Jeanette were really the ones I should blame for causing the incident. After all, it was them who chose to spoil the children with expensive gifts every time they visited Naples. On this particular occasion, they handed over two, never-before-seen-in-Naples, pump-action water guns! These were something special to the boys and the envy of all their young friends.

As the boys retold the story, the details fell into place. It was about the second or third night Mo was away, and for the first time, as best as I could remember, the boys were misbehaving. They had gone to bed but clearly had no intention of going to sleep. I had given them a couple of verbal warnings, and threatened that if I had to come into their room again there would be punishment.

They didn't heed the warning. The noise of their giggling and shouting filled the house. I stormed into their room only to face complete havoc. All the bedding had been pulled off the two beds and both the boys were lying on soaking wet sheets, as a result of their water rifle fight.

Dominic interrupted Kieran, recalling that I didn't say a word. I simply grabbed both rifles, snapped them over my thigh and handed back the broken plastic parts. Their expressions, which I could still easily recall, told me it couldn't have been worse if I'd beaten them within an inch of their lives. What had I done to their favorite toys! Of course, I immediately felt horrible as I turned off the light and walked out of the room. The muffled sobs could be heard for hours afterwards. Fortunately there was a humorous twist to the story.

On Dominic's twentieth birthday, as was a family tradition, Mo had composed a funny poem about the major events that had happened in his life. She was reading the poem to the family and a few friends who had gathered to help us celebrate the occasion. The end of the poem ended with a reference to the water rifle incident, at which time we all pulled out concealed water guns and soaked Dominic.

For me, I was delighted the sad incident had finally been turned around and now, on that special night and many times since, made us laugh each time it was mentioned. It seemed appropriate somehow that it was revived in full detail this happy night in the restaurant.

As arranged, we met up with our lawyer outside the immigration building a few minutes before 8:00 the following morning. It was a hot and humid start to the day, the air thick and heavy as we left the air-conditioned car in a parking lot near to the main entrance.

As we approached the building we came across a sight I will never forget. A line of people was already surrounding the entire drab-looking government building. It started at the front door and snaked its way right around the corner. New people were joining the line where it reappeared to our left.

As we looked on with amazement, our lawyer directed us past the long lines and led us quickly through the guarded glass doors. He must have noticed the puzzled looks on our faces. Once inside, he began explaining that those at the head of the line had probably been waiting since 3:00 a.m. and it was like this everyday of the week! While most waited patiently, others chose to pay someone, usually children, to wait in line for them. Anyone joining the line after 6:00 a.m. had no chance of seeing an immigration official that day. The unlucky ones would simply try again the following morning, choosing to arrive a little earlier. This process would go on until they were fortunate enough to be included in the allotted group that would be handed a number, which entitled them to speak with an official and begin their immigration process. Our situation was different. We were given an appointment time because we were here just to pick up our cards. No more lines for us to join. But then we had been waiting fifteen years!

Inside the gray stone building, the large hall was dark and depressing but that hardly mattered to us. While we sat on cheap plastic seats and joked about the surroundings, our lawyer walked over to speak with an official seated at a table at the front of the hall. We could see him hand over a package which we knew contained the important documents approving our applications. He appeared to be exchanging a few friendly words with the official before returning to our group. Ten minutes later we were summoned to a side room where we were photographed and fingerprinted by a friendly black man dressed in a starched white shirt on which he wore a shiny badge that indicated he was from the Immigration and Naturalization Department. The irony of the surrounding hadn't escaped any of us. All the notices around the room were in Spanish, and we all confessed later we had difficulty understanding the heavy accents of each government official we met.

And suddenly it was all over! After going back to our seats and waiting just a few more minutes, we were summoned to the front desk one more time when each of us was handed a laminated green card. "Why are they pink?" asked Kirsty.

An incredible feeling of joy and relief swept over me. As I walked towards the exit and looked at others still seated, waiting their turn to pick up their cards. I couldn't help but wonder how many would feel as excited as me. But then, how many others had waited those fifteen long years, and spent nearly $30,000 to be in this position?

We walked quickly from the building and, after saying our goodbyes to our attorney in the hallway, we made our way out into the bright sunshine to find an appropriate spot to take a celebration photograph. There were masses of people all around. The line had now made a complete circle of the building and it was difficult to find a vacant spot where we could take a picture. Eventually, Susan and Shelley Dee lined us up near a side entrance where we stood under the gold Department of Immigration and Naturalization sign. With excited giggles we all waved our little paper cards in the air. I suspected that those waiting in line couldn't help but be a little envious of our situation, while those passing by on their way to work had probably witnessed our joyous scene many times.

"Hold them higher," shouted Susan. *Click!*

EPILOGUE

Today, eight years later, Mo and I have lost our green cards. Instead we have become American Citizens and for the first time voted in the Presidential Elections. We wasted no time making the application for citizenship once the regulatory, five-year wait period was up. Mo and I have always known that Naples would remain as our permanent home, so it seemed right to become American citizens as soon as we were able. Now I'm looking forward to celebrating my 60th birthday.

It's Friday evening and Mo and I have returned to the beach. We came here as the sun was setting and we strolled up and down in the warm surf. We brought along a small picnic of sandwiches and beers and we are enjoying dinner while watching another beautiful sunset.

While most others leave, we settle down on our straw mat. As darkness rolls in we find ourselves alone. We feel the beach has been left for us to enjoy. Perhaps we have earned that right.

Long after the sun has set we make our way to the wooden steps leading to the car. Despite the late hour, it is not cold but the surrounding darkness makes it feel that way. Mo reminds me that we shouldn't stay here too much longer as I have an early start time tomorrow at the Ritz. I have been working there for over five years now, but I don't know for how much longer. Last year I passed my Florida Real Estate license, and I am now selling real estate three days a week at a local luxury home development. I don't want to put all my eggs in one basket so I'm choosing to ease in slowly into my new career. Last week I sold one of the models for nearly $750,000. It wasn't a difficult sell. Naples is enjoying a real estate boom.

We still haven't given up on the idea of pursuing more business projects. Two years ago I watched a late night show on television about buying real estate with no money down. We have now managed to buy five, low-cost rental units. Our real estate portfolio is certainly starting to look a lot better than most other investments we've tried...including our pension plan in England that nearly went bust!

Decades back, when the signs indicated our original publishing operation back in England was going to be successful, Dennis, Rob and myself decided to invest a sum of money into a *safe* pension fund. Through the years, Mo and I had always believed that whatever else happened in our lives, this fund would be there to ensure we had a comfortable retirement.

I had urged our children to do the same; to try and get into a position where they could invest a sum of money into a pension fund and have it working for them over the ensuing years. At the time I thought I was giving them sound advice. They, on the other hand, thought it was quite amusing when they heard about the contents of a letter we received from our pension company in London, one of the world's oldest and most respected pension societies. The letter informed us that because of a ruling against them in the House of Lords, the company was being forced to pay out billions of pounds in bonuses to a group of newer policy holders who were not receiving equal bonuses. This costly action would force the company to regroup. They were facing financial disaster, until they were saved by another pension society. But the financial aid did not come without strings. The new arrangement would mean the value of our pension funds would be drastically reduced.

"Nice one Dad! Any other financial advice?" the two boys joked.

The irony of returning to real estate investing hasn't escaped me. I don't have to be reminded we lost half the money we brought over from England in the real estate market. Didn't I vow to myself that I would never get involved again, only to witness real estate investors making big profits over the next twenty years?

But this time around, inspired by the television course, we are approaching the market in a completely different way. We are now locked into fixed mortgages. The local rental market remains very strong so we see little or no problem collecting enough income from rents to cover our expenses. If we can maintain a positive cash flow then we are confident that we have made a wise decision. We shall see!

Two boys married, one daughter in a committed relationship and our first grandchild born just a year ago. What next? I had given some consideration to training for a year and attempting an Ironman race on my coming birthday. I was inspired after watching my daughter's boyfriend, Pete, compete successfully in Hawaii. Watching the finish of the eighteen-hour event was one of the most emotional experiences of my life. Fortunately, my orthopedic doctor convinced me my knees wouldn't stand up to either the training or the race itself so that idea has been abandoned. Instead, I will continue to play my soccer for as long as the knees hold out.

This was never intended to be a sad or self-pity story, just a truthful one about some interesting events that were weaved into our lives. We really do consider ourselves a fortunate family. With each difficulty came a solution. While there were many tears shed, there were also many smiles.

It's such a beautiful view up here on top of our mountain!

ISBN 1-4251-2690-1

9 781425 126902

Edwards Brothers Malloy
Oxnard, CA USA
October 3, 2013